THE GOSPEL ACCORDING TO
NATURE

ALSO BY ZACK MASON

Killing Halfbreed
Shift
Chase
Turn
The Gospel According to Nature

THE GOSPEL ACCORDING TO

NATURE

ZACK MASON

Dogwood Publishing
Lawrenceville, Georgia

ISBN: 0988652412
ISBN-13: 978-0-9886524-1-5

Printed in the United States of America.
9 8 7 6 5 4 3 2 1
First Edition: January 2014

Cover Design by Matt Smartt

This book is dedicated to my Author

THE AUTHOR OF CREATION

READ THIS FIRST

"For since the creation of the world
His invisible attributes are clearly seen,
Being understood by the things that are made,
Even His eternal power and Godhead,
So that they are without excuse..." (Romans 1:20)

W hy is the sky blue?
A simple question every child at one time or other asks their parents. The explanation that usually follows is one involving the refraction of sunlight and the atmosphere, but the question remains: Why *is* the sky blue?

God could have chosen purple. So, why *blue?* He could have made rain fall up and trees grow horizontally instead of stretching their branches up toward the heavens.

Rocks could have been soft. We could have been given three eyes instead of two. Why didn't He give us wings?

God literally made trillions upon trillions of specific decisions as He created, deciding one thing would be a certain color or size, and another would be a certain shape.

Why did He make each decision as He did? Why *didn't* He make the sun green?

This book was born of a similar, yet much larger question.

A question regarding God's revelation of Himself in Creation as described in Romans 1:20. From Creation, we easily recognize God's existence, if only because of its sheer complexity. The astronomical number of features of our planet and the Universe that had to be just right for life to exist shouts the existence of a Creator so forcefully it's impossible to ignore.

We also notice how well each plant and animal is provided for on a daily basis. That the climate on earth is suitable not only for survival, but even for comfort. Every bird has enough to eat. Every fish finds its food. God's love and provision shines throughout.

Theologians refer to this as *general revelation*. General revelation is God's revelation to man through nature of His existence and certain aspects of His character. This type of revelation is called general because it has been available to all mankind throughout history as opposed to *specific* revelation, such as the Bible.

But is that the extent of general revelation? Does it bear witness to God's existence and love and nothing more? Or are there deeper levels to Creation's testimony?

Did God make all those decisions on a whim, or did He have a reason for each and every choice?

The question itself states the only two possible answers. Either God made His design decisions on a whim, or for a reason.

If you believe He decided everything on a whim, you might as well stop reading now.

The God I know always has a reason for everything He does. In fact, He usually has three or four (if not a hundred)!

Therefore, if God has reasons behind His design, what are those reasons?

To answer this we cannot appeal to the necessities of the laws of Physics, for God created those too. Which means to answer why gravity exists, we cannot say He did it because the universe needs gravity to hold it together. God could have created the universe so it would not need gravity to hold itself together, so necessity is never an answer for God's actions.

No, everything God does is because He wants to.

Reason means purpose. He had a purpose for making the sky blue, as He did for every other design decision, and in Scripture, His purposes almost always have something to do with us. Logically, then, His purpose could only be communication. Communication with us.

INTRODUCTION

Is it possible that God encoded a
symbolic message in Creation that can be interpreted?

Sure, it's *possible*. A lot of things are possible. A better question would be: *Did* He encode a symbolic message?

What other reason could God have for the myriad of design decisions He made if it was not to communicate some spiritual message to us symbolically? I can think of no other.

So, what we know is as follows:

1. God made many design decisions.
2. He always has a reason for everything He does.
3. His reasons usually involve us, which, in this case,
    could only mean communication with us.
4. Such communication would have to be symbolic in
    nature.

Yet, if He did encode such a message, how could we know we were interpreting that message correctly?

1. The message would have to be symbolically coherent.

If there is a message encoded in Creation, then as we interpret it, the symbolism revealed must be consistent across all of Creation's aspects. In other words, if we interpret trees as having a certain symbolic meaning with respect to the soil, we cannot give trees a different meaning with respect to the seasons.

Our interpretation of the symbolism must be consistent and true throughout every aspect of nature, or we have made a mistake somewhere in our reading of the message.

2. The message cannot conflict with Scripture.

God has already spoken clearly through the Bible, which is *specific* revelation, His Word to man. Therefore, if the message we interpret from natural symbolism contradicts any clear teachings of Scripture, we would know that we have made an error. So, for those readers who are gifted by the Spirit to be theological watchdogs, don't worry, Scripture is supreme. Not because there is no message in Creation, but because Scripture is easier to interpret without error.

That said, there may be places where our personal spiritual beliefs conflict with the understanding we are gleaning from God's symbolic revelation in nature. While it would be tempting at those times to assume the symbolism we are pulling from nature is in disagreement with the Bible, the reader should step back and honestly ask themselves if it is our natural interpretation that is unbiblical, or if the problem might be personally held beliefs that are not truly supported by Scripture.

We must always remember that God is the author of both Creation and Scripture. He will not disagree with Himself. The problem with interpretation always lies with man. We misinterpret both science and Scripture. We can also misinterpret this natural symbolism. The problem never lies with the Author, but with us, the readers.

3. The message will agree with Scripture.

If we do a good job interpreting God's message in nature, then there will not only be an absence of conflict between the natural message and Scripture, but Scripture will also affirm and agree with the message.

4. The message is symbolic.

As we pull symbolism from nature, we should never confuse the symbols with the thing they represent.

For example, when Jesus told the parable of the wheat and the tares, the wheat stalks represent believers. But the wheat stalks are not *actually* believers, they're just symbols of believers. In Scripture, the wind is a symbol for the Holy Spirit, but that's all wind is, a symbol. The physical movement of air is not to be worshipped as we would the Holy Spirit.

God is not one with nature. Nature is just a book that God has written testifying to His glory. We do not worship the symbols we find, we read them as words.

So, it's time to get started. If you find yourself still balking at the idea of a symbolic message in God's Creation, then you should stop reading and first settle within yourself once and for all whether God's design in Creation is whimsical or purposeful. If He made every decision on a whim, there is no message.

If He had a purpose, then we just have to decipher His message — and if He encoded a message, then *He meant for us to read it.*

In fact, that's what we'll find as we begin this journey together. God's message to us through Creation is much deeper, much more coherent, and much more detailed than I ever imagined when these questions first arose within me.

This book is really nothing more than a commentary on a much bigger book, the book that is Creation, and our efforts here will barely scratch the surface of what God has to say. It is no stretch to say that literally thousands, if not tens of thousands of books could be written on *Ketisology,* the study of His message in Creation.

TABLE OF CONTENTS

PART I

Section 1 - God, Truth, & Man

- The Sky   19
- Light   23
- The Sun   27
- Heat   34
- Darkness   36
- The Law of Gravity   38
- The Wind   40
- Oxygen   42
- Carbon   46

Section 2 - God's Power & the Kingdom

WATER   51

- Oceans (Salt Water vs. Fresh Water)   55
- Natural Springs   57
- Rivers   59
- Water Table   63
- Evaporation   65
- Clouds   66
- Rain   67
- Rainbows   69

LAND   73

- Rocks, Stone & Soil   75

-Rocks (Boulders)		77
-Stones		79
-Soil		81
-Types of Soil		83
-Erosion		84

SKY

- The Moon   87
- Stars   97

Section 3 - Believers in the Kingdom

TREES   107

- Photosynthesis   111
- Capillary Action   114
- Tree Rings   115
- Tree Mass   116
- Tree & Plant Growth   117
- Roots   118
- Trees & Soil   119
- Wood   122
- Fire   125
- Forest Fires   128

TYPES OF PLANTS   135

- Evergreens   135
- Deciduous   139
- Fruit/Seed   143
- Fruit Trees   144
- Vines   145

- Bushes   147
- Grass   148
- Flowers   152
- Crops   155
- Sea Plants   157
- Rock-Eating Plants   161

Section 4 - Churches

CLIMATES   165

- Desert   165
  - -Desert Rain   168
  - -Desert Life   169
  - -Oases   170
  - -How to Make a Desert   171
  - -A Blooming Desert?   172
  - -Arroyos   174
  - -Sandstorms   178
- Forest & Jungle   182
  - -Rain Forest   184
  - -Deciduous/Temperate Forest   189
  - -Boreal/Evergreen Forest   193
- Arctic Regions & Snow Caps   196
- Mountains & Valleys   198
- Plains & Grasslands   202
- Swamps   205
- Beaches & Coastlines   208

Section 5 - Spiritual Cycles & Judgments

SEASONS 215

- Spring 215
- Summer 219
- Autumn 222
- Winter 224

WEATHER 227

- Sunshine 227
- Rain (again) 228
- Storms 229
- Lightning 233
- Snow 236
- Fog 240
- Dew 242

DISASTERS 243

- Earthquakes 243
- Landslides 246
- Earth's Core 247
- Volcanos 251
- Tsunamis 261
- Floods 264
- Tornados 268
- Hurricanes 270

PART II

ANIMAL KINGDOM

Section 6 - The Lost & the Body of Christ

THE SENSES   278

- Vision   278
- The Blind   279
- Hearing   281
- Smell   281

FISH   283

- Salmon   290
- Freshwater Eels   292
- Great White Sharks   293
- Bull Sharks   295
- Flying Fish   296
- Fishing   297

MAMMALS   299

- Lions   307
- Carnivores (1st Order)   309
- Dolphins (2nd Order)   311
- Whales   315
- Hoofed Animals (3rd Order)   316
  - -Even-Toed Hoofed Animals   319
    - -Sheep   320
    - -Pigs   322
    - -Giraffes   328

-Odd-Toed Hoofed Animals   333

    -Horses   335

    -Camels   338

- Dogs   341
- Cats   344
- Rodents (4th Order)   347
- Bats (5th Order)   349
- Primates (6th Order)   352
- Marsupials (7th Order)   355
- Elephants (8th Order)   360
- Final Note on Mammals   369

Section 7 - Angels & Spirits

BIRDS   373

- Eagles   380
- Doves   381
- Owls   382
- Ravens   384
- Songbirds   385
- Hummingbirds   387
- Carrier Pigeons   389
- Birds vs. Mammals   389

REPTILES   390

- Crocodiles   393
- Snakes   394
- Turtles   395
- Conclusions on Reptiles   398

AMPHIBIANS   399

INSECTS   405

- **Locusts**   410
- **Cockroaches**   412
- **Bees, Wasps & Ants**   413
- **Butterflies**   413
- **Final Note on Insects**   413

COLORS   415

- **Blue**   415
- **Purple**   417
- **Red**   417
- **Yellow**   419
- **Green**   419
- **Orange**   420
- **Black**   421
- **White**   422
- **Brown**   423
- **Pink**   423

Errors: A Window to Viewing   425
Correct Interpretation

In Conclusion   429

Author's Note   435

Glossary   439

Index   449

PART I

THE BASICS

Sky, Light & Gravity:

GOD, TRUTH, & MAN

THE SKY

"He who builds His layers in the sky, And has founded His strata in the earth; Who calls for the waters of the sea, And pours them out on the face of the earth— The LORD is His name."
(Amos 9:6)

"So that they should seek the Lord, in the hope that they might grope for Him and find Him, though He is not far from each one of us; for in Him we live and move and have our being..."
(Acts 17:27-28b)

W hen we look for God, why do we always look up? Is it just a reflex ingrained in us from childhood? Do we subconsciously absorb the idea that God is "up above us" from some innocent moment when we first ask 'Mommy, Daddy, where is God?' and they point upward in reply?

Not likely.

All cultures, even and especially primitive ones, have always associated the sky with God. In fact, many languages use the same word for "sky" and "Heaven." Even in English, we sometimes substitute the word 'sky' with 'heavens'. In polytheistic cultures, the supreme, all-powerful Creator God is almost always the one associated with the sky.

I, for one, cannot take in the view of a crystal blue sky without thinking about God. Which is intentional on His part. He built that sense, that intuition, into every man and woman.

When you find yourself inspired by a beautiful landscape, which part of the view inspires you the most? Are you most inspired by closely examining the rocky clefts in the side of a mountain, or does your spirit soar more when you see at that same mountain framed by a beautiful sunset above it? Is it the river or the canyon by itself that inspires you, or rather the whole picture of that same river or canyon topped by a wide, azure heaven?

Picture in your mind a close-up photo of a field of grass and nothing more. Now, imagine a photo of the same field overshadowed by dark, angry thunderclouds. Which photo would fill you with a greater sense of awe?

Be it a clear summer blue, a stark winter gray, or the black of night littered with stars, it is the sky in nature that most inspires us.

The sky is God's symbol for Himself.

It is one of God's principal testimonies to man of His existence. Man has always known there was a God *primarily because of the existence of the sky.*

Why? Because the sky is so vast, so immeasurable. It has an incomprehensible depth. It is unattainable. Man can reach and reach but will never grasp it. He stretches himself to his limits and jumps as high as he is able, but will still never touch it. He can build a tower, a skyscraper even, yet that tower will never truly scrape it. The sky remains just out of reach, outside our grasp.

In the same way, God is immeasurable and incomprehensible. He often seems unattainable, unknowable, and unreachable. Mysterious.

At one time or another, we've all witnessed moments like the cover of this book when sunbeams pierce a hole in a blanket of clouds and illuminate the landscape below like a spotlight. It's a rare sight, but a beautiful and familiar one, and I never tire of seeing it. Who can look upon such a view without strongly sensing God's presence? In that moment, you can't help but believe that God is somehow peering through the clouds at the earth below.

It demonstrates how strongly we associate the sky with God.

Throughout the history of the world, how many have trembled before the deep rumbles of thunder rolling through the heavens? As it rattles our very bones, we imagine we are hearing God's voice powerfully pronouncing judgment. A strong thunderstorm inspires fear and awe, and even repentance in spirit for sins committed.

All of mankind's provision comes from the sun and the rain, without either of which, there would be nothing to eat. Both the sun and the rain are obviously of the sky. Therefore, man has always known his daily bread was dependent upon the blessings given from the sky and has looked to the sky for his sustenance. This speaks to God being our Provider.

Interestingly enough, as man has increased in his scientific knowledge of the sky, the things we have learned correspond exactly to things the Christian learns as he or she grows in their knowledge of God.

For example, to ancient man, the sky seemed unreachable and unattainable. While modern man retains that sense of awe before the sky, he also knows the sky is made of a mixture of nitrogen, oxygen, and a few other gases, which he is constantly breathing. He knows if the oxygen were not continually flowing in and out of his lungs, he would quickly die.

So, while the sky remains distant and vast, modern man has learned it is also extremely intimate and close. We cannot grasp it, yet it flows through our veins and resides in every one of our cells. The sky is our very life, for it is our breath.

An unbeliever (symbolized by ancient man) only knows of God as distant and far away — they have no concept of His nearness. Yet, once a person believes (increased knowledge, modern man), they become acutely aware of how close God has always been, and how constantly dependent on Him they are for their very existence.

Without Him, we cease.

Another thing modern scientists have learned is how much the sky protects us. It incinerates falling meteors before they can strike, and its various layers, such as the ozone layer, protect us from the powerful rays of the sun.

Likewise, the Christian learns as He grows in his knowledge of God just how much God protects us from harm on a daily basis.

While in a state of ignorance, we think life continues for us just because it always has. Once we know God, though, we become increasingly aware of how intimately He's involved as our Protector and just how many accidents, mishaps, and tragedies He saves us from.

These accidents would be the meteors.

What about a man whose car breaks down on the way home from work? Cursing because he's going to be late for dinner, he will never know that had he continued, he would have been in a major crash.

What about the myriad of accounts of people running late for work in the Twin Towers the day of September 11th 2001, many of whom swore they were rarely ever late. Many said their alarm clocks had mysteriously failed to sound that morning.

How many times does God save us from unseen dangers of which we're not even aware?

He also protects us from Himself, from his own righteousness and power. If we were exposed directly to the power and presence of God (i.e. no ozone layer for protection), we would burn like hot dogs left on the grill for hours.

So, we gaze up at the sky, and we can see God the Father. From it, we learn that God is the source of all inspiration. He is the source of all sustenance and provision. He is vast, unattainable and invisible, yet simultaneously intimate and close. He bestows blessings and comes in judgment. He is the Protector. All of these things we learn from the grand symbol that is the sky.

It is no accident the ancients chose the color blue to represent God in art. Blue is the color of God in the Bible as well. (Exodus 26:31)

One last thing. Note that all plants, bushes, and trees strain up toward the sky as they grow. They fight the law of gravity to do so, aspiring to reach for God in spite of the heavy load burdening them and pulling them down. Thus should all perfect members of creation strive to do.

So far, we have only scratched the surface of the symbolism built into the sky. If you find yourself wanting to dive in deeper, don't worry, we'll be going into much, *much* more detail in many of the chapters to follow.

Lesson: *We can fully trust God for our provision, our protection, and our very breath.*

LIGHT

*"Then God said, 'Let there be light'; and there was light.
And God saw the light, that it was good..." (Genesis 1:3-4a)*

You're standing in a room, immersed in complete blackness. Suddenly, a single, tiny pinprick of light is revealed. That tiny pinprick of light immediately becomes the focus of your attention. It's easily seen by you and anyone else with you in the room.

The very first thing God created was light. It represents Truth and Goodness. I don't think I need to work real hard to establish this association — we are all used to using light as a symbol for truth — but the reason God created light first was to symbolically establish the foundation of Creation. Truth is the foundation of existence. If nothing is true, then there is no true existence, because to say something exists is to attempt to state a truth.

In fact, in a room without light, you cannot tell if anything exists. Since light represents Truth and Goodness, darkness represents deception and evil.

Just as the tiniest, minute spot of light can pierce absolute darkness, so does the smallest truth or good work pierce a society filled with lies and evil deeds. Just as light holds tremendous power over darkness, which has no ability to retaliate, so does truth trounce lies wherever it finds them.

However, darkness does hold one power over light in that a tiny light is not capable of banishing darkness completely. A small light cannot brighten an entire room. A stronger lamp is required for that.

Imagine the hell that was the concentration camps in Nazi Germany. In such places, where one could find nothing but misery, murder, and depravity at every turn, the smallest good deed performed would have riveted the attention of all present like a strong magnet. It would have been starkly visible in contrast to the evil surrounding it.

When compared with Nazi Germany, however, there is an abundance of truth and goodness available in modern day America (though admittedly these are dwindling at an alarming rate). That same small good deed which would have pierced the darkness of Nazi Germany would be hardly noticed today. Yet, as our society declines, these small good deeds will grow more noticeable, though this is not to be considered a good thing since it only means our society will have fallen further into darkness.

There is a level of light that will be sufficient to banish darkness from a room or other enclosed space. Similarly, when sufficient levels of truth are projected into a society, Truth pushes out the lies, and the lies cannot resist.

A person lost searching for help in the darkness of night will be drawn to and walk toward any light they see. In a similar way, those who are spiritually lost will naturally be attracted to the nearest person demonstrating the love, goodness, and truth of Christ.

Light gives off warmth, but very little in comparison with its intensity (With the exception of sunlight, of course.) This is analogous to the fact that being in the presence of truth will emotionally warm us a little bit, but truth alone is not sufficient to comfort us if we're "in the cold." Truth and goodness keep us from stumbling in the dark, but they do not "warm" us significantly. Truth lights the way, but it does not make us feel loved.

Light exposes flaws.

Nightclubs, bars, and restaurants are kept dim for a reason. Flaws cannot be seen, which heightens the "romance" of the place. Visit a bar during the day with all the lights turned on, and you'll suddenly see the chipped wood, the grimy, unpainted trim, the dingy carpets, stained ceiling tiles, and a multitude of other flaws not seen in the "ambiance" of the night before.

Truth similarly exposes error and misdeeds just as powerfully.

Light exposes the flaws in our skin and bodies.

As the truth and goodness flowing within us increases, it has a tendency to expose more and more of those elusive flaws that remain inside our hearts. As truth and goodness flow out from us, it tends to expose flaws in others as well, whether we want it to or not.

The reaction to the truth shining from us, when that truth is unwelcome, can at times be similar to the hiss and shriek of a vampire struck by sunlight. For others, it is as healing as the kiss of the sun after being locked in a dark room for months on end.

Light can be blocked, as evidenced by the shadow you create every time you stand in front of one. This means Truth can be blocked. We can place obstacles in front of people so they cannot see the truth. However, there still remains, in these cases, an outline of light, a remnant of the light if you will, surrounding the form of the obstacle. While this corona of light is minuscule in strength of intensity, it's still sufficient to alert the observer who cares that some light is indeed behind the obstacle, and if they will move themself to a new position, they will see it unblocked. The same with Truth.

A person who has been in a darkened building for an extended period of time will experience minor pain or discomfort when suddenly exposed to a much brighter light. It takes a few minutes for this discomfort to dissipate while their eyes adjust.

If a mature Christian suddenly exposes a worldly person, or even a new believer, to intense amounts of goodness, love, and truth, that person may "wince" spiritually and retreat back into the darkness for a time, not being used to such brightness. The new believer, while feeling discomfort, will stick around and let his "spiritual eyes" adjust to the new levels of truth and love.

Light energizes us.

We feel more energetic on sunny days than we do on rainy ones. When you first wake up in the morning, if you turn on all the lights in your home, you will instantly feel more awake and energized than a moment before.

In the same way, in life, when we find ourselves surrounded by lies, evil, and hopelessness, we feel despondent. When truth pierces those lies, we are revived.

When people act in love, it brings us joy, regardless of whether their kind act was directed toward us or someone else. We are happy just to be in the presence of goodness.

White light is the sum of many different colors (frequencies) of light. I interpret this to mean that there are many smaller truths that together compose the grand Truth. In other words, Truth can be broken down into smaller truths for analysis, but each "frequency" is still truth.

The speed of light is the fastest velocity known to man.
The laws of physics indicate it may not be possible for anything to travel faster than light.

In the same way, Truth impacts very quickly when not blocked by an obstacle. I'm sure you've had at some point in your life one of those *discussions* where you were utterly convinced of your position, even adamantly so — until, that is, you received that single piece of information you hadn't known, changing your opinion quicker than you can bat an eyelash.

One undercover video can transform the mood of an entire society in a matter of hours. Truth penetrates quickly when it is not blocked.

Lastly, light is as difficult to understand in some respects as it is easy in others.
To this day, physicists are *still* unsure whether light is actually a particle, a wave, or somehow both. It is also not clear what would happen to objects traveling at the speed of light. There are other issues that puzzle scientists too.

This means that while there are many truths and aspects of Truth that I am easily able to understand, the Whole of Truth is too great and complex for my mind to fully comprehend. Only God can understand it in its full extent.

Lesson: *Seek God's truth. Truth and goodness are essential for life and freedom.*

THE SUN

"...and He was transfigured before them.
His face shone like the sun,
and His clothes became as white as the light."
(Matthew 17:2)

When the sun rises, the whole world is flooded by its light. Its brilliance is so great it renders every other heavenly object invisible in the daytime. All else, including the moon, is supremely eclipsed by its power, brightness, and glory.

So, what does the sun represent?

To be frank, when I first considered the sun as a symbol, I was mystified.

The sky and light are somewhat obvious, but not the sun.

Until we examine its basic characteristic. Then, what it represents is easily seen. The piece clicks into place.

(Throughout this book, we'll be using this method. Whenever an object is not immediately obvious, examine its characteristics.)

Life would not be possible without the sun.

The Earth would be a cold, dead rock otherwise. It's *the* source of *all* the warmth, and almost all the light, we experience, even at night when it's removed from our sight.

The sun is located in the sky.

It is the *sole active agent of the sky* which produces life and sustains it. If we were to personify the sky and say it had a favorite son, would it not be the sun?

God's active agent is His Word.

Through the power of His Word, God created the universe. Through His Word, He gives life, sustains it, and takes it back again. Of course, Scripture tells us that Jesus is God's Word, His *Logos*.

The sky represents God, and **the sun represents Jesus**. The sun is part of the sky, yet it is also a separate entity that lies within the sky. Just as the Son is one with the Father yet also abides in the Father. Jesus is God, yet He is a distinct person in the trinity. The interaction of the sky and sun picture this.

When Jesus is present with us, like during His ministry on earth, His brightness, His glory, and the truth and goodness that emanate from Him supremely eclipse that of all others.

Life would not be possible without Jesus.
We know this not only from Jesus' role in Creation, but also because of the Resurrection. It is only through our hope and trust in Jesus that we can have eternal life.

Jesus is the source of all love (warmth), truth and goodness (light) on Earth.
Even when Jesus is not physically present with us (nighttime), He is still the source of the love, truth and goodness we experience, though He be hidden from us.

Indeed, the teachings of Jesus are well-known (though I would protest not well-known enough). Are not the teachings of Jesus universally recognized as the supreme instruction with regards to how to love, even among non-Christians?

If every person in the world suddenly chose to consistently do the opposite of everything Jesus taught, would not the world quickly become a cold, dark place? All truth and love comes from the Word, just as light and warmth originate with the sun, even at night.

If you were to view the sun from outer space, you would see a bright, *white* sphere, not a yellow one.
Our sun burns so hot, it actually emits white light. White light is the sum of all frequencies of visible light. The truth and goodness that shines from Christ is complete and pure.

When white sunlight enters Earth's atmosphere, blue light, which is one of the frequencies contained in white light, reflects off particles in the sky, making the whole sky appear blue. At night, when direct sunlight is not present, the sky becomes invisible, transparent against the blackness of space.

Again, blue is the color of God in Scripture.

Therefore, symbolically, we see in this that when Jesus was on earth with us (daytime), we were able to clearly see who God is, what He's like. The truth (light) shining from Jesus illuminated God the Father for us, showing us God's "color" if you will. Christ's presence revealed God to us, making Him visible during His time on Earth. If you have seen the Son, you have seen the Father.

As this blue light is "subtracted" from white sunlight when it enters the atmosphere, the remaining sunlight is redder in color. This is what makes the sun appear yellow, except when it's setting or rising. At sunset and sunrise, sunlight has to pass through more of the atmosphere. Then, it may look completely red.

Red is the color of man. In Hebrew, Adam means "red," or "red ground."

It could be said that as Jesus illuminated God for us (blue), His own humanity (red) became that much more apparent. Especially as Jesus' time on earth was "rising" and "setting." His humanity was most revealed at the times of His birth and death. He looked most human (red) and bloody as He hung on the cross, dying for us.

Another part of sunlight is ultraviolet light. Ultraviolet light cannot be seen by the human eye, but it has several beneficial properties, one of them being antiseptic. UV light is an easy way to kill bacteria.

As we shall see, bacteria are a symbol for spiritual disease. **Thus, the truth of God's Word (sunlight) is an especially effective tool for eradicating spiritual illness (bacteria).**

When sunlight strikes our skin, a chemical reaction begins that produces Vitamin D.

Vitamin D aids in bone growth and density, helps our body fight off cancer cells, and aids in kidney and liver function (which control excretions of waste products in the body).

The symbolism here is in what happens to a person who is not being exposed to truth. They have trouble "excreting" their sin and instead begin retaining it (poor kidney and liver function), they become spiritually weak (poor bone growth and density), and generally become spiritually sick (possible cancer cells take root).

So, if we wish to be free of sin, be strong spiritually, and be clean from spiritual sickness, we need do nothing more than expose ourselves regularly to Truth.

Ultraviolet light is a form of light invisible to the human eye.

However, with the right instruments, it can be seen and looks purplish in color. Purple, historically, is the color of kings. So, while the kingship of Christ may not be immediately visible to the ordinary human eye, with the aid of the Holy Spirit, His royalty becomes quite clear.

It is through our submission to His kingship that we are rid of spiritual illness, rid ourselves of our daily sins, and are strengthened spiritually.

We depend on the sun to provide our daily bread.

Our crops will not grow without it. In the same way, we depend on God's Word for our daily spiritual nourishment.

The sun is *extremely* powerful.

So much so, we are not truly capable of comprehending its power. It's a tremendous, fiery furnace, hundreds of times larger than Earth. We can only experience a tiny fraction of its fullness, or we would be consumed by the fire within it. We're protected by distance and by the protective elements of the atmosphere (sky).

In the same way, Jesus' presence on earth is always a small, diminished form of God, for if we were to experience the full power of God up close, we could not survive it.

Yet, just as the smaller image of the sun that we see from earth is a true representation of what the sun looks like, so is Jesus a true and accurate image of the Father.

God (represented by the sky) protects us from Himself (represented by the sun), from His full presence and power. For our own good.

The sun traces a figure 8 through the sky each year.

If you plotted the sun's position in the sky at noon each day for one year and then connected the dots, you would see a figure 8.

Most people believe the number 7 is God's number. While the number 7 does appear quite often in Scripture, it is actually the number of completion or perfection, but not necessarily the number of God. Man is assigned the number 6 in Scripture because he is "less than complete" or "less than perfect," i.e. less than 7.

In fact, a more detailed study of Scripture reveals that there is another number that is considered to be the number of God, and that is the number 8. It does not appear in Scripture as often as 7 does, but it is no less significant when given. Since God is the only being who could be described as "more than perfect," 8 is a quite fitting number for Him.

E. W. Bullinger's book, "Number in Scripture," does an excellent job of exploring the uses of 8 in the Bible.

It is a neat confirmation then, that as we interpret the sun to be a symbol for Jesus, we discover the sun actually traces a figure 8 through the sky.

The sun rises in the east.

The sun rising in the east and setting in the west is one of the surest events in nature. For the sun to stop rising, the earth would have to stop spinning.

Zechariah 14 tells us that when Jesus comes back, He will appear in the eastern sky. He will first set foot on the Mount of Olives, which is east of Jerusalem. He will enter the Temple Mount through the Eastern Gate. When Jesus comes back, He will rise in the east.

And Jesus' return is as sure as the sunrise each morning. More sure in fact.

The sun is the center of our solar system and the earth revolves around it.

For millennia, mankind believed very firmly that *the earth* was the center of the universe and that the sun actually revolved around us, rather than the way it really is.

Today, many people think this earth-centric belief came out of Christianity and that Christianity opposed science as science began to discover the truth. This is historical garbage.

The idea that the sun revolved around the earth was a very common idea among *pagans*. In fact, the Greek philosophers Plato and Aristotle were both major proponents of this teaching. When the Catholic church originally challenged Galileo's theories, they were attempting to preserve the philosophies of Aristotle, not the Bible.[1]

Also, non-Judeo Christian cultures often claimed the earth was flat and rested on the back of a giant turtle. It is references in the Bible that actually allude to the earth being round and suspended over nothingness. (Job 22:14, Isaiah 40:22, Job 26:7)

It was only natural the authority structure of any society would have reacted negatively to such a core understanding of reality being up-ended. To the credit of the Church, it didn't take them but a few decades to become convinced of their error and correct themselves. (See Hugh Ross' book "Creation and Time")

How natural for the egocentric nature of mankind to elevate himself to this level of importance. From earth, we can only see how the sun interacts with us and seems to revolve around us, so we decide this is the reality. As men, we think we're so important. We see how God interacts with us and seems to be focused on us and we begin to believe that God is revolving around us.

Throughout history, there have been those few scattered, enlightened individuals from societies all over the world who successfully escaped their earthly perspective enough to perceive the truth, that the earth was actually revolving around the sun and not the other way around.

They are also few, those rare individuals, who correctly perceive that God is the center of the universe and that we revolve around Him, not the other way around. Such people have always tried to share this great understanding with the population at large, only to have their

---

[1] http://en.wikipedia.org/wiki/Geocentric_model (accessed October 15th, 2013).

efforts rejected and ignored as were the heliocentric philosophers like Galileo of every age.

Lastly, sunspots.

These are visible to any astronomer who observes the sun through a telescope. Large, darkened spots of cooled material marring the otherwise unblemished surface of the sun that look like wounds or even scars. These symbolize the scars that Jesus would bear after enduring the cross.

We know the sun's internal activity level is indicated by the frequency of sunspots, and that the earth grows warmer when there are more sunspots due to increased solar radiation. Recently, we experienced a general cooling of global temperatures because of a prolonged absence of sunspots.

This connection between sunspots and temperatures on earth would symbolize how the scars of Christ are connected to a greater love.

Many more aspects of the sun are yet to be discussed, but since they also relate to other pieces of creation, we'll wait and address them in those sections, including solar eclipses and the sun's corona which will be discussed in the section on the moon.

Lesson: *Make God the center of your universe.*

HEAT

"For as the heavens are higher than the earth,
So are My ways higher than your ways,
And My thoughts than your thoughts." (Isaiah 55:9)

Heat represents love.
Next to light, heat is the primary thing we receive from the sun. Just as Jesus transmits the Truth and Goodness (light) of God to us, He is also the main way we experience the warmth of God's love.

While the sky protects us from the full power of the sun during the day, it also retains the sun's heat for us at night when the sun is no longer present.

In the same way, it is God (sky) that makes it possible for the love of Jesus to continue to spread throughout the world while Jesus is not here with us (night).

This is actually a very natural interpretation. Love just *feels* warm.

Apathy and hatred feel cold. We often describe someone as being "cold" who does not show much emotion, especially affection. On the other hand, if someone is affectionate or loving, we describe them as a very warm person. A house filled with love we'd refer to as a warm home, etc.

Now, God's Love is different from human love. It is more similar to the love of a parent than romantic love. It is a very mature love.

Because God loves us, He challenges us. He refines us, shapes us, and molds us — and to shape a piece of pottery requires a tool. The challenges in our life are often God strengthening us or making us better because He cares about us. Those challenges are the tools He uses.

Truly, to continue to believe this can require great levels of faith when you are in very trying circumstances, yet it remains true.

So, returning to our symbolism, a gentle warmth corresponds to a light affection on God's part, but when He pours out His love, because He loves, there are necessarily challenges that burden us in a way more similar to an oppressive heat.

When we are overheating, we turn to water to cool off. (Both water and fire will be discussed later.)

I'll never forget this one day while I was in college. I came back from class hungry and found I was out of money — literally. Nothing in the bank account, nothing in the dorm room to eat, and my friends were all going to the Baptist Student Union to get lunch for $3.50. It looked like my growling stomach and I were going to be staying behind.

I scraped all the loose change I had off my desk (which was all I had to my name) and the grand total came to $3.47. Not enough.

I'm sure the good people down at the BSU probably would have pardoned me the three cents, but when I opened the front door to my dorm room to leave, I saw three pennies laid out on the carpet right in front of my door, neat as could be.

A warmth flowed through me.

As unimportant as I am, as unimportant as that one lunch was, and as unimportant as three cents ever is when paying a bill, I knew then that God cared so much about me He arranged for those three pennies. I saw He cared.

I remember another time when I thought my business was on the verge of failing, and I'd done everything in my power to produce the best results I could. This actually went on for years, and the entire time I did not feel "warm," but overwhelmed, beaten down, *burned out*. I constantly turned the issue over to God, but He did not relieve the pressure as He had with the pennies.

I will freely admit, it was very difficult to maintain faith through the midst of it at times.

Yet, I never went hungry, and at long last, I did experience a breakthrough where God seemed to release His power and free me from the burden. When that happened, a flood of warmth filled me that far eclipsed the warmth of the pennies because I realized He had been loving me through the entire process, but in His maturity, He cared more about my growth and building my faith than giving me a life of ease.

Lesson: *Enjoy the warmth of God's Love when you feel it, but trust when you can't see His love through your burdens.*

Darkness

As previously mentioned, darkness represents deception and evil deeds. Darkness is really just the absence of light.

Nature abhors a vacuum. When there is no truth, no goodness, no love, and no God, then lies, selfishness, and depravity quickly fill the void.

Darkness is vulnerable to the light.

Lies and evil cannot stand against the power of the truth. Darkness itself *cannot extinguish light*. It's pierced by it every time.

No, an independent agent, something other than the darkness itself must extinguish the light in order to restore the darkness. In the same way, lies cannot extinguish truth — truth pierces lies every time. The lies themselves are powerless, but people, acting as agents of the darkness, can extinguish the light, whether it be through martyring, banishing, or seducing the agents of light (the saints), thus restoring the former lie.

Criminals thrive and prosper in the darkest hours of the night. They are usually hesitant to act in the bright of day, and when they do, people are even more scandalized by their crimes because of their brazenness.

Similarly, when a society is a "good" society, one that is filled with truth (full of light), those members who would wish to act in deviant ways usually restrain themselves and hide their desires. The few that dare to act upon their desires are demonized by society.

But, as a society declines morally, as lies take hold, the darkness sets in and these deviants become much bolder. As the darkness grows, condemnation of their acts decreases because *their acts cannot be seen*. Their deeds can no longer be contrasted with the deeds of light, so acceptance grows and condemnation fades.

There are those people who we might call "creatures of the night." No, they aren't vampires or werewolves. They're people who love the nighttime and hate daylight.

I don't mean "night owls." I myself would plead guilty to being one of those.

No, I mean those pale-skinned individuals who rarely see sunlight, who party all night at clubs, or at the homes of like-minded friends and then sleep it off the whole of the next day. They are often heavily involved in drugs, alcohol, sexual depravity, occult practices, pagan/gothic trends, and/or maybe all of the above.

Similarly, in the spiritual realm, there are normal-looking people who are spiritually "creatures of the lies." They may live next door or be a politician in Washington D.C. They seek cold power, not love. They scheme and plot. They thrive in deception and anger and will attack anyone who threatens to expose them to truth. As John 3:20, says *"For everyone practicing evil hates the light and does not come to the light, lest his deeds should be exposed."*

Those who actively struggle against temptation know that temptation usually comes on much stronger at night.

Within an evil society full of deception (darkness), a person is more likely to give in to temptation. When you are surrounded by "good" people who know the truth, you are less likely to succumb to the same temptation.

We stumble in the darkness. Light helps us navigate our way.

Lesson: *Live in the truth.*

The Law of Gravity

"If we say that we have no sin, we deceive ourselves,
and the truth is not in us." (1 John 1:8)

Why do parents always bring up jumping off a cliff when talking about peer pressure?
"C'mon, Mom! Everybody's doing it."
"If everybody else leapt off a cliff, would you leap too?"
Maybe because we instinctively sense the similarity between a cliff and putting ourselves in a place where we're vulnerable to sin?

Put yourself on a spiritual ledge and if you start to fall...well, you're just as likely to stop the fall into sin as you are to stop yourself from splatting on the floor of a canyon.

The Law of Gravity is an irresistible law of Physics to which all things on Earth are subject. It's what weighs us down, keeps our feet on the ground, and prevents us from soaring away into the heavens.

Once, when I was a kid, I remember racing down the sidewalk behind my house when I tripped and fell. It scraped my knee all up, and in the following burst of sudden pain, I remember getting really mad at God for allowing that to happen to me.

Obviously, though, it was truly *my* fault.

Gravity is just waiting for us to slip up and get careless so it can introduce us to hurt.

Gravity is not something we like very much.
It's what makes us so tired at the end of our day. We feel better when we can lie down and get relief from its effects.

Gravity makes us work.
We strain against it with every movement of our body. Without gravity, we wouldn't need cars — instead we could bound our way across the land, leaping hundreds of feet in the air with each step. We

could lift furniture, trees, and even houses with a finger. Gravity prevents us from being Superman or Superwoman.

Gravity is what causes us the most pain growing up.

From the moment we begin crawling, we fall and things fall on us. As we grow, we learn to manage our bodies in ways that avoid the pain gravity so easily brings, yet even as adults we'll have our momentary spills.

Gravity holds us prisoner.

We cannot leave this Earth; we are held prisoners here by this mysterious force. Only in recent years, and with tremendous amounts of cost and energy, have astronauts been able to escape Earth's pull.

So, there is a strong force that keeps us from the sky, holds us prisoner on Earth, causes us great amounts of pain (especially when young), causes us to work, makes us tired, and even makes us less attractive over time as body parts begin to sag.

The law of gravity is a symbol for the sinful nature of man.

Just as gravity holds us prisoner and keeps us from the sky, so does the sinful nature hold us prisoner and keep us from reaching God.

Try to jump straight up in the air, as high as you can. Take note of the pitiful height you achieve, and the force with which you come back down. The sinful nature is just as strong in keeping us spiritually away from God.

Our sinful nature causes us a lot of pain, especially when we're spiritually young. As we mature, we learn how to manage ourselves so we don't get hurt by the sinful nature, but we always remain vulnerable if we slip.

Without the sinful nature, the curse of work would not have been given. We must constantly battle the sinful nature to overcome. These struggles tire us spiritually just as we tire physically fighting the law of gravity.

It is a fact that almost all muscle building occurs doing exercise (which is resisting gravity in some way), whether it's lifting weights, doing aerobics, jumping rope, or jogging. **Spiritual muscles are also built by resisting the sinful nature.**

Yet there is an aspect of gravity that may not be immediately apparent. While gravity holds us "prisoners" on Earth, it also keeps us alive. Gravity holds the Earth together as a planet. It keeps the Earth revolving around the Sun, the Moon going around the Earth, and us from floating off into space and dying.

This is the *one* positive benefit of the sinful nature. **It keeps us humble before God,** dependent upon Him for truth and love. It is what holds us revolving around Him. Without the sinful nature keeping us humble, our egos would cause us to fly off into cold, dark space away from the life-giving presence of God where we would die spiritually.

Lesson: *To grow spiritually strong, we must fight the sinful nature. We are all subject to its power, whether we like it or not.*

THE WIND

"The wind blows where it wishes, and you hear the sound of it, but cannot tell where it comes from and where it goes. So is everyone who is born of the Spirit." (John 3:8)

Since Jesus Himself compared the Holy Spirit to the wind, we don't really have to try very hard with that one:
Wind symbolizes the Holy Spirit.
So, what did Jesus note about the Holy Spirit? That like the wind, where He goes and moves cannot be predicted. Meteorologists to this day cannot accurately predict the weather, which is for the most part determined by the winds (i.e. movements of air over land and water). Experts among men cannot predict where the wind will move next.

Neither can theologians predict any better the movements of the Holy Spirit. The Spirit has a Will.

Wind cannot be seen, but we see its effects on things around us. Leaves blowing on trees, a paper tumbling across a parking lot, and a sailboat pushed across the sea — these otherwise unexplained movements are firm evidence for the existence and acts of an unseen force. We can even feel it on our skin.

Similarly, we cannot see the Holy Spirit, but we can feel Him, experience Him within us, and we can see His effects on the world around us.

The Spirit is invisible, but where He is moving and what He has done are not. His presence is known by His acts.

The wind is of the same substance as the sky — air.

In the same way, the Holy Spirit and the Father are of one substance, they are both God. God is Spirit (air) and no man has seen Him.

Further proof the Holy Spirit is symbolized by air (the wind) is the language used in the Bible. In both the original Hebrew and Greek, the Holy Spirit is actually referred to as the Holy *Breath*, which in Hebrew is *ruach* and in Greek, *pneuma*. It doesn't have to be pointed out that breath and wind are of the same essence.

Wind is powerful.

The Holy Spirit is more powerful than anything we can imagine. For the most part, the Spirit deals with us gently, like a refreshing breeze blowing inspiration, joy, and love into our dusty hearts.

Yet, the Spirit is also capable of moving as powerfully as a hurricane, uprooting everything in His path.

Like the sun, wind is also highly involved in various interactions in nature, so we will be discussing it more in future sections.

Lesson: *Respect the Spirit.*

OXYGEN

"The Spirit of God was moving
(hovering, brooding) over the face of the waters."
(Genesis 1:2b, Amplified)

Oxygen is the primary element in the atmosphere necessary for life. Oxygen is the part of the air that would be considered our true *breath*, since this is the part of air that functionally supports our life.

Fires need oxygen to burn.

Fires ignite at the moment a substance reaches a temperature where its atoms are able to bond with oxygen in the air. As the substance bonds with the oxygen, energy is released. The flames and heat are the released energy.

Removing all oxygen from a fire is the surest and quickest way to put it out. So, suffice it for the moment to say that the Holy Spirit (oxygen) is necessary for the burning of all spiritual "fires."

The atomic number of oxygen is 8.

This is derived from the number of protons in its nucleus. As previously mentioned, 8 is the number of God, of new birth, in Scripture.

In liquid form, oxygen has a light, sky blue color.

Blue is the ancient color for God, evidencing further that oxygen is intended to be a symbol for God the Spirit.

However, scientists now know the light blue color of oxygen is not what gives the sky its color. We're not seeing sunlight reflecting off of oxygen molecules. Rather, when sunlight strikes the atmosphere, a phenomenon called Rayleigh Scattering occurs. Because of the natural characteristics of blue light and its wavelength, blue light is the color we primarily see scattered across the heavens.

The interpretation is this: Jesus (the sun) illuminates the Father (sky) so we can see the Father's "color." While the Spirit (oxygen) aids in this illumination, Jesus does not illuminate the Spirit (oxygen), but the Father (the sky). Since the coming of Christ, the nature of God the Father has become clearer, but the Spirit still remains mysterious.

Oxygen (air, wind, breath) is the third most abundant chemical in universe. The Holy Spirit is the third member of the Trinity.

In 1857, God spontaneously birthed the Third Great Awakening in the United States. Some call it the Prayer Revival of 1857, others the Businessman's Revival.[2] Either way, it was arguably the most significant, most impacting of the three awakenings in our history and completely transformed our society.

It began with a single, tiny prayer meeting in New York City. Yet, within two months, 10,000 businessmen were attending. The movement of God spread to other states and soon witnesses were reporting a continual 2,000 mile-long prayer meeting extending from Omaha to Boston. One ship reportedly docked in New York Harbor with all the sailors on board having converted to Christ while still at sea.

The result of this awakening was a transformed United States. It spiritually prepared us for the looming Civil War that would tear our country apart. Brand new ministries dedicated to reaching all kinds of groups of people, from lawyers to prostitutes, were launched. Social movements initiated, from giving women the right to vote to enacting child labor laws.

Such a spontaneous movement has no natural explanation.

The word oxygen means "Sharp Producer" or "Sharp Birther." While the name originated from beliefs in early Chemistry regarding the relationship of acids to oxygen, it remains, of course, a very apt description for the Holy Spirit.

The Spirit is the energizer of the universe.

---

[2] Peter Marshall, *Sounding Forth the Trumpet* (Grand Rapids, MI: Fleming H. Revell, 2002), pp. 416-437.

Genesis 1:2 says the Spirit moved, or hovered, over the waters. The Hebrew word translated as "moved" more closely means "vibrated" or "set into motion." The Spirit is who opens our minds to understand and know God. It is through the Spirit's movement that revivals begin and cease. God's Spirit is who breathes life into every creature and keeps us breathing. He is the Great Producer, the Sharp Birther.

The most common forms of oxygen compounds are water ($H2O$), sand (silica, $SiO2$), and rust (ferric oxide, $Fe2O3$). Sand and water will be discussed later in this book; rust will have to wait for another volume.

Oxygen reacts and easily bonds with all kinds of elements.
In fact, very few elements can *resist* bonding with oxygen. Or, to say it another way, oxygen refuses to bond with only three elements. They are fluorine, gold, and platinum. Fluorine will be discussed at another time, but there is an obvious symbol in oxygen refusing to bond with gold and platinum. The Holy Spirit will not bond with money.

Why? Because money represents human power. It is our labor in tangible form that allows us to do things, to buy and create.

God's Spirit won't compete for glory. Therefore, if someone could say a tremendous work of God came about just because a lot of money was put into it, the Spirit may choose to withhold His power. This is why God chooses the weakest among us to do great things. He performs amazing works through believers with no resources and no power, and He challenges those who do have resources in other ways so that in both cases, the glory belongs to Him.

It's notable that in addition to a large percent of our atmosphere being oxygen in its most natural state (O_2), **Ozone (O_3) is also made solely of oxygen**. The Ozone layer in the upper atmosphere is what protects us from the full power of the sun. This implies that it's the Holy Spirit that protects us from the full power of God's Word. The Spirit has mercy toward us.

Our immune system produces ozone and peroxides to kill bacteria. This is a symbol for the Holy Spirit working within the body of Christ to root out harmful, foreign organisms.

The biggest industrial uses for oxygen are in cutting metal, welding, in rocket fuels, and for water treatment.

Scripture compares men to metal when it says men sharpen each other as iron sharpens iron. Without a doubt, the Holy Spirit sharpens us.

He also welds us together (fellowship). He is the fuel, the power, behind any mission or project we do (rocket fuel) and He purifies our life (water treatment).

In 1999, researchers thought that it might be possible for oxygen to become a solid under extremely high pressures. Remember, *liquid* oxygen, which looks blue, had already been observed, but no one knew if oxygen could become a solid. They called this potential solid molecule O_4.

If we follow the symbolism through, identifying oxygen as a symbol for the Spirit, then gaseous oxygen (Spirit) taking on the form of a solid would be analogous to God becoming a man. God in tangible form.

To achieve this with oxygen requires extreme *pressure*. Do we have any doubt that God underwent extreme pressures in order to become a man and live among us for a time? He gave up His glory to take on the humble form of a normal man. The blood that poured from his sweat glands in the Garden of Gethsemane gives an indication of the level of pressure He endured.

One thing that stood out to me about O_4, however, is its number. 4 is the number of the "world" in Scripture.

Now, as we dive into this symbolism, I do not expect, nor is it a requirement that every number that shows up in chemistry will match its symbolism in Scripture. If that were even possible, only God could purposefully pull off such a thing. Still, in this particular case, given the importance of the symbolism in our interpretation in oxygen, it seemed a little odd that the number 4 (the world) would be associated with Jesus if our understanding is correct.

However, in 2006, it was discovered by X-ray crystallography that this stable, solid phase of oxygen, known as red oxygen, is not in fact, O_4, but O_8. When I first read that, I laughed out loud.

Red is the color of man and 8 is the number of God. So, oxygen placed under extreme pressure to become a solid was originally and mistakenly thought to be O_4, but was actually O_8. Just as Jesus was under extreme pressure to come to Earth in the humble form that He did, and He was mistakenly assumed to be part of the world, but was truly God Himself, as was learned later.

Red O_8: Fully God, fully man.

Lesson: *The Holy Spirit is active and powerful.*

Carbon

"...and had no need that anyone should testify of man, for He knew what was in man." (John 2:25)

We're not going to delve into all the elements in this book, but before we can begin any discussion of trees, we have to comment briefly on Carbon. You know...that black stuff you get on your hands after messing with a burnt log? It's what coal and diamonds are made of.

Truthfully, it's what *you* are made of.

In fact, all life forms on our planet are carbon-based. Whether it be plants, animals, or people, all forms of life have carbon as their most basic building blocks. Carbon has 6 protons in its nucleus, thus its atomic number is 6.

Since you and I are made of it, a natural interpretation would be to associate it with man. When we recall that the Book of Revelation identifies 6 as the number of man (Rev. 13:18), this association is strengthened significantly.

As Oxygen is the element that represents God, Carbon is the element that most represents man.

We'll be encountering carbon and its characteristics often as we continue, but for now, I'd like to bring up the formation of diamonds.

Diamond is the hardest substance on earth. Everyone is familiar how brilliant and transparently pure diamonds can be.

Remember when Superman squeezed a lump of coal in his fist and made a beautiful diamond? Yes, subjecting carbon to intense pressure and heat will create a diamond.

Black coal represents the darkened, unrighteous natural man. As God subjects a man or woman to spiritual pressure and challenges out of His love (heat), a diamond of a believer is slowly formed.

However, most lumps of coal cannot be made into diamonds because they contain too many impurities. Only graphite, which is considered the highest-grade coal (fewest impurities) can be made into diamonds that way. And graphite, unlike diamond, is extremely soft.

Therefore, God takes the unrighteous man (coal) and begins removing impurities — a process that make him softer and more malleable (graphite). Then, God subjects this believer to high pressure until they become a strong, beautiful work of art, fit to decorate the clothing of the King of Kings.

Lesson: *Without God, you are incomplete.*

WATER & LAND:

God's Power &
The Kingdom

WATER

Many would agree that water is a symbol for life.

Life, however, is a tricky thing to define. A quick search of the dictionary reminds us of its many different definitions and uses, such as: "You only get one life," "Life is funny," "She's my life," and "Life on Earth is biologically diverse," etc.

We will define life as being that *active, energetic, transforming force of God at work in the world.*

Before God ever said "Let there be light," Genesis 1:2 says the Spirit of God "fluttered" over the waters. The Hebrew word translated in English as flutter means to "set in motion" or "to vibrate." The idea presented in Genesis 1:2 seems to be that before anything else, the Spirit of God set matter (the waters) into motion, maybe even starting the flow of electrons that makes life possible.

A shorter way of saying water symbolizes the *active, energetic, transforming force of God at work in the world* is to say it symbolizes God's power. Stepping back, we can see this interpretation for water makes much more sense.

Take Noah's flood, for example. If water is just a symbol for life, then how do we understand the symbolism of that global catastrophe? Did God drown the world through a flood of *life*?

Instead, if we translate water as a symbol for God's *power*, then all of God's uses of water in nature make much more sense. When God's power flows in great torrents, it is in judgment like a flood, but when He applies His power gently like a summer rain to cracked soil, it produces life.

Understanding this, the interpretation of floods becomes a lot easier. It explains why water was the method of judgment in the days of Noah.

God destroyed the world through an immense release of His power (Great Flood).

This also adds depth to the symbolism of baptism. We've always understood baptism as being symbolic of being buried with Christ and resurrected into Life as a new creation. Through this deeper under-standing of the symbolism of water, we could say that baptism was more specifically symbolic of being buried into God's *power*, which is the same power that regenerates the new man into life in Christ.

This giving of life should not be confused with God's Spirit, His breathing of spirit into man. The spirit, or *breath*, that God breathed into Adam was distinct from the "life" that transformed Adam's body from inanimate matter into animate flesh. Animals are alive, bacteria are alive, but God does not breathe spirit into them as He did man and woman.

All biological life on earth needs water to live, and it needs it regularly.

Even the most desert-adept creatures must have water or they perish. When searching out the possibility of life existing somewhere else in the universe, water is the very first item scientists look for on a potential planet. No matter how creative Sci-Fi writers want to be, there's never been a scientifically observed organism that did not require water to exist. Where there's no water, there can be no life.

Jesus Himself alluded to water being symbolically tied to life. *"Whoever drinks the water I give him will never thirst. Indeed, the water I give him will become in him a spring of water welling up to eternal life." (John 4:14)*

Man is very keenly aware of his desperate need for, and dependence on, water. Within mere hours of being denied it, a person can become desperately thirsty. Go without it for two to three days, and you die.

This means that we cannot go very long without being exposed to God's power, the Life that He gives, before we die spiritually.

Water refreshes us.

Close your eyes.

Imagine turning up a glass filled with clinking ice and taking a deep drink of the cold water inside. Can you feel the cool liquid filling your mouth, trickling down your parched throat? There is nothing more refreshing than that sensation, especially after a long, hot, dry day.

True Life in God is like that refreshing glass of water. So many of us are bored stiff with our daily routines. The ennui drives us to seek thrills and new experiences in an attempt to fill our lives with something exciting and interesting. We believe "life" lies within such things. Yet, they give us nothing of the sort.

The latest TV shows, movies, parties, clothing styles, cars, electronics, sky diving, base jumping, sex, pornography, drugs, alcohol, cigarettes, gambling, name your thing here, none of it satisfies, none of it leaves us refreshed for any extended period of time after the experience. In fact, all of these things are like eating spoonfuls of sugar, not water. You get an immediate "rush," a stimulating excitement that is clearly distinct from the previous boredom, yet, you quickly crash thereafter. "Sugars" like the items in the list above may have a fascinating taste, but when the sugar rush has left, you lie there on the couch feeling less healthy than before you ate.

A cool glass of water is very different from sugar. The opposite in fact. Those who aren't used to drinking water never desire it. It sounds like a boring, tasteless idea. Why drink water when there's Cokes and Sprites and Gatorade and Sweet Tea and every other kind of sugary drink you can imagine to titillate the taste buds?

However, those who are accustomed to drinking pure water cannot do without those simple, cool glasses. There's nothing like it. While drinking water doesn't send you on some sugary rush, it doesn't take but a couple of glasses before you feel cleaner, more healthy, like your body has been cleansed and weighs just a little bit less. Nothing refreshes like a glass of water.

The Life that God offers, True Life, is like that. To outsiders, those who've never experienced Him before, His ways sound boring, tasteless, and bland.

Yet, those of us who have partaken know differently. We know the Life that refreshes, the Life that leaves us electrified, with a sense of well-being and spiritual healthiness. It truly is an abundant spring of "water" that takes away your thirst for that something you've always felt was missing. It's not some sugary drink. It's True Life.

Water is a cleanser.

Water washes and purifies like few other cleaning agents. Bleach damages and even chemically alters objects through its cleansing. Water lifts dirt off an article, leaving behind the original, often times as good as new.

God's power cleanses us. Sin is a powerful stain, and it requires something of power to remove it. Only God's power is sufficient.

Water is a solvent.

It's actually often referred to as the universal solvent. This means that just about everything, solid, liquid, and gas, will dissolve in water. Some items may take longer than others, but they all eventually break down.

God's power is just as effective in "breaking things down." To come in contact with Him is to be humbled by His power. Through His power, He breaks down both physical and spiritual walls and softens up people's hearts. He dissolves the will of His enemies and disintegrates contaminating impurities.

Lesson: *Partake regularly in the Life that God offers to feel clean and healthy.*

Oceans
(Salt Water vs. Fresh Water)

"...and on the earth distress of nations, with perplexity,
the sea and the waves roaring;" (Luke 21:25b)

"Then he said to me: 'This water flows toward the eastern region,
goes down into the valley, and enters the (Dead) *Sea.*
When it reaches the sea, its waters are healed.'" (Ezekiel 47:8)

I've stood for hours on the beach staring out at the dark, endless seas, their waves crashing in, one after the other, driving themselves up the sand only to recede back again. It's fascinating to watch.

The expanse of the oceans is so vast and without end, your mind inevitably leaps to thoughts of bigger things, of the immensity of the world. The waves' action is so repetitive and fruitless, you are pulled into thoughts of eternity and how many waves have crashed on that shore over the centuries, and how few people have noticed. Just like the millions of lives that have gone before us that are now long forgotten, so are the waves that are no longer known.

Salt water does *not* have the same symbolic meaning as fresh water in Scripture. Salt water deceptively looks like fresh water, but it's not drinkable. Drinking fresh water results in life; drinking salt water will eventually lead to death.

Salt water represents the world.

The Dead Sea in Israel is so salty, nothing can live in it. Thus, its name.

Ezekiel 47 and Zechariah 14 both prophesy of a beautiful symbol embedded in Christ's future Kingdom. These prophecies say that a deep, freshwater river will spring up from under the Messiah's throne and flow down and eastward into the Jordan Valley where it will transform the salty Dead Sea into a large freshwater lake teeming with fish and life. Trees of Life will line the shores of this river.

The interpretation of this is clear. When Christ comes back, Life flowing from His Kingdom will be so powerful that it will finally transform the world (salt water) to life (freshwater).

Sometimes, people stranded at sea give in to the overwhelming temptation to drink the ocean water. After several days under a glaring sun, the soft lapping of waves against your boat would begin to drive you crazy with a desire to cool your swollen tongue. Yet, once a person begins to drink sea water, they grow thirstier and thirstier until they die, completely dehydrated by the salt content. Your kidneys require more water to remove the salt than you drank.

This is so similar to the effect the world has on us.

If we partake in the wonderful, crystal-clear Life that God offers us, we will live and flourish. Yet, when we partake of the world, our spiritual thirst is not only unsatisfied, it becomes more intense. The more we drink of the world, the thirstier for God's Life we become, though we remain deceived and do not understand why our thirst is not satisfied.

If we do not come to understand what is happening and break the cycle, we will die. If we stop drinking from the world, but then do not partake in God's Life, we still die.

The oceans are boring.

I mean, if you really think about it, aren't they kind of... *blah*?

Yeah, yeah I know you Jacque Cousteau types who want to go on and on about the marvelous wonders of the seas and how we've not even begun to explore their mysterious depths. There are obviously some exciting and scary things in the oceans — like sharks, and beautiful things — like coral reefs, but those are the things *in* the oceans. The endless grey waters themselves are just plain boring. It's the same view mile after mile.

The same is true in the Spiritual realm. There are some fascinating people in the world, neat people with neat personalities that God loves.

But the world itself is just kind of boring and same old, same old when compared with the dynamic life we experience in the Kingdom.

The oceans were not designed to be our dwelling.

You can't build a house on top of the waves and you can only tread water for so long.

In the same way, believers in Christ cannot survive in the world long term. We can float for a time, playing and frolicking, but we cannot live there without perishing.

If we understand the oceans represent the world, then land obviously symbolizes God's Kingdom.

The sky is present over both the oceans and continents. In the same way, God rules over both His Kingdom and the world, but the Kingdom (land) is the only place we as believers can dwell and survive.

Lesson: *If you find yourself living in the world, move back into the Kingdom.*

Natural Springs

"...But the water that I shall give him will become in him a fountain of water springing up into everlasting life." (John 4:14b)

Natural springs are a lot more important and common than you may realize. Some rivers are formed by simple runoff from rain, but rain doesn't *always* produce a river. Rain soaks into the soil but does not runoff in a flow until the soil becomes overly saturated. Rain may also produce *temporary* creeks or streams that dry up when the rainfall stops.

Natural springs, on the other hand, almost always become streams and then rivers. The most consistent of rivers have natural springs as their source.

Clearly, spring water emerges from within the earth.

Symbolically, this pictures "life" bubbling up from within the Kingdom, forming a "stream of life" which then combines with other streams to form a "river of life." This river of life waters the soil near its banks and flows on until it penetrates the ocean.

Looking at it from a different way, natural springs don't water the majority of the land. The limit of their irrigation effect is within close proximity of the banks of the river they form. Rain is what waters the entirety of the land.

Therefore, natural springs do not symbolize God's giving of life to the whole Kingdom, but rather His power bubbling up from within the Kingdom, forming movements and flows of His power to specific parts of His Kingdom.

I feel like my church is built upon such a natural spring in the Kingdom. Wherever you turn, life is abounding in our body. Sometimes, our biggest challenge has been keeping up with growth. From a human perspective, we might point at this pastor, or that practice, and say that is the reason for the life we experience, but the truth is it's the movement of God, the flow of His power that is producing the growth. All the elements we do "right" are actually a symptom, not a cause.

I know we're blessed with excellent leadership, humble men and women of God who are truly about God's Kingdom and not their own glory, but I think God decided to move, to let flow His power, and He brought all the right elements together rather than the other way around.

I must confess, I've lived in "desert" churches before, and frankly, it's nice to be in a church located by a spiritual natural spring for a change. It's a lot less work getting the water, and much more refreshing.

Lesson: *God has put His power within the Kingdom.*

Rivers

*"All the rivers run into the sea, yet the sea is not full;
to the place from which the rivers come, there they return again."
(Ecclesiastes 1:7)*

Rivers, streams, creeks, and brooks represent the currents of God's power which flow through God's Kingdom.

While most of creation is well-watered by rain, historically civilizations have located themselves next to rivers simply because it's the easiest way to access fresh water. London has the Thames, Paris, the Seine, and Washington DC, the Potomac. Most large cities in the world are centered on large rivers due to the simultaneous advantages of the access to fresh water and the ability to navigate or transport cargo via the river.

So, what exactly are these currents of power, or Life, which flow through God's Kingdom?

I don't think we can *see* them, since they are spiritual currents, but we can experience them. Most readers have had the experience of attending a church where the people seemed very nice, but the church itself just felt "dead." Like nothing was happening there.

On the other hand, many readers will have also experienced attending a church, large or small, where things just seem to be "happening." There's a certain crackle in the air, an excitement. These churches just *feel* alive, though the reasons we feel this way about such a church are not always clear, and we usually will analyze them to death trying to identify what programs or philosophies this church has put in place to achieve this.

God demonstrated through Moses that He can bring a river of water gushing from a rock in the middle of a desert.

Instead of trusting this truth, we break our backs trying to produce these rivers of life in our churches through man-made efforts. We analyze ad nauseum the characteristics of a good river, what their river beds look like, where they're found.

Knowing that most rivers are found in valleys, we will expend great effort to dig out the flat terrain around us. We dig until we think its low enough, then we dig out a nice looking river bed. Then, we go get water elsewhere and carry it back up to the start of the empty river bed we've dug. We pour it into the top of the river bed and watch it flow. We will exhaust ourselves doing this over and over again in a vain and senseless effort to make this man-made river flow.

True rivers cannot be created by man.
Their source always originates with powerful forces from within the Kingdom that are much greater than our meager abilities.

Still, it *is* possible for men to discover a small, trickling natural spring, dig it out, and then suddenly have a gushing river on their hands.

In such a case, the source to supply the river was always there, the rocks blocking its flow just had to be removed.

This means it is possible for us to locate a place where God is moving in a small way, add our own efforts, and succeed in amplifying the movement until God is moving powerfully. What *must* be noticed here though is that God was always ready to move and He always remains the source of the power and life. **Our work can be nothing more than to remove obstacles.**

So, just as it would be foolish to pick some random place in the desert to start digging and hope a river will flow, it is equally foolish to begin work in a new part of the Kingdom and expect God to move powerfully when He's given no indication He wished to do so there. If, however, we already see Him moving somewhere in a small way, or He tells us to dig in a certain place as He told Moses to strike the rock, then we can be much more certain that our efforts to clear the way for God to move will be successful.

Rain waters most of the land on earth with regularity, but before the advent of modern pump technology and electricity, it was impossible to found a large city without the presence of a decent-sized river.

In the same way, God waters His entire kingdom with spiritual rainfall, sustaining every church that acknowledges Him. But, large, influential churches, just like large cities, can only be established around large spiritual "rivers." These are bodies of believers who have purpose-fully aligned themselves next to where God is moving powerfully.

Civilizations flourish around such rivers, and the bigger the river is, the bigger the civilization can be surrounding it.

When a river dries up, the people who depended on its flow to live will find themselves suddenly migrating elsewhere to another source of water.

The same with our churches.

The spiritual "rivers" in God's Kingdom are not geographical, appearing in one town and not another. No, we experience God's rivers when we align ourselves spiritually with Him. This is what Henry Blackaby was referring to when he said to find where God is already working and join Him.[3] When we stand next to God, we will find ourselves next to the river, with plenty to drink.

When a church moves herself out of sync with God's movement, believers find themselves standing around a dried-up spiritual riverbed, and her people will quickly move on in search of life.

Just as animals can smell water from miles away, believers have a natural instinct for detecting life within a church. When it dries up, they can smell the life elsewhere and migrate on.

Rivers are beautiful.

We love to sit and stare at the moving current, whether it be a small creek or raging rapids. The view constantly changes. While there are patterns to be seen in the flow of the water, the swirls and eddies are in constant flux. This dynamism fascinates us, fixating our eyes.

God's movements of power are also beautiful. We are fascinated by them and want to sit next to them. The sound of gurgling water is a sound of life to us. We love to see God move.

And there are patterns to His movement, but He's also so dynamic it's never boring to watch.

---

[3] Henry Blackaby, *Experiencing God* (Nashville, TN: Broadman & Holman, 1998), p. 122.

If a river is large enough, it can serve not only as a source of food and water for the people, but also as a means to transport goods.

Churches could be compared to towns that grow up around a river. Churches grow up around a spiritual movement of God. Smaller movements of God are adequate to feed and meet the thirst of small churches.

But large movements of God (large rivers) can support a large enough church that "goods" can be brought into the church in addition to the normal water and fish. For example, smaller churches would have a tough time getting a national speaker like Dave Ramsey, Joyce Meyer, or Beth Moore to come and speak to their congregation. Large churches have the size, resources, and contacts to bring in all kinds of ministries and opportunities that a smaller church just doesn't have access to.

This larger size also allows more of the members to be on staff, to earn their livelihood bringing these ministries, opportunities, and teachings to their congregations. These are comparable to dockworkers importing goods from the river for the benefit of the rest of the town.

Rivers flow from many different sections of a land, and as they descend in altitude, they combine to form larger rivers. Finally, they empty into the ocean.

In the same way, the Life that God gives constantly flows from the Kingdom into the world.

Rivers deposit sediment in the ocean, and over time, they success-fully create deltas. A delta represents a small gain of territory from the ocean. This pictures God's movement within the Kingdom acting to redeem some of the world and transforming it into *new* Kingdom (land).

Comparatively, however, rivers make very little progress against the ocean as a whole. Small bits of the Kingdom are constantly being deposited in the world, but for the most part the world just covers them up. There are small progresses made in increasing the *proportionate size* of the Kingdom versus the world, but in the end the overall size of the world does not decrease.

We know this is true by confirmation in prophecy.

According to the Book of Revelation, the large majority of the population of the world does not repent and turn to Christ, but is destroyed in the events of the last days.

I do not say this to discourage missions and evangelism. On the contrary, you will find few greater advocates than I for Christians getting off their collective rear ends and doing missions with a passion. Jesus commanded us to go to the ends of the earth and make disciples. We must obey that Great Commission with a passion.

I am simply interpreting what I see imbedded in the symbolism of rivers and their interaction with the ocean. I believe Scripture confirms this interpretation. Just as the oceans will always be larger in size than the continents, so will the world always have more members than the Kingdom.

"Enter by the narrow gate; for wide is the gate and broad is the way that leads to destruction, and there are many who go in by it." (Matthew 7:13)

Lesson: *Align yourself with God's movement.*

Water Table

"And Isaac dug again the wells of water which they had dug in the days of Abraham his father..."
(Genesis 26:18a)

One of the earth's wonderful features is the water table. It's an amazing provision of God that in most of the lower lying places on the planet, a person can dig a well and, at some reasonable depth, reach this water reservoir, ensuring access to that life-giving liquid.

The depth at which this water table can be found varies from place to place. Sometimes, it lies right at the surface, which results in a natural spring. Other times, it is necessary to dig down hundreds or even several thousand feet to reach water.

The truth symbolized in this is that no matter where we find ourselves in the Kingdom, we can find the Life that God gives *if we are willing to dig deep enough.* Sometimes, it's easy to find Life, as in the case of natural springs and rivers, but sometimes, we have to really dig for it.

Digging into the soil means digging into the Kingdom. We'll discuss rocks and soil later, but they represent the truths of God and the body of Christ. If we dig into the truth of Scripture and fellowship with other believers, we will find True Life no matter where we are.

As we grow in our understanding and knowledge of Him, we find Life. We don't find Life by just being in the Kingdom. We must either move ourselves to where the water is flowing freely, or we must dig for it.

Once we've dug our well, once we've found Life (water), we don't have to dig again. The well is there. Still, *we cannot abandon our well.* Digging the well is comparable to learning how to seek God by digging into His word, but you still must go to the well every day to get water out. If you stop getting the water out, you die, even though you've dug the well.

We do have to be careful about pollutants, making sure nothing foreign falls down into it. Once we've dug into the truth of God, learning how to find Life, we must guard our minds against pollutant thoughts and philosophies that will cloud our "water" and make it undrinkable. If this happens, we must "clean" out our heart, just as we would a well.

Lesson: *Seek God and His Kingdom daily to access His living water.*

Evaporation

"As water disappears from the sea,
And a river becomes parched and dries up,
So man lies down and does not rise"
(Job 14: 11-12a)

Heat from the sun evaporates water and raises it back up to the sky again. *This symbolizes God taking back the life He gave.* To interpret this cyclical process of precipitation and evaporation as being symbolic of reincarnation would be an error. Water is symbolic of *life force*, not individual lives. The water present in the atmosphere and on the earth is not divided into separate units; it is one substance that is distributed across the earth by the sky and collected by the same. A single drop of rain cannot be followed through its cycle, for it combines with others and mixes and separates again into new drops. There is no consistent *identity* for a piece of water.

Therefore, this cycle is nothing more than symbolic of the fact that God is constantly giving and taking life. To be more accurate, He is giving and removing His power, which results in the giving and taking of life.

Especially interesting is the fact that it is the *heat* of the sun that lifts the water back up. So, is it the *love* of God that removes life from the earth? I believe this is true.

This world is in a fallen state; it is not heaven. It's full of anger, hatred, lust, greed, pride, violence, and all other kinds of selfishness. It would actually be *un*loving of God to leave us here on earth forever when He's prepared a perfect Heaven where there is no more suffering.

A loving God would remove us from this painful place once our purpose here has been fulfilled.

(Note that evaporation occurs from both oceans and land. God gives and takes life from both realms.)

Lesson: *Work to see things from God's perspective.*

Clouds

"Do you know how the clouds are balanced,
those wondrous works of Him who is perfect in knowledge?"
(Job 37:16)

C louds are the result of evaporation.
They're always found in the sky. They testify to the abundance of Life and power present in God. Clouds testify to the fact that God is the source of all Life, just as the sky is the source of all rain.

Clouds are generally white, except when preceding storms.
The whiteness of clouds symbolizes the purity of the life to be found in God.

As water evaporates, it leaves behind all the impurities it picked up while on earth. When we leave this earth, we too will finally leave behind all the impurities we picked up and be clothed in white as we reside with God.

The whiteness also testifies to the general benevolence and beauty of God's power. We love to see Him operate in creativity. It's beautiful. Knowing that God is all-powerful, and that He wields that power in love is a wonderful thing.

Dark thunderclouds also testify to God's power, but in that case they symbolize His power in coming judgment.

Clouds give the sky character.
On cloud*less* days, the sky is no less awesome, but it's difficult to perceive its dynamism. It's still immense and beautiful, but you cannot perceive its character. There's nothing to break it up, to distinguish its parts, to make it interesting to look at.

In the same way, it's the actions of God in our lives, in history, in Scripture, His movements of power that reveal His character. How and when He moves distinguishes many of His characteristics to us. Without the stories of the Old Testament and God's activity in the lives of men like Abraham, Moses, and David, much about God's nature would remain invisible. It's His power that is most interesting to us.

Rain

"Then Elijah said to Ahab, 'Go up, eat and drink;
for there is the sound of abundance of rain.'"
(1 Kings 18:41)

Water comes to us from two sources, rain and natural springs. Ground springs turn into rivers, but they do not water the greater portion of the land.

Rain is by far the greatest contributor to irrigation of the land. When deserts are created, it is not because natural springs are lacking, but the rain. Death Valley is the hottest and driest place in North America, yet there are a number of natural springs to be found there. It's the lack of rain that makes a desert.

Rain comes from the sky.

The symbolism is blatant to the natural man. Life is given from God. This was always understood in ancient cultures. Their error was worshiping the sky instead of understanding the sky was merely a symbol for their Creator, just as water is not life, but a symbol for life.

The message is this: God is the source of our life. He gives it regularly, though sometimes sparingly and sometimes in abundance, but we are completely dependent upon Him for it. We cannot force rain from the sky. Similarly, we cannot force God to give life, nor can we predict *when* He will give it.

We should wait patiently and be thankful for His gracious gift when it is given.

On rainy days, a certain melancholy sets into my heart that I never feel on sunny days. An unusual feeling to associate with the giving of life, to say the least.

I think this mild sadness we all sense on gray, dismal days may be God sharing with us how He feels about giving life back to the earth.

Just as it is His *love* (heat) for us that removes us from this earth in death (evaporation), could it be that He is saddened somewhat by births?

Would it really be a stretch to say once again that God has an opposite perspective on things than we do? Or shouldn't we expect this? His ways are not our ways.

Now, there's a difference between a sweet sadness and *depression.*

Imagine yourself in a cozy mountain cabin, sitting in front of a wide window with a clear view of a mountainside. As rivulets of rain dribble down the glass, you cup your hands around a warm coffee mug to take away the slight chill on your skin. Maybe there is even a soft song playing in the background.

Rainy days lend themselves to melancholic contemplation of the world.

When I feel this way, I don't feel depressed. I don't want to bawl my eyes out and mourn. No, the feeling is not like that at all, more of a light melancholy, a sweet kind of sadness that I actually enjoy.

So, if God is saddened as He returns life to the earth, as new babies are born, He doesn't mourn, for He's still greatly pleased with the birth, the new life that He's created, but maybe His potential joy is tempered by a sweet melancholy. A melancholy that flows from His knowledge of everything that baby will have to suffer during their short life.

Could this also be said of being born again spiritually? We know all of Heaven rejoices when a sinner comes to Christ, but we also know that everyone who truly follows Christ will suffer as they imitate Him.

He died for us, of course, so we are to take up our cross and follow. Is it too much of a stretch to think God might feel a twinge of sadness along with the joy of a person coming to Christ, knowing what they will endure during their Christian walk?

Lesson: *Contemplate the many ways in which God moves in power to produce life.*

Rainbows

*"And God said... 'I set My rainbow in the cloud, and it shall be
for the sign of the covenant between Me and the earth.'"*
(Genesis 9:12-13)

Rainbows bring to mind thoughts of Toto and the Tin Man, and Judy Garland singing in her melodic voice, "Somewhere, over the..."

If not that, then it's images of little Irish Leprechauns scampering around with their pots of gold, filling boxes with Lucky Charms cereal for all the kids of the world to eat.

Yet, rainbows really are a serious matter. The rainbow is one of the few things in Creation that God specifically said He was creating to serve as a symbolic reminder of something. Every time we see a rainbow, God wants us to remember His covenant with the earth to never again destroy it with water.

Therefore, rainbows are an awesome sight to behold.

Rainbows are created by sunlight passing through water droplets in the sky.

The drops refract the unified, white sunlight into a spectrum of different colors. Each color has a different wavelength, so it refracts at a different angle. The observer sees a beautiful, orderly band of colors: Red, orange, yellow, green, blue, indigo, and violet.

This pictures God's power (water) breaking down God's truth (sunlight), making it possible for us to perceive its different aspects (colors). Through His power, God helps us see into His truth and understand it better. This is why the rainbow is symbolic of God's covenant to never again destroy the Earth through water (God's power). In order to understand a covenant God makes, we first need to be able to understand some deeper truths about God and His power.

At first glance, God's power is simply terrifying and powerful. A random force to be feared.

How do we understand and respect a covenant, a promise, made by a God who is unpredictably mean, terrible, and even whimsical? The answer is we can't. Without understanding the truths behind God's power, why and when He wields it, we can't understand His covenant.

Through that same power, however, God opens men's eyes, revealing to them aspects of it that were not immediately visible otherwise.

For example, we see that He waits long periods of time before moving in judgment in spite of much provocation on our part. We see that such judgments often result in a breaking down, which produces growth, like the pruning of a bush, rather than a devastation that permanently destroys. These things reveal that His power is based in His merciful, compassionate, patient, and loving nature. That His power is used more for creative purposes than destructive ones. We see that His power gives life. That His power wielded in judgment is for the purpose of establishing justice, not because of some random, destructive impulse. Without a deeper understanding of the nature of God, we cannot understand His covenant.

God uses His power (water droplets) to refract the unified truth of God (sunlight), so we can perceive more detailed truths about Him (different colors), so we can remember the covenant.

The rainbow is a circular arc.
Circles are symbols of things that have no end. Rainbows truly have no beginning or end. They disappear mysteriously into the earth, or fade out of sight into the sky.

God has no beginning or end. His truth has no beginning and no end, nor does any covenant He establishes have an end. The rainbow reveals this.

The rainbow has 7 colors that we can perceive with the human eye. Seven is the number of completion and this represents the completeness of God's truth.

We perceive the rainbow's colors in order from red to violet.

This represents how *we* perceive God's covenant with us through Jesus Christ.

Red transforming into blue and violet. When we first encounter Jesus, we see Him as a man (red). After more exposure to His words and life, we see that Jesus is full of light (yellow). A little more and we realize He's the way to Life (green). Finally, we understand that He is God Almighty, in the form of a man (blue), which brings us to the conclusion that He is King over all (purple).

Now, under the right conditions, a fainter, second rainbow can be seen hovering in the clouds above the first. This rainbow will be higher in the sky, i.e. "closer" to God. It's not as easily seen and its colors are always in *reverse order*. The violet and blue colors are on top, and red is on the bottom.

This second rainbow represents God's perspective on the matter, which is fainter, harder for us to see. His perspective starts from the opposite place as ours. Violet-Blue becomes red in His view. The God-King becomes man.

Rainbows are most often seen right after rainstorms.

The truth of God's merciful, trustworthy, and gracious nature is most easily seen right *after* (not during) a time of judgment or struggle in our lives (thunderstorms and rainstorms).

Lesson: *God's complete truth is a beautiful thing. If we study His truth, we will know Him better and be more able to trust and rest in His grace, mercy, and love.*

LAND

"Or who shut in the sea with doors? ... I said, 'This far you may come, but no farther, And here your proud waves must stop!'"
(Job 38:8;11)

Land is the only place we can exist.

You can't live in the waters of the sea (no matter how much some surfers would like to). With the exception of whales and dolphins, air-breathing creatures cannot survive in the ocean. Air-breathers live on land, water-breathing organisms live in the sea.

Therefore, symbolically speaking, *those who breathe the Spirit (air) live on land*, and those who breathe the world, live in the world.

Oceans symbolize the world.

Therefore, Land represents the Kingdom.

Land is firm.

It lies steady beneath our feet. Land is able to support an unlimited number of people, animals, trees, and buildings without collapsing. It remains so stable we can build skyscrapers without them shaking under normal conditions.

That means God's Kingdom is firm. It's rock solid, capable of supporting an unlimited number of "structures" built by God's people, as long as they're architecturally sound.

Land is fertile.

Plants, shrubs, and trees sink their roots deep to extract nutrients from it. We, in turn, eat the vegetation, or we eat animals that have eaten vegetation.

Any way you cut it, the nutrients we need come directly from the soil. One way or the other, all our nourishment comes from it.

We truly are made of earth, as the Bible says. We're dirt and clay. Our bodies consist of the exact same elements as are found in the soil around us. This shouldn't surprise us, especially when we understand the process described in the preceding paragraphs, but it is eye-opening to rethink this fact when considering the symbolism God intended.

Yet, nobody I know is capable of scooping up a handful of dirt, stuffing it in their mouth, and getting the nutrition they need from it. We can't eat dirt to live. We have to eat plants, or animals that have eaten plants, to get what we need.

The Kingdom is fertile. It's the source of *all* our spiritual nourishment; it contains the spiritual "nutrients" we need to live. In fact, we are the Kingdom, and the Kingdom is us, just as our bodies are essentially dirt and dirt is our bodies. However, we cannot partake directly from the nebulous Kingdom (eating dirt), but we partake in it through fellowship with God and other believers (plants).

Land is not a uniform place.

Deserts, jungles, mountains, valleys, plains, glaciers, *et al.*, there are all kinds of varying terrains and topographies scattered across the continents.

On the other hand, the oceans are very uniform (the world is uniform). Sure, there are some interesting and colorful things to see underwater, but we're not speaking of creatures or corals that inhabit the ocean, merely the ocean itself. Most of what you see is just more and more of the same — dark blue water.

When it comes to variety, land has got the oceans beat hands down.

In the same way, God's Kingdom is not a uniform place either. It's made up of a wide variety of believers and churches from all different cultures, all over the world. In fact, you'd be hard pressed to find any two churches exactly the same in character and personality.

On the other hand, the world is pretty uniform. You can find ennui, materialism, dissatisfaction, oppression, lies, and distrust evenly distributed across all cultures.

Continents and islands do not have straight shores.

Coastlines are jagged, irregular, and unpredictable in shape. Just as there is a clear distinction between the beach and the ocean, so there is always a clear distinction between the Kingdom and the world, but, when looking at the Kingdom from a distance, you don't see clear, straight lines.

For example, one cannot say "every person in such and such denomination is a believer, and nobody in that other denomination is." That would never be true.

You *could* say that a lot of people in such and such a denomination are believers, or that such and such denomination is likely to have fewer believers than others, and this could be proven by how much a specific group of people publically aligns themselves with the clear teachings of Scripture. Churches that don't elevate the Bible as authoritative always have a higher percentage of nominal Christians and fewer true believers.

Still, even among Bible-believing churches, there are always a few in the congregation who don't sign on to the publicly stated beliefs of the group, even though they remain in the group.

The coastlines are jagged.

The ocean will never overtake the land.
In the same way, the world will never overcome God's Kingdom.

Lesson: *You can trust in the firmness of God's Kingdom. Partake in fellowship with other believers to be healthy and don't make blanket judgments about others.*

Rocks, Stones, & Soil

I freely admit that correctly identifying the symbolism behind rocks, stones, & soil initially threw me for quite a loop. My instinct was to see them all as representative of truth, i.e. the firm truth of God. The admonition of Christ to build upon a firm rock foundation seemed to bolster this interpretation.

Yet, something nagged.

That interpretation didn't quite mesh with a few of the other meanings we've already identified. If we are to correctly interpret God's message to us in nature, it *must* be a complete picture, a *coherent* picture. One that meshes seamlessly.

Also, being well aware that Jesus is the Rock of our salvation and that many times in the Old Testament, God is called our Rock, another interpretation identifying rocks as symbols for Christ, and by extension other believers in the Kingdom, seemed probable.

Jesus' parable regarding the sower of seeds appeared to support this. After all, Jesus Himself declared the soils in that parable to represent different types of people who receive God's Word (the seed).

Scientifically speaking, soil is basically rock that has been weathered down by erosion. It's the same material. Yet, then, why in the very same parable does the seed not take root in rocky soil?

Searching Scripture for references to rock and stones used in metaphorical ways revealed many interesting and clarifying things.

It turns out, the correct interpretation is a hybrid of the two theories.

Keep in mind, human *perception* of nature is an important factor in determining God's message imbedded in nature. God's witness through Creation was designed for all generations, not just this one that has special access to scientific knowledge.

To mankind, unaided by microscope or chemistry lab, there was always a marked distinction between rocks or stones and soil. Previous generations had no idea that soil was the same material as rocks. To the naked eye, they seem very distinct. So, a different interpretation for rocks and soils is not only possible, it should be expected.

Rocks (Boulders)

"The LORD lives! Blessed be my Rock!
Let God be exalted, The Rock of my salvation!"
(2 Samuel 22:47)

There is a huge boulder jutting from the side of the hill in the woods behind my childhood home. I and my friends used to take turns hanging from our finger tips, pretending we were adventurers caught in a precarious position. Then, we'd take turns saving each other's lives.

That boulder stood out as a landmark to us, something special, distinct from the rest of the terrain. We all knew where it was and we marked our paths by it.

A search of Scripture for references to "rocks" reveals that there is *not one instance* in the Bible where a rock is used in a metaphorical sense to refer to a truth. Almost every single time the word rock is used symbolically (meaning a large rock, i.e. boulder), it refers to a person, and that person is almost always God Himself. Furthermore, when the word rock is used of God, it is usually in the context of the "Rock of our Salvation," which would seem to imply more specifically the Messiah, Jesus Christ.

There are a few instances where the term rock is used to symbolize other people, usually prominent leaders such as the twelve sons of Jacob represented by the twelve rocks set in the Jordan River after Joshua led Israel across.

The one exception to rocks representing people, specifically Jesus, is possibly Matthew 16:18. *"And I also say to you that you are Peter, and on this rock I will build My church, and the gates of Hades shall not prevail against it."*

This is the only passage in the Bible that could seem to use a rock as a symbol for truth. While Catholic teachers will maintain that Jesus was saying here that he would build His church on Peter, most Bible scholars are aware that the Greek words for Peter, *petros* (meaning "little stone"), and rock, *petra* (meaning "boulder"), are completely different in meaning. Thus, Protestant scholars have interpreted this verse as the *petra* referring to the truth that Peter had just confessed, that Jesus is the Christ.

I believe it's bigger than that. The *petra* does not refer to Peter's statement, but to Christ Himself. Jesus is not building His church upon a statement of truth, but upon Himself in His fullness.

When Jesus said that the wise builder builds on a foundation of rock, He was not advising us to build our homes or our churches solely on a foundation of truth, but upon Himself. Jesus is truth, of course, but He is much more than just truth. He is the truth, the light, and the way. He is good, He is love, He is wisdom, He is faithful. We must build upon the whole person of Christ, the actual person of Christ, not just statements about Him.

Wherever boulders are found in nature, they have two primary uses for us: *foundation stones* **or** *navigational landmarks.*

Jesus serves in both functions in the Kingdom. He is to be our foundational rock for every building project. He is also our guide, the visual aid to help us find our way back to the path when we start to stray.

We haven't yet mentioned bedrock, but underneath all the soil you see outside, underneath all the layers of sedimentary rock, if you keep digging you will eventually hit bedrock. Bedrock underlies the upper, softer soils of every single region of the earth's crust. As bedrock is the solid foundation of all land, so is Jesus Christ the solid foundation of the entire Kingdom.

Jesus Christ is *the* rock.

Lesson: *Build your life on Christ.*

Stones

*"So when they continued asking Him, He raised Himself up
and said to them, "He who is without sin among you,
let him throw a stone at her first." (John 8:7)*

S tones are smaller versions of rocks — pieces of larger rocks, if
you will.

If boulders symbolize the entire person of Christ, then stones
would represent a smaller "piece" of Him. Perhaps an *aspect* of Him
would be a better description as He surely cannot be divided. That
aspect is truth.

Stones represent those hard, sturdy truths of God that we find
strewn throughout His kingdom.

We can sharpen a stone into a weapon and use it to wound or kill
somebody. Or we can use them in the construction of a building.
Historically, these are the two primary uses man has found for stones,
either to make some kind of tool or weapon, whose purpose is to grind,
crush, pound, or cut — or we use them to build.

God's truths can be used, and have been used, in the same ways.
**Some Christians take the truth of God and they misuse it to cut or
crush others**. Yet there will always be times when it *is* necessary, even
a good thing, to use God's truth as a cutting tool. After all, every day
scalpels are used in surgery for the benefit of the patient.

Still, many times when Christians take up the sharp, stone knife of
truth, they do so to attack and harm, not for the benefit of a patient in
need of surgery. Rather than initiating a healing process, as through a
surgery, when it's all said and done, the victim of their attack lies
wounded on the ground, bleeding out.

Let all Christians apply God's truth to their brethren in a careful,
loving way, for the purpose of healing, not hurting.

Stones are often used to build foundations, just as larger boulders
are. However, these foundations are very weak when compared with the

massive foundation rocks used in some of the larger building projects of antiquity. Before the advent of concrete, it was common to erect homes upon small stacks of these foundation stones.

Yet, it's impossible to build any kind of larger building using only smaller stones in a foundation. There's a strict limit to the size of the structure that is possible.

This is symbolic of building a church solely on the truth of God (stones), and not on the person of Christ (boulder).

This would mean we build our church by firmly declaring the truths of God as revealed in Scripture, but we neglect the weightier matters of love and mercy, etc.

Many churches do this, and in an interesting "coincidence," these churches are always smaller in size.

It's impossible to build a large church on cold truth alone without *all* of Christ as the foundation.

Traditionally, stones have also been used in boundary walls, such as the low stone walls one finds all over Ireland, dividing field from field, showing where one property ends and the other begins. The limits of where we may go.

Truth serves this role in the Kingdom as well. Ancient believers long ago built these walls, recorded in the pages of God's Word. Scripture has clear lines of demarcation, limits and boundaries indicating where believers should stop and go no further.

Finally, stones are used in the construction of the walls of buildings, not just foundations. For example, cathedrals.

The strongest of churches do this, building their *walls* with the truths contained in Scripture upon the person of Christ (boulder) as their foundation.

Just as the great cathedrals are awe-inspiring, yet cold in ambiance, these churches must take care to adorn the inside of their church home with warm adornments of love, lest the visitor perceive it to be sterile and frigid.

Today, many "stone" buildings are not actually stone at all, but rather steel or wood framing with large air gaps between the studs, covered over by a thin facade of decorative stone. These buildings are not much stronger in the face of a storm than a normal stick-construction home.

Today, many churches mimic this. Giving lip service to truth (decorative stone), they appear strong and firm from the outside, but inside their walls are mostly air. The reality of their weakness is shown when faced with a true storm of significance. In the aftermath, while the cathedral will still stand, the pretend stone structure will have fallen.

Lesson: *Build the structure of your life with truth, but do not mis-use truth to abuse others.*

Soil

"And the Lord God formed man of the dust of the ground..."
(Genesis 2:7)

Soil is very distinct from rocks and stones. Yet, it's also the same. To the unknowing eye, dirt looks nothing like rocks, but in reality it's of the same substance.

Broken-down soil is where most plants get their nourishment.

Soil is of the same exact material as rocks, but it has been broken down enough that plants can interact with it.

Of course, as plants pass through their life cycles, they deposit decaying vegetable matter in the soil that helps even more with fertility. Yet, since this *humus* is just recombined forms of the same elements originally present in the soil, it can be viewed as just another form of broken-down minerals/rocks.

Stones are broken down by a combination of water and heat, and sometimes with the aid of very hardy plants, and without that process, plants would have a very difficult time.

In the same way, many Christians find it difficult to take spiritual nourishment directly from the hard truths of God, and if that is all they are surrounded with, they find themselves struggling.

So, God applies His power (water) and His love (warmth or heat) and suddenly these truths which seemed so formidable are broken down and transformed into the Body of Christ, where all believers can take nourishment.

It turns out, soil is *not* just the dark granules that run through your fingers as you plant a flower.

Soil is technically three parts: mineral particles, water, and air.

Soil so compacted that the air has been squeezed out cannot support life. Roots need these mini air-gaps in order to have room to grow.

Dry soil is similarly sterile. Water must be present.

Soil represents the body of believers in the Kingdom — the Body of Christ.

We identify with Christ in our humanity (rock material). To produce fruit, however, we must be filled with the Life that flows from God (water) and the Holy Spirit (air).

Lesson: *Stay rooted in the Body of Christ.*

Types of Soil

"But others fell on good ground and yielded a crop:
some a hundredfold, some sixty, some thirty."
(Matthew 13:8)

Around the world, top soils are infinite in their variety, yet all types fall within a triangular spectrum that varies between the three extremes of *sand, silt, and clay*. Those are the points on the triangle and every soil type falls somewhere in between them, meaning it is a combination of the three.

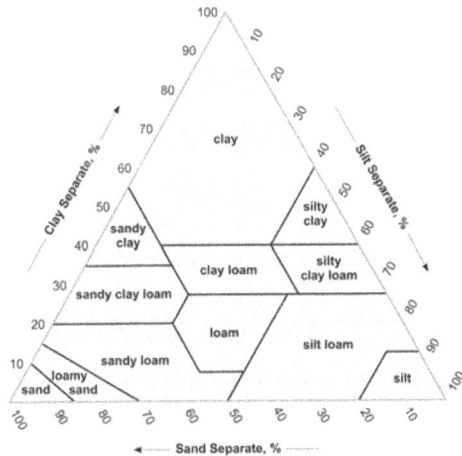

Source: USDA

The basic difference between the extremes is the size of the granules. Sand is the coarsest. Its grains are the largest, the least weathered. Clay is the most weathered. It consists of very fine mineral grains. Silt is a medium-sized granule, halfway between sand and clay.

Pure sand does not support much life because the grains are so large it does not retain water well. Sandy soil has plenty of air trapped in the gaps, but it can't hold onto water.

Clay is the opposite. Its grains are so fine, it grips water like there is no tomorrow, but it's so compacted, there's no room for air.

The ideal soil, the most fertile of every type, is called *loam*. Loam is a perfect balance between sand, silt, and clay. It retains the best amount of water in proportion to the air gaps and allows plants to prosper more than any other type of soil.

The different sized granules of soil represent believers that have experienced different levels of "weathering" in the course of their lives.

Rough believers (sand) are those who have not had enough harsh experiences in their life to be humbled yet. They receive much inspiration from the Holy Spirit (large air gaps), but they cannot hold onto God's power (water) because they have no need for it. Everything is fine.

Broken-down believers (clay) are the opposite. These believers have been so weathered, so humbled by the harshness of their life that they hold fast to God's power (water), desperately aware He is their only hope for overcoming. Yet, because they have been so broken, receiving inspiration from the Holy Spirit (air), stepping out in faith, becomes very difficult for them.

Believers in the sandy or clay states are not bad, it's just their current condition is not the most fertile, though producing some fruit will still be possible.

The most fertile believers will be like loamy soil. They will have been weathered by life enough to depend on God's power, but no so much they feel broken and uninspired.

Lesson: *Culture relationships with believers who have been weathered by life, but are still inspired by the Spirit and His joy.*

Erosion

"But as a mountain falls and crumbles away, And as a rock
is moved from its place; As water wears away stones,
And as torrents wash away the soil of the earth;
So You destroy the hope of man." (Job 14:18-19)

Imagine a Christian driving down the road, on top of the world, happy that his life seems to be running smoothly. Work's going well, his family is at peace, success seems to be on the horizon. Maybe a little bit of cockiness is creeping into his spirit right before he hears a strange clanking under the hood.

He pulls to the side of the road in a cloud of steam. The tow truck says they'll be there in forty minutes, but four hours and five phone calls later, they still haven't arrived.

He misses a very important ministry meeting, embarrassing himself and his church, and now he's going to miss a deadline on something he promised to have done by the end of the day. The day finishes, and he is frustrated, but also humbled.

He is now more "consumable" by the average man. Coarse, arrogant believers are less able to connect with others, less able to retain God's power in their life. They are the sandy soil.

This process is water erosion.

As water pours through a soil, it pounds the particles against each other, breaking them down and rounding their edges. This type of erosion is symbolic of the way believers are bumped against each other under the pressures of life (water). The process results in a general humbling of the believers involved, and a softening of their sharp "edges."

Wind erosion is similar, but instead of believers being humbled and softened through the course of their daily lives, this erosion occurs during movements of the Holy Spirit. As the spirit moves, believers are often uprooted and blown into one another. The result is the same as water erosion, a humbled and softened spirit.

This time, imagine a large church moving along the path the pastor and his staff perceive as the will of God for their body. Suddenly, the Spirit of God begins blowing in a new way, showing the church God has something different in mind. The result is a jostling about of believers. Staff members change departments or roles, or they leave. Others are hired, leaving behind Christians elsewhere who didn't want them to go, and the staff into which they're entering is not ready for their arrival. Amidst all the turmoil, the members of the congregation are similarly moving about, some leaving the church for another, some coming into the church for the first time, others simply finding their new place in the new plan. In most cases, this "wind erosion" of believers causes a humbling of the spirit just like water erosion.

Plant erosion is when a plant absorbs minerals and nutrients from a granule, thus reducing the granule's overall size. The plant uses these nutrients for its benefit, but eventually dies, decomposes and the nutrients are returned to the soil, but more eroded than before.

This kind of erosion occurs as believers serve one another. As one believer serves another, loving them in Christ, the believer being served is able to partake of the spiritual fruit being produced by the other. As believers voluntarily serve others, they give of themselves and are reduced in the size of their spirit, not meaning that they are reduced in strength or potency, on the contrary. They are reduced by becoming more humble through their service, which allows them to become more "consumable" to more "plants" in the Kingdom.

Whatever the kind, erosion is symbolic of the humbling processes believers regularly go through, which is not normally pleasant at the time, but nevertheless results in the softening of their hearts. It is a good process.

Lastly, it has been proven that increasing the ambient temperature in an environment by 20 degrees Fahrenheit, increases the rate as which rocks and soil weather by 2 to 3 times.

This would indicate that when believers can better perceive God's love for them (warmth) in the midst of the bumping and jostling they're experiencing, they are humbled faster than when they feel like God's mistreating them.

Lesson: *Remembering God's love will soften you faster in the erosion process.*

The Moon

"Now a great sign appeared in heaven:
a woman clothed with the sun, with the moon under her feet,
and on her head a garland of twelve stars."
(Revelation 12:1)

The moon represents God's people.

God's people means just that: People who belong to God.

Formerly, that was primarily Israel. Now, it's the Church (Gentiles and Jews), and in the end times it will probably be Israel again. Whatever your views of the Israel-Church relationship, please suspend them during your reading of this book. The symbols built into the moon apply to God's people throughout the ages. For simplicity's sake, I will refer to God's people as the Church from here on out.

The moon illuminates the world at night.

Yet, on certain mornings or evenings, the moon may remain visible while the sun is up. At those times, the moon's light is hardly noticeable.

Just so, when Jesus (represented by the sun), is *not* present with us (night), it is the Church that shines truth (light) into the world. Once Jesus returns, however, the Church will pale in comparison to the extraordinary levels of truth and light emanating directly from Him. At that time, the church will be barely noticeable next to Him. When He is present (daytime), He is the overwhelming source of light.

Just as God's purpose for creating the moon was to provide
light at night, so His purpose in creating the Church
was to illuminate the world while Jesus is absent.

The moon does not create its own light.

It merely reflects the light shone onto it by the sun. In the same way, the Church is truly not a *source* of truth or goodness, it can only *reflect* the truth and goodness shone onto it by Jesus.

Obviously, the moon is "in" the sky, just as the sun is in the sky. Therefore, just as Jesus abides in the Father, so the Church abides in the Father. Held by Him, if you will.

The moon is made of the perfect material to reflect white light upon the earth.

There are a plethora of other materials God could have used to make the moon that would have bathed the earth in reflected red, blue, green, or other color light. But, he didn't. He chose a material that would reflect white.

Similarly, God has also made the Church of the perfect material to shine the complete and full "white" light of truth and goodness into the world, not just one aspect of God's truth (a color).

When the moon is in its fullest phase, the moonlight cast upon the earth has a bluish appearance to the naked eye.

Remember, blue is the color of the sky and the color associated with God in Scripture.

So, when the church is *fully* shining the light of Christ into the world, when the church is in its fullest phase, it is then the world can catch a glimpse of God in the church and not just the normal reflection of truth and goodness.

The moon passes through various phases each month.

These phases begin with a New Moon, which is a completely darkened moon. Next, it grows into a crescent moon. Then follows a half moon, a three-quarters moon, and finally a full moon. It passes through these phases repeatedly, every month.

The Church has also passed through cyclical phases like these over the centuries. There are times when the Church is in its "full" phase, when God's people are fully committed to Him and they reflect His light, truth, and goodness to the world in full, so much so, the people can feel they're seeing a little bit of God Himself in them.

Then, lamentably, there have been times when the church seemed so dark that not a trace of God's truth or goodness could be seen, and those "new moon" phases of church history are the darkest of times.

There's also been every phase in between when the Church was in the process of rising up to its fullness, or waning into darkness.

Israel passed through these same phases over and over just as the church has. (The Book of Judges comes to mind.)

We can take comfort in two aspects of this cycle. First, the lunar phases continually repeat. They always have and always will.

Also, Jesus promised the gates of Hell would never prevail against His Church. So, even when the Church appears to be waning, when it seems dark and disappointing, we can take comfort in the fact that God will not let His Church remain in such a state. He will raise it back to its fullness once again.

The Church is not static, it is always either increasing in holiness, or it is waning.

The second comforting aspect of this cycle is the knowledge that while the moon appears to us to have differing levels of light during these phases, the truth of the matter is that a *full half of the moon is always illuminated.* It's only the visibility of the illuminated side of the moon *to us* that increases or decreases.

In my opinion, this means God *always* has people in the Body of Christ who reflect His truth and goodness fully. When those people are visible to the world, the Church appears bright indeed. During the times when the Church has seemed dark, there were still those faithful "reflectors," the faithful remnant, they were just not generally visible to the public at large. They may have been doing a good job of reflecting the light — they just weren't seen.

No matter how dark the church may seem, there is a faithful remnant.

The moon was the timepiece of ancient man.

We watch the moon through its phases to mark the passage of time. One full lunar cycle was the ancient definition of the length of a month.

Similarly, God's people have been used by God as a sign for the rest of the world to mark time, to know whether the end was approaching, or whether God was doing something new. This is especially true for Israel, but has been true for the church as well.

Passover begins with a full moon.

Passover is a feast designed by God to symbolically foreshadow Christ's sacrificial death on the cross for us. This full moon would imply that right at the time of His death and resurrection, God's people were in their fullness, prepared to reflect the light of Jesus after His ascension. A reading of the Book of Acts confirms just how powerfully Christian Jews and others reflected Christ into the world in the years immediately following His ascension.

The moon completes one rotation in relation to the sun every time it revolves around the Earth, which means *we* always see the exact same side of the moon.

Thus, there is a far side of the moon nobody ever sees. We tend to think of the far side of the moon as always being dark, but this is not so. The far side of the moon is not the same thing as the dark side. The illumination on the far side varies inversely with how much light is on our side. When we have a new moon, there is a fully lit moon on the other side we can't see.

The interpretation is that there is a portion of God's people who are always seen, and a portion who are not, and the level of faithfulness in both varies. It seems natural to identify the near side of the moon as the leaders among God's people. Leaders are the *face* of God's people, the face of the moon. They *are* the part of God's people that always remains visible. Pastors, priests, prophets, scribes, and teachers.

The far side of the moon would then represent lay people, regular members of the congregation. Their light is not as easily seen in the world as a whole, but they are part of God's people and do shine just as much light.

I admit the previous paragraphs may be stretching, but it does seem the best interpretation. Perhaps it symbolizes the cycle of revival that goes on in the Church.

At times, when we lack faithful laymen, God raises up strong leaders to preach to the world. As the Word goes out from these leaders, disciples are made and the average lay Christian grows in their faithfulness. As the leaders are successful in their discipleship efforts, they tend to relax, no longer feeling the heat of the battle. It is ironic that as the lay people increase in faithfulness due to the hard work of the leaders, the leaders become more susceptible to a fall with the scent of success in their nostrils.

Countless times, a congregation full of faithful followers has suddenly been faced with a great fall in their leadership. Then, out of this same congregation of dedicated followers, new faithful leaders will step forward, but usually after significant time has passed and the faithfulness of the congregation begins to wane once again into complacency. The new leaders rise up to lead their people back into faithfulness again.

God perfectly designed the size of the moon.

The moon is large enough that its light successfully brightens the night. Any smaller and its light would be too insignificant to make much of a difference. If it were any larger, the light would begin to rival the sun's, and we'd start to lose the stark difference between night and day.

Just so, the Church is always the perfect size to accomplish God's purposes. God wants the church to illuminate the night, but He never wants it to rival the glory of His Son.

Let us turn to solar eclipses. It may seem odd to bring up solar eclipses in the middle of our discussion of the moon, but *the moon* is what moves in front of the sun to block its light during an eclipse.

We'll note the dark side of the moon is what we see during an eclipse (not the far side, but the dark side), and the eclipse quickly passes.

"Now from the sixth hour until the ninth hour there was darkness over all the land. And about the ninth hour Jesus cried out with a loud voice, saying, 'Eli, Eli, lama sabachthani?' that is, 'My God, My God, why have You forsaken Me?'" (Matthew 27:45 -46)

The solar eclipse represents the death of Jesus.

Though it's probable that particular solar eclipse was actually a large asteroid blocking the sun's light instead of the moon as would normally happen, the miraculous event was still a solar eclipse and all solar eclipses since that time have been caused by the moon, reminding us of what happened in that crucial moment in history.

Two thousand years ago, Jesus was eclipsed from the sight of the earth, for a short time, by the religious leaders of His day, who by any earthly definition were supposed to be part of God's people, yet they were obviously darkened ones, not reflecting God's light. These darkened leaders were the dark side of the moon we see during an eclipse, the face of God's people.

Just as a solar eclipse passes quickly, so did Jesus' death last but for three days before He rose from the dead. One day for each hour of eclipse when He died.

Notice also that a solar eclipse can only happen during the day. Jesus' death occurred between His ministry and His resurrection, both periods of time when He was present with us, i.e. daytime.

During a solar eclipse, the sun's corona becomes visible.

This corona is not visible at other times. The word "corona" means *crown* and it even looks like a golden crown, a flaming halo around the sun.

Jesus' crown, His worthiness to be our King, becomes visible to us through His submission to the cross.

One last interesting fact: It was a solar eclipse that allowed scientists to finally verify a prediction of Einstein's General Theory of Relativity. The prediction was that gravity bends light, and in 1919, through observing a solar eclipse, astrophysicist Arthur Eddington was able to verify that prediction.

The principle rings true symbolically. Our sinful nature (gravity) does bend truth and goodness (light). This was never more visible than when we put Jesus to death. We took God's Son and declared Him a blasphemer punishable by death.

Now, lunar eclipses are very different animals from solar eclipses. A solar eclipse occurs when the moon gets between the sun and the Earth, **but a lunar eclipse occurs when Earth gets between the sun and the moon**. When this happens, and a lunar eclipse is full, the moon takes on a deep reddish glow.

Numerous prophetic passages in the Bible predict moments when the moon will turn to "blood." These prophecies more than likely refer to an occurrence of a lunar eclipse.

It pictures the world (earth) eclipsing the Church (moon), turning it to blood. *This can only represent a time of martyrdom.* It's no accident, then, that the biblical prophecies referring to a red moon are associated with the Day of the Lord, which is a time of great judgment for the world. In that day, the bloody moon will stand as a sign and a witness to the world for what it has done to God's people.

The moon stabilizes the earth's rotation.

If there were no moon, our planet would wobble severely, which would result in all kinds of chaos. The church similarly acts as a stabilizing force on the world, preserving it from chaos. (*"Ye are the salt of the earth..."*)

Any discussion of the moon's impact on earth wouldn't be complete without discussing ocean tides. The oceans represent the world, therefore, tidal effects on the ocean by the moon represent the way in which the Church affects the world.

Tides are created by the moon's gravity.

Wherever the moon is, the ocean "bulges" up toward it, attracted by its gravity. This is what is known as high tide.

But if this is true, then why are there always two high tides per day if the moon only passes over one time every twenty-four hours. The scientific explanation is that as the ocean is "bulging up" towards the moon on one side of the earth, the ocean on the opposite side of the planet is experiencing the least amount of the moon's gravity. The earth at that point is actually pulled more by the moon's gravity than the ocean water covering it and so the ocean seems to rise relative to the earth, but the earth has actually been slightly pulled away.

The ocean in between is lowered as water is drawn toward one "bulge" and left behind by the other, and these are the areas of low tide.

So, what does this mean? It means the Church has a tremendous impact on the world. On one hand, it attracts a significant portion of the world to it through its mere presence (high tide), and on the other, an equal portion of the world is constantly rushing away from it (opposite high tide), with neutral portions in between (low tides). The only difference between whether the world is attracted or repulsed is *its proximity to the Church*. I would not interpret this to be geographical proximity, but spiritual proximity.

Non-believers who are spiritually closer to believers will be naturally attracted to the church. Some of those who warm the benches in our churches are these kinds of non-believers. They are those lukewarm persons who sit in a church for decades thinking they're part of the Kingdom while they've never truly accepted Christ as their Lord and Savior. Yet, their hearts are near the hearts of believers, so they feel comfortable. They have just never humbled themselves before God, confessing their sin, abandoning any hope of earning Heaven through works, and asking for forgiveness through Christ.

Militant atheists and worldly leisure-suit Larry types are repulsed by the church. Their hearts are spiritually very far from the heart of the average believer, and they want nothing to do with the church. They will run away as fast as they can.

Tidal currents cleanse shorelines.

They regularly scour out shipping channels, keeping them useable by boats.

In the same way, the Church's influence on the world causes the world (ocean water, waves) to interact at a higher level with God's kingdom (Land). This interaction cleanses the "driftwood" and "garbage" from the shorelines of the Kingdom. The world's waves repeatedly conduct mini-assaults on the Kingdom, cleansing the Kingdom of its waste products and lukewarm believers. A nominal or lukewarm believer has no strength to withstand even a tiny assault by the world. They are easily washed away.

These assaults on the Kingdom are at their highest levels when God's people (moon) are exerting their fullest influence or their least (high tides). Only when the Church is neither hot nor cold but instead lukewarm does the world recede its attacks (low tide).

Some places near the coast are too shallow for a boat to cross during low tide, but it may be able to navigate perfectly well during high tide.

Sailors are inhabitants of the Land who are traveling the seas in boats. They represent Kingdom missionaries going out into the world. Just as boats can get around easier near shore during high tide, the ability of these missionaries to navigate is greatly increased when the Church exerts its full influence. We know this is true. When the Church is fully engaged, prayers are offered up, people go, money flows, and missionaries find their work facilitated. When this is not happening, missionaries find the work more difficult.

Lastly, ancient pagan religions of the Middle East worshipped the moon-goddess. To them, she was the *mother* of the sun god. Worshiping *either* is idol worship and sin, but it's especially telling they would flip the relationship in such way, declaring the moon a parent of the sun, when in the physical context of the universe and even our human experience, the sun is obviously so much more powerful.

Why was this done? *Why would pagan religions limit the more powerful sun to be a child of the moon?*

Because pagan religions have always been about controlling God instead of submitting to Him. Their rituals are always designed to exact a desired response from their god. Need rain for your fields? The sinful nature of man prefers to be able to do some fertility rite to secure what he needs rather than having to depend on transcendent God for provision and wait upon His mercy, which they do not trust. People want to be in control.

The sun *is* a very powerful entity when compared with the moon. In the mind of ancient man, it seemed much more plausible that he would be able to influence or control the moon than he would the sun.

So, in their delusion, to better control the spirit world, these pagan minds exalted the moon as being in authority over the sun. Then, instead of trying to control a powerful entity through their little ceremonies and rituals, they believed they could control a lesser one which would then in turn control the more powerful one. Beliefs born of a combination of spiritual insecurity, a need to control, and a lack of faith.

The symbolism here is worshiping people (moon) before God (sun).

Like pagans, secular liberals today say the Church created Jesus, rather than the truth, which is that Jesus birthed the Church.

Another current parallel is the worship by some of the Virgin Mary and the preeminence given to her in prayer instead of Christ. When those who practice this are asked to explain why, the response is usually something along the lines of "A son will always listen to his mother." They fear the power of Jesus, so instead of praying directly to Him, they pray instead to his "mother." They feel they will have more influence with her, and she in turn will influence Him. Just like the ancient pagans.

In ancient Babylon, one of the common names for the pagan moon goddess was *Sin.* Coincidence?

Lesson: *Let us never worship any created thing, but simply recognize them for the blessings and symbols that they are, blessings and symbols given by God Almighty.*

Stars

"Then He brought him outside and said, 'Look now toward heaven,
and count the stars if you are able to number them.'
And He said to him, 'So shall your descendants be.'"
(Genesis 15:5)

Sparkling, glittering stars twinkling like diamonds against a backdrop of velvety, black night, their tiny lights filling the soul with a sense of eternal peace.

During a darkened new moon, drive far out into the country, away from the artificial light produced by the world, and gaze up into space. The sight is beautiful to behold. The ethereal glow of the Milky Way belt, the crystal clarity of these pin-prick sized lights, and the sheer quantity of their number create an awe-inspiring view.

Stars are made of the same material as our sun, but they're so far away, they're not capable of warming and lighting the earth anywhere near the level our sun does. In spite of the fact millions of stars are potentially visible to the naked eye, starlight has almost no impact on the earth when compared with illumination from the sun, or even the moon.

In Genesis 15:5, God promised Abraham that his descendants would be greater in number than the stars of heaven.

Stars are symbols for individual believers.

In the same way that stars and our sun are made of similar materials, so are believers constantly being conformed to the image of Christ. Believers have also been indwelled with the fiery power of the Holy Spirit, just like Jesus.

Like the stars compared with the sun, the impact of an individual believer on the world is virtually non-existent, yet the impact of Christ is so great, God Himself has to shield the world from His full power.

Stars represent believers as individuals and the moon represents believers corporately. When believers work together as one body, and when they are reflecting the light of Jesus well, they can, unlike individual stars, successfully light the world to some degree. But even then, this "moonlight" is not much when compared to the light Jesus shines throughout the earth when He is present Himself.

Individually, believers can be beautiful, like stars, but they have no power on the earth by themselves.

The multitude of stars spread across the night sky reveals the beauty and vastness of the heavens, the universe.

In the same way, the multitude of believers spread across history testifies to the beauty of God, His immense and infinite size, and the vastness of His creativity and plan.

A super majority of stars (85% or more) are classified as Red Dwarfs.

Red Dwarfs on average have only 40% of the mass and emit only 10% of the light and energy of our sun. So, even up close, most stars would appear pitifully weak and small if compared side by side with our own powerful sun.

Red Dwarfs emit a primarily red-colored light. Here we would remember that red is the color of man. The fact that almost all stars are red, small, and weak when compared to our sun reaffirms symbolically the large difference between Christ and His followers even up close.

There are other types of stars, some that look closer to our sun in size, and some that are called giants. I would note that the "giants" are considered to be dying and also do not give off as much light and energy as our sun in spite of their enormous size. Many giants also emit red light.

That said, I do not believe that God intended every single star in the universe to be interpreted symbolically. There are 200 billion billion of them after all, and most of those cannot be seen with the naked eye. I believe God's primary intent was the symbolism already described which would have been discernible to ancient man without the aid of powerful telescopes and other tools. The additional symbolism that becomes visible with increasing scientific knowledge is just gravy.

By far, the number one reason for such a variety in the kinds and types of stars that scientists can observe is to give witness to the incredible creativity and greatness of God. He has left astrophysicists without excuse.

Stars are "in" the sky.

In the same way, true believers abide in God.

Stars are distant.

When a believer dies, they are no longer near to us, but have become unreachable, just as a star is unreachable. In contrast, Jesus (represented by the sun) always remains near, even at "night" when we cannot see Him.

This is a hint that stars may more specifically represent believers who have passed on and received glorified bodies, as they are distant and in the heavens.

Stars twinkle.

Their light wavers, blinks on and off, at least with respect to our eyes.

This can be interpreted in two ways. First, it could be a symbol of how all believers struggle with sin and obedience, and as their faithfulness wavers or oscillates, their ability to shine the light of Jesus wavers or "twinkles" as well. Meanwhile, the sun blazes away constantly, with no faltering.

The second possible interpretation comes from a proper scientific understanding of why stars twinkle. Stars "twinkle" because they are so far away their light reaches us as a single point of light, even through powerful telescopes. As our atmosphere slightly bends the light waves, the receptors in our eyes fail to detect stars' light momentarily since their brightness is so slight.

This could be interpreted by noting that we are as distant from the inner spiritual lives of our fellow believers as we are from those stars. Only God understands and knows the hearts and minds of other believers. We cannot. So, as other believers pass through spiritual struggles that may cause their light to appear to cease for a time "in our eyes," perhaps their light remains constant in God's.

I think both interpretations are probably accurate.

Stars are not evenly distributed across the sky.

They are clustered together in galaxies and other, smaller groups of stars. In a similar way, God has not evenly distributed His children in the earth, or throughout history. Both geographically and through time, God has clustered His people.

Some portions of history have had a famine of believers, and others have been chock full. The contrast in the number of believers between different nations and periods of time can be shocking.

Why has He done it this way? Why *doesn't* He evenly distribute believers around the world, and in all ages and eras upon the earth?

The answer lies in the skies.

If the stars in the nighttime sky were evenly distributed, north and south, east and west, what would it look like?

It would be a grid, made up of points of light. While this light grid might be of momentary interest just because of its orderliness, it would not be beautiful. In fact, it would probably bore you after just a few minutes.

God is painting a beautiful picture on the canvas of time, *and you can't paint a beautiful picture using straight lines.*

Men have used stars for thousands of years to orient themselves while on land and to navigate by ship at night.

At night, wherever men found themselves lost, they only had to look to the stars to determine their position and find their way home again.

As we travel through life, what is one of the most effective means we have of ensuring we don't get off course as believers? Well...we look to other believers as examples.

Other believers serve as guiding beacons as we travel, whether we're studying the lives of Christians who've gone before or following the stellar example of our godly parents.

We model our behavior based on the words and deeds of others. An act of faith seen in the life of a saint is a beacon calling us to imitation — a bad decision serves an omen of warning.

We even use the lives, actions, and words of our current brothers and sisters in Christ to correct ourselves. This is a large reason why the Book of Hebrews exhorts us to never abstain from the fellowship of believers. We use the examples we see in the lives of other believers as guideposts, landmarks, and indicators as to which way we should go, how we should behave.

What discussion of the stars would be complete without mentioning astrology? Astrology, of course, encompasses horoscopes and the zodiac and believes that the locations of celestial bodies (planets and stars) affect and influence events here on earth. It is obvious to most rational-minded people that astrology is a false religion, a cult even, with no basis in reality.

Some, however, would say their trust in horoscopes is a matter of faith. These people would not expect their belief to be validated through science. To any reader who feels astrology may have some truth to it, I would say this: For your belief to be true, you must not contradict what God says. If we disagree with God, what we say is false.

As we've seen throughout this book, God has revealed Himself to us in two ways, General Revelation (which is Creation) and Specific Revelation (His Word).

As far as General Revelation is concerned, astrology is in violation of the symbolism God incorporated into creation, for to believe that stars influence the world is to symbolically say that individual men and women have more influence over this world than God. A faith in horoscopes is not only a symbol of worshiping men instead of God, but it is an indicator that in reality you probably place a lot more faith in people than in God Almighty. Astrology is the equivalent of worshiping the saints instead of Jesus.

Of course, God did not leave it up to us to interpret the symbols in creation correctly to discover His displeasure with astrology. In His Word (Specific Revelation), God clearly condemns it. Deuteronomy

4:19 and 18:10-12, among other passages, demonstrate how much God hates astrology and horoscopes. They are not a game to Him.

Lesson: *May we view the stars, not in false worship or some futile attempt to manipulate God, but in the way they were intended, as a wonderful testimony to the greatness of our Creator.*

Question: What can we infer from the fact that stars are dimmed by city lights?

REVIEW	
Sky	= God the Father
Sun	= God the Son/Jesus Christ
Wind	= God the Spirit/Holy Spirit
Oxygen	= The Holy Spirit
Light	= Truth
Darkness	= Lies
Heat	= Love
Gravity	= Sinful Nature
Carbon	= Humanity
Oceans	= The World
Land	= God's Kingdom
Fresh Water	= God's Power
Rain	= God's power that gives life
Rivers	= God's power moving through the Kingdom
Water Table	= God's power lying within the Kingdom
Clouds	= God's power visible within Himself
Boulders	= Jesus Christ
Stones	= Truths
Soil	= Body of Christ
The Moon	= The Church
Stars	= The Saints (Believers who have passed on before us)

TREES & PLANTS:

Believers
In The Kingdom

TREES

"Let the field be joyful, and all that is in it.
Then all the trees of the woods will rejoice before the Lord."
(Psalm 96:12)

"And he looked up and said, "I see men like trees, walking."
(Mark 8:24)

I f you could be a tree, any kind of tree, what kind would you be? Barbara Walters is famous for asking that question in interviews, though she really only asked it one time, and that was in response to Katherine Hepburn saying that she wanted to be a tree.

But the question remains an interesting one. There is such a variety of trees in the world, and they all seem to have their own personality. The oak with its thick, strong trunk and hard wood. The willow weeping gently by the side of a creek. A majestic cedar towering high over the rest of the forest.

Trees are the fruit of the Kingdom. They take root in the land and receive nourishment from it. **Trees represent individual believers, faithful followers of Christ, rooted in the Body of Christ (soil).**

There are many places in Scripture where trees are used as symbols for people (I have referenced a number of these verses at the end of this section). They can represent an individual believer, or even God's people as a whole. (i.e. fig trees, olive trees, in various prophetic dreams and visions, etc.)

Trees thrive on sunlight.

In a process called photosynthesis, their roots extract water from the earth and then they combine that water with the sunlight to produce energy.

Believers not only thrive on the truth and goodness (light) that Jesus (the sun) provides — *they need it.* If a believer doesn't get enough truth, they begin to wither spiritually, just like a tree whose leaves start to brown.

The lack of sunlight is comparable to neglecting God's Word.

Or if a believer is not tapped into water, the life that God gives through the Kingdom (earth), then they also begin to wilt and "turn brown."

Finally, a believer who does not stay in fellowship with other believers by spending time with them is like a tree that's pulled its roots out of the soil. Tapping into the Life of God through fellowship is equivalent to sinking one's roots into the soil in search of water.

Trees also absorb water through their leaves from the air. This is equivalent to receiving Life, or God's power, through prayer.

A lack of water is comparable to neglecting fellowship with God (through prayer), or God withholding His power from the life of a believer.

"So his heart and the heart of his people were moved as the trees of the woods are moved with the wind." (Isaiah 7:2b)

Wind moves trees.

Leaves flutter, branches sway, and sometimes, when the wind is strong enough, even the trunks will rock back and forth. In fact, it's really the movement of trees that primarily reveals the presence of wind when we're not standing in it, feeling its brush on our skin.

In the same way, the Holy Spirit moves believers, sometimes just a little, sometimes a lot.

It is primarily through the movements and actions of other believers that we know the Holy Spirit is present and moving. At least, when He's not moving within *us*.

The waving of branches in the wind resembles the act of worship on the part of a believer. This metaphor is fortified by Isaiah 55:12, which declares that the trees will "clap their hands" in worship of the Messiah.

Naturally speaking, at what do the trees wave their branches when moved by the wind?

The sky.

It is an image of believers being moved by the Spirit to worship the Father.

Trees reproduce according to their own kind, and this is the *only* way trees can reproduce.

An oak tree cannot spawn a weeping willow, and a weeping willow cannot seed a pine tree. Genesis goes out of its way to confirm this in its first chapter (Genesis 1:12).

Similarly, in disciple-making, a believer will produce a disciple after his or her "own kind." A believer is not capable of producing a disciple that is anything different than themselves. Every disciple bears their discipler's stamp.

If you want to make obedient disciples, you must be obedient yourself. If you want passionate, generous disciples, you must first be passionate and generous.

More examples of Scripture using trees as symbols:

"And even now the ax is laid to the root of the trees.
Therefore every tree which does not bear good fruit is cut down
and thrown into the fire." (Matthew 3:10)

"To console those who mourn in Zion, To give them beauty for ashes,
The oil of joy for mourning, The garment of praise for the spirit of
heaviness; That they may be called trees of righteousness" (Isaiah 61:3)

"And all the trees of the field shall know that I, the Lord, have brought
down the high tree and exalted the low tree, dried up the green tree and
made the dry tree flourish; I, the Lord, have spoken and have done it."
(Ezekiel 17:24)

"Then the trees of the field shall yield their fruit, and the earth shall
yield her increase. They shall be safe in their land; and they shall know
that I am the LORD, when I have broken the bands of their yoke and
delivered them from the hand of those who enslaved them."
(Ezekiel 34:27)

"Then I answered and said to him, "What are these two olive trees — at the right of the lampstand and at its left?...So he said, "These are the two anointed ones, who stand beside the Lord of the whole earth."
(Zechariah 4:11-14)

"And I will give power to my two witnesses, and they will prophesy one thousand two hundred and sixty days, clothed in sackcloth. These are the two olive trees and the two lampstands standing before the God of the earth." (Revelation 11:3-4)

"Listen to me, you men of Shechem, That God may listen to you!

The trees once went forth to anoint a king over them.
And they said to the olive tree, 'Reign over us!'
But the olive tree said to them, 'Should I cease giving my oil,
With which they honor God and men, And go to sway over trees?'

Then the trees said to the fig tree, 'You come and reign over us!'
But the fig tree said to them, 'Should I cease my sweetness and my good fruit, And go to sway over trees?'

Then the trees said to the vine, 'You come and reign over us!'
But the vine said to them, 'Should I cease my new wine,
Which cheers both God and men, And go to sway over trees?'

Then all the trees said to the bramble, 'You come and reign over us!'
And the bramble said to the trees, 'If in truth you anoint me as king over you, Then come and take shelter in my shade; But if not, let fire come out of the bramble and devour the cedars of Lebanon!'"
(Judges 9:7b-15)

Photosynthesis

"It is the Spirit who gives life; the flesh profits nothing.
The words that I speak to you are spirit, and they are life."
(John 6:63)

D o you remember your high school biology teacher droning on and on about photosynthesis? Were you bored to tears? I bet when you saw the title of this section you might have even groaned inwardly in anticipated apathy.

Yet, what if we renamed it *energy*-synthesis? Still kind of boring with that "synthesis" part, huh? Okay, how about *Get Energized!*

Photosynthesis is the process plants use to create energy, and if we realize trees are symbols for believers, then that means photosynthesis describes the way you as a believer get spiritual energy.

Hopefully, most of those reading this remember the basics from school, but I'll refresh you.

During photosynthesis, plants absorb sunlight, water, and carbon dioxide from the air. Within the plant, these three things recombine to form glucose, water, and oxygen.

Trees breathe it in, but carbon dioxide is a waste product that we humans breathe out. We inhale the pure Spirit of God (O_2) and combine it with human pollutants (carbon) in our lungs. Carbon dioxide (CO_2) is the result and it's the perfect symbol for the spirit we humans put out into the world.

Call it a form of godliness that falls short, an altered version of truth, or some other description of what is most properly termed the "Human Spirit," but it remains obvious that we take what God gives us and mess it up with ourselves, polluting the world with what we exhale. This respiration process is representative of what natural man does with what he receives from God.

CO_2 is not a breathable gas for humans or animals. It's not necessarily poisonous, but it will suffocate living creatures or extinguish a fire.

Trees perform the opposite respiration process. They take in carbon dioxide and put out oxygen. Trees (believers) receive this carbon dioxide, this waste product that men put into the world, and within them, the oxygen is freed back up through a reaction with sunlight and water.

In other words, believers (trees) breathe in the human spirit (CO_2) polluting the world and, within them, God's truth (sunlight) and the life He gives (water) redeem this human spirit, stripping off the human element (carbon), and the believer exhales back out God's Spirit into the world. This "believer respiration" decontaminates the world.

Trees keep the earth's air breathable.

Without trees, carbon dioxide would continually build up in the atmosphere until everyone suffocated.

In the same way, without believers, the world would quickly begin to suffocate under the oppression of the human spirit (CO_2). Believers keep the world clean of spiritual impurities, falsehoods, etc. Without their presence, non-believers would not survive long.

Let's highlight something here: *Trees don't consciously perform this service*. It's a natural, automatic process that God built into them.

Believers also don't *choose* to redeem or filter out impurity from the world. It is an automatic process that happens within them as they are tapped into God's truth, love, and life. Believers purify the world through their mere presence, not by their skill or decision, so they cannot take credit for this blessing any more than a tree can take credit for giving us oxygen to breathe.

God is the only one deserving of credit in both cases.

There are three ways for a tree to die.

First, if you keep a tree in the dark, photosynthesis *immediately* ceases — and if you keep it there long enough, it will die.

Second, trees can survive in very cold climates and even withstand long, snowy winters, but if the ice and snow never melt, they will eventually die.

Third, if you cut a tree off from water, photosynthesis will stop, not quite as immediately as in the case of zero light, but it will cease nevertheless. After an extended drought, the tree will also die.

Of the three scenarios, depriving a tree of light will kill it the fastest, a lack of water second. They can survive the longest without warmth.

So, a believer will quickly wilt and perish without access to God's truth (sunlight).

If they have the truth, but don't experience the life that God gives His children (water), they'll wilt under the scorching power of that truth.

When believers are exposed to God's truth and His life is flowing through them, but they are out of touch with His love (no warmth, arctic region), they will still wither, though it takes a lot longer.

In the absence of truth or life, the believer immediately becomes unable to purify the "atmosphere" of this world. Spiritual photosynthesis ceases.

Therefore, if you want to fulfill one of your primary purposes as a believer, which is to purify the spiritual atmosphere of the world, you must bask in God's truth, sink your roots into the Life of the Kingdom, and allow His Love to envelope you.

Finally, one of the byproducts of photosynthesis is glucose.

Glucose is a sugar that plants use for energy.

Also, a plant typically puts back into the soil about one-half the amount of water it needed to do the reaction in the first place.

So, as believers actively redeem the world, transforming its atmosphere, they receive energy for themselves from the process, and of the life God gave them (water), they return a significant amount back to the Kingdom.

And the energy we get from this process (glucose) is "sweet."

Lesson: *Practice the 3 habits regularly: Pray, Read the Word, and Fellowship with other believers. Those will ensure your spiritual growth and health.*

Capillary Action

*"As His divine power has given to us all things
that pertain to life and godliness..." (2 Peter 1:3a)*

Have you ever wondered how a tree is able to pull water from the soil and move it all the way up to the very tip top of its branches without a pump?

The truth is trees and plants don't have any kind of pumping mechanism that pushes the water up. They also don't suck it up like a vacuum.

Instead, water moves *itself* up through a phenomenon of physics called *capillary action.* Water has a high surface tension, which means it tends to "stick" to any surface it touches.

In fact, this surface tension causes the water to act as if it is attracted to other surfaces. Water molecules will move themselves until they can touch and adhere to another surface, not as strongly as a magnet on metal would, but the principle is similar.

If a thin tube, such as a test tube or a capillary (vein) in a tree, is narrow enough, water will actually defy gravity and begin to flow upward into the tube because the molecules are drawn to move to a place where they can adhere to the side of the tube rather than other water molecules.

Capillaries in trees are so narrow that water will flow all the way to the tops of the uppermost branches before gravity has enough pull to counteract it.

This physical principle keeps Creation running well in a number of other ways too, not just in trees and plants.

In other words, water has a property that allows it to defy gravity and rise up into trees of its own accord.

The symbolic interpretation of this is the life that God gives (water) is so pervasive, it rises up into believers under its own power *in spite of our sinful nature* (gravity).

Water's high surface tension that defies the laws of nature symbolizes just how powerful God's power is.

`**Lesson:** *God's power can overcome our sinful nature.*

Tree Rings

W e're all familiar with the phenomenon of tree rings which can be used to determine a tree's age. Trees usually develop one ring per year.

Each ring consists of a wide section of soft wood and a thinner section of denser, harder wood.

In the springtime, when light (truth) is new and water (life) is plentiful, the tree grows rapidly. Because of the rapid growth, the wood is soft. During the summer and fall, when conditions are a little tougher, the hard, dense portion of the ring is created.

The spiritual growth of believers follows the same pattern. We do not experience constant, equally distributed growth. On the contrary, we repeatedly experience alternating periods of ease and difficulty.

There are easier times when we are exposed to much of God's truth and life. Circumstances allow us to focus on those things, taking them in ample supply, and we experience significant and noticeable spiritual growth.

In times of difficulty, however, we are hardened, more deeply strengthened. Our growth then is not as visible, but it is more durable.

Both types of growth are necessary.

Tree Mass

Where do trees get their mass?

From the soil, right?

The buzzer just sounded. You would have lost the Daily Double. Sorry, not soil.

Almost the entirety of a tree's mass comes from the air, not including its water. Yes, as we've already reviewed, a tree respires in CO_2 and respires out O_2, keeping the carbon atom for itself. This carbon, which is taken from the air, is what gives the tree most of its mass.

Since we've already established that carbon dioxide is a symbol of the "human spirit" which has a somewhat negative connotation, I have to confess this little biological fact at first threw me for a major loop.

If trees are believers, then how can we say that they are filled with the "human spirit" as opposed to God's Spirit?

Yet, here is an important distinction: Trees are not *filled* with carbon as a believer is filled with the Holy Spirit, trees *are* carbon.

The alternative would be for trees' biomass to be made of oxygen. Since your mass is essentially what you are, the symbolism in such a case would be that believers are of the same essence as God. Which, of course, is not true.

Tree mass being primarily carbon is a statement to the fact that believers are human, carbon-based.

Spirit and breath are spiritual synonyms. Believers (trees) get their humanness from God the Father, their Creator, breathing their human spirit into them. This is the tree receiving carbon dioxide from the sky.

Believers then retain their humanness (carbon) and are capable of "breathing out" God's Spirit into the world. This symbolism clarifies and confirms that believers are not God in essence, they are not His Spirit in essence, they are just human (carbon). But as trees respire and retain the carbon, the remaining oxygen "fills" them, as God's indwelling Holy Spirit fills the believer. The tree also breathes out the oxygen as the believer exudes the fruit of the Spirit into the world.

We receive our essence from God, but our essence is not God.

Once more, notice the symbolism in *human* respiration (the opposite process from photosynthesis), taking in O_2 and breathing out CO_2. While trees take the carbon and make it their essence, humans do not retain the oxygen in their biomass. The human breathing process has nothing to do with the mass of our bodies. Human breathing is very different from that of trees in that we do it primarily to get energy, while the tree is getting its mass.

For the first time, let's connect human and tree respiration symbolically. Lost men and women (humans) receive energy and life force from God, but breathe out a fallen human spirit, crying out in brokenness, pain, and tragedy.

Believers (trees) take in that same brokenness, which humbles and gives them their humanity (carbon) in a heart-felt identification with the lost, then they breathe out words of God's healing back into the broken mass of humanity, giving natural man a little more "air" to breathe, which does not transform him, but allows him to keep going for a time.

Tree & Plant Growth

No one can make a plant grow. We fertilize and water, but only God grows the tree.

Same thing with us. No one can make a believer grow spiritually. We can plant spiritual seeds, water, and fertilize the soil, but only God can make people grow.

Lesson: *Do not believe you have the power to make someone grow spiritually. Do not be frustrated with those who grow slowly. Just plant seeds and water and trust God to do the rest in His timing.*

Roots

"For I am persuaded that neither death nor life, nor angels nor principalities nor powers, nor things present nor things to come, nor height nor depth, nor any other created thing, shall be able to separate us from the love of God which is in Christ Jesus our Lord."
(Romans 8:38-39)

Have you ever tried kicking over a tree? I have. Granted, it was in my more youthful, senseless days, but for some reason I thought it would give — at least a little. To my shock, and also to the great shock of my leg bones, it didn't give at all.

I vaguely remember trying a lesser bush at some point, maybe a crepe myrtle or something, with, of course, no better results, just an aching foot. You would think that something as flimsy as a sapling could be knocked over, but it can't. If it's thin enough, you might be able to break it in half, but you won't be pulling those roots out.

Just pick a random bush in your yard and try to yank it out of the soil by your own strength. (Now, to be fair, it can't be one you just planted yesterday.) You won't have any luck. For goodness sakes, it's hard enough to pull up a little weed or a clump of grass with the roots intact.

Plants are rooted firmly in the earth and that firmness is symbolic of the firmness with which God roots us in the Kingdom. *Nothing is going to pull us out.* Nothing will separate us from God's love.

A tree can be cut down by others, and so can a Christian, but no created thing can *uproot* a tree, and neither can any created thing remove our foundation in the Kingdom.

Only water. Flooding, a super-saturation of the soil is the only thing that can topple a tree from roots to tip. A flood does not represent God's release of His power in life-giving ways like a gentle rain, but as judgment.

This means that God can and does sometime release His power to judge sin and topple believers who've strayed, to make them fall, even the very mature ones. This does not represent a loss of salvation, or to be more specific, this does not represent a loss of our legal "justified" status before God granted to us through faith in the work of Christ. Such a symbolism would include a transformation of the basic nature of the tree when it is uprooted by the flood, and this does not occur.

No, the toppled tree simply represents the believer being uprooted from Kingdom life, i.e. a pastor who has sinned so badly he is removed from his position of influence, or an unrepentant layman who is expelled from his local church body. These people continue to be believers in essence, but their interaction with the Kingdom, their influence has ended.

Lesson: *Take joy in the secure firmness with which God has rooted you in His Kingdom.*

Trees & Soil

"And let us consider one another in order to stir up love and good works, not forsaking the assembling of ourselves together, as is the manner of some." (Hebrews 10:24-25a)

There is an old story that is often told about a man who had stopped coming to church. One day, his pastor paid him a visit at home, and the man welcomed him in.

The pastor sat next to him in front of the fire, but did not say a word.

After a few minutes, the pastor picked up the tongs and quietly removed a flaming coal from the heart of the fire, placing it by itself to the side. A time passed and the coal turned grey and cold. Finally, the pastor lifted it with the tongs and placed it gently back into the fire where it very quickly flamed a bright orange again.

The pastor stood and left, again without saying a word, but the next Sunday, the man was back in church and never stopped attending again.

Rumor has it that years later, he told his pastor that the most powerful sermon he'd ever preached was the one where he'd never said a word.

Trees being rooted in the earth are a symbol for *fellowship* between believers and the Body of Christ.

Every believer (tree) is rooted in the mass of believers (soil) that makes up the Kingdom.

Remember, a tree gets 90% of its mass from the air, and only 10% from the soil. So, a believer receives the vast majority of their spiritual growth through interaction with the Holy Spirit (air) while only a small percentage is due to fellowship with other believers.

Regardless, a plant does receive *some* nutrients from the soil. You can pluck a flower and keep it alive in a glass of water for a week or two, but it will eventually fade and die. Christmas trees can last about a month, as long as you keep them in water.

In the same way, if a believer is removed from fellowship with other believers, they can remain alive, spiritually speaking, for a time, but they will soon wither. Fellowship is one of the three basic habits of a Christian.

Just as a coal removed from a fire will soon cool off by itself, so will a believer wilt when separated out from the rest of the Body. No Christian is an island. We must be rooted in the Body or we fade away.

Of all the things you can deprive a tree, taking away soil will kill it the slowest. Just so with us believers. The Holy Spirit (oxygen), truth/ goodness (light), life (water), and love (warmth) are all more essential to our spiritual health than fellowship (roots in the soil), but without fellowship we die all the same, even if it takes longer.

Trees could be considered the fruit of the soil.

In other words, each believer is a fruit of the Body of Christ.

Individual trees then drop their fruit, their seed, back into the Kingdom, and through interaction with the Kingdom, that seed grows into a new believer, equal in kind to the believer who sowed them. Disciple-making 101.

Wood resting on bare soil, without a stone foundation, soon rots.

Wood (dead trees) symbolizes the lives of Christians who have gone before us, their testimony of the work of Christ in them, if you will.

If we study the history of the church, which is the sum of the historical events combined with testimonies of past believers, yet we do not have the foundation of Christ (stone foundation) on which to rest this understanding, the substance of those testimonies soon rots to us, no longer useful for building. But, if we build with those testimonies upon the foundation of Christ, they endure.

This is evident in the different ways people from different backgrounds interpret the history of the church. Non-Christians looking out over the past two thousand years, who do not have a foundation in Christ built in their heart, see nothing but the Crusades and the Salem witch trials, and they condemn.

On the other hand, believers who know Christ see those same events and recognize that those events represent the failure of certain believers to follow the teachings of Christ, which actually accentuates how great Jesus was because it highlights the purity and goodness of His teachings when contrasted with the actions of some in history who have professed His name. It also illustrates to most believers that those who participated in such events are less likely to have actually been part of the church because of their straying from the teachings of Christ.

Believers are not blinded by these singular events and are able to see the entire history of the church, the majority of which is excellent and filled with a love for the lost and self-sacrifice. Believers can see the hospitals begun, the orphans sheltered, the improvement of the lot of women, the liberations of slaves, etc. while non-believers can't get past the Crusades and the Inquisition.

Wood

"Where there is no wood, the fire goes out"
(Proverbs 26:20a)

Dead trees are useful too.

Wood is an excellent building material. For thousands of years, people have used wood to build homes, furniture, and all kinds of tools and equipment. It's sturdy and firm, strong enough to bear great weight, yet more flexible and easier to cut than stone.

Wood is no longer alive, so it represents the lives of believers who have gone before us. While we build lots of different structures with wood, let's focus on the construction of a church where the symbolism is more obvious.

For centuries, churches have been primarily built of wood, or other similar materials, sitting atop a stone foundation. If trees represent believers, wood represents the lives of deceased believers, and stones represent the truths of God, then the symbolism becomes clear.

We build our foundation with the firm truths of God, and the lives and testimonies of believers who have gone before us provide the structure and shape of the church. We, today, are not isolated from those brothers and sisters in Christ who passed centuries ago, but we are inheritors of their legacy. This symbolism is not limited to deceased believers, but could apply to the influence of other living believers too, since wood is the essence of the tree.

However, if we fail to build our church upon the truth of God and instead make other believers the foundation of our church, this is the equivalent of resting the wooden walls of our church directly on wet soil with no stone foundation.

Very quickly, we'll find our church rotting and infested with termites. Such a building would also be highly susceptible to earthquakes and floods. Founding a church on people rather than the truths of God results in a weak, rotten, and short-lasting structure.

Cathedrals of stone are the most enduring of churches.

They are stronger, can be built much larger, and last forever (barring a tremendous earthquake). This type of construction symbolizes building the entire church purely from the grand truths of God, rather than the testimonies of believers. (This does not mean churches built of stone are built on true doctrines and smaller wooden churches are not, we are simply commenting on the symbolism of the building materials).

The very first image of this would be the enormous Temple of God built by King Solomon.

While much stronger, longer-lasting, and even, it could be argued, more majestic, building a church purely of stone (truth) is much more expensive, more time consuming, and requires great expertise. I might also point out that while a stone cathedral may tower majestically, at the same time, it feels colder and less homey. A wooden church generally feels warmer and cozier.

There is nothing wrong with building a church from the lives of believers (wooden church) as long as its foundation is still Jesus (stone). Wooden churches are warmer (more loving), easier to build, less costly, and more flexible. It's easy to make an addition to a wooden church, whereas it's fairly difficult to alter a cathedral.

Wooden churches are symbolic of the normal church, built upon the foundation of Christ and built up through its members' lives as a family.

Cathedrals are majestic monuments, testifying to God's glory, yet they rarely house a close-knit loving church family. These "cathedral" church families are built wholly upon God's truth, not so much the testimony and fellowship of its members.

Unless these "truth-focused" church families are large, they feel uncomfortable and unpleasant, like a tiny stone house in the woods. Once inside, the thick walls feel like they're going to close in on you.

With great effort and expertise on the part of the builder, these truth-focused church families can be built into large church families. Once a large size is achieved, the truth-focused church now inspires awe in its grand austerity. A lack of comfort remains but gives way to an overwhelming atmosphere of reverence.

Another positive aspect of this kind of construction is that it is not subject to rotting. It is much easier to build a church centered around the fellowship of believers, but the truth-focused church family is sturdier and won't be swayed by changes in the fellowship dynamic.

Both types of construction are valid and have "truth" as a foundation. It's their wall and roof materials that differ.

Jesus is the master builder.

Wood can be carved into beautiful sculptures and other artistic pieces.

This pictures God carving the lives of His children into beautiful works of art.

I love sitting around a campfire with friends, staring at the flames and stoking the coals, telling ghost stories and cooking s'mores.

When the conversation has petered out into silence and that fire finally burns low, when people have stopped throwing on new logs and that cold seeps in, you know it's time to say good night.

We burn wood, usually in order to cook food or keep warm at night.

In the cold, dark night of the world, when we find ourselves surrounded by lies and hatred, we can look to the lives of believers (wood) around us, or of those that went before us, for comfort.

God, through the Holy Spirit (oxygen), combines with the essence of those believers' lives (wood) to create "fire." This fire provides us with a small measure of warmth (love) and illumination (truth and goodness) in an otherwise dark night.

These fires are small in nature, controlled, and are usually built within our homes, which represent our minds. When we feel overwhelmed by darkness, hopeless, the Holy Spirit brings to mind the lives of Abraham, Moses, David, and Peter, and maybe even our parents or grandparents, and we remember what God did for them and how the darkness is never permanent. This combustive act of the Holy Spirit illuminates us with truth and the goodness of God through these remembrances, and warms us with the reality of God's love.

In fact, the night can get so cold, so dark, that if we do not bring to memory what God has done in the past, we can easily perish in the belief that God has abandoned us, that His love is no more, or never was, and we freeze to death for a lack of it. It is this remembering that bolsters our faith and allows us to experience Him in the middle of the night.

Fire

"And suddenly there came a sound from heaven, as of
a rushing mighty wind, and it filled the whole house where
they were sitting. Then there appeared to them divided tongues,
as of fire, and one sat upon each of them." (Acts 2:2-3)

Images of those tongues of fire resting on the apostles' heads easily come to mind when we remember Pentecost. Yet, we tend to forget the "rushing mighty wind" that preceded the fire.

Fire is considered by most to be a symbol for the Holy Spirit Himself, but I feel a more specific definition is required. Fire seems to actually be a symbol for the *activity* of the Holy Spirit.

The mention of wind in Acts 2 coming before the tongues of flame supports this idea. The Holy Spirit (wind) came and acted upon the disciples (fire). In other places, when God's presence is represented by fire (burning bush), or we are told the face of Jesus glowed like molten metal (Book of Revelation), these glows are the *effects* of the Holy Spirit within.

Furthermore, as we dive in deeper to the various symbols of fire in nature, this distinction of interpretation becomes more obviously important.

Our sun is a blazing ball of fire with temperatures that range from six thousand to one million degrees Fahrenheit. What burns is the sun's internal substance, and from this great fire great amounts of light and heat flow.

Jesus was perfectly filled with the Holy Spirit. The Holy Spirit was His "internal substance," and all the truth, goodness, and love that shone from Him then, and that still shine today, flow from the Holy Spirit within Him, yet He and the Spirit are one.

Most natural fires on earth are caused by oxygen combining with other elements.

To clarify, we'll examine more closely how wood burns, though the process is the same for most objects.

Scientifically, as wood gets hotter and hotter, it eventually reaches a temperature at which it becomes capable of combining with oxygen in the air. As oxygen combines with the wood, new and different molecules are formed from the wood. While that's happening, great amounts of energy are simultaneously released from the former wood molecules.

This energy released is the fire we see.

Fire is a renewer.

Fire takes the old and reforms it into something completely new. Spiritual revivals throughout history have acted in the same way. When the Holy Spirit sweeps through a society, He burns up the culture and old institutions, and leaves behind a brand new society that grows out of the ashes.

Ashes, of course, are a great fertilizer. Mixing them with soil can greatly increase its fertility, and, as we discussed earlier, the earth is a symbol for God's Kingdom.

Fire is powerful...*and it can be a very scary thing.*

My first dog was named Bandit, and I loved him dearly. For some reason, when I was thirteen, I got into playing with candles and wax (yes, yes, I know, not real smart). So, one day, I decided I was going to melt a bunch of candles in a pot on the stove and try to make a statue of Bandit.

Well, the candles melted all right, but then the wax caught fire, and I'll tell you what — I've never seen flames that big inside a house!

Panicked, I rushed the pot to the sink and, forgetting all about those middle-school fire safety lessons, I turned on the faucet...

The resulting explosion would have seemed magnificent if I hadn't been so freaked out. Flames shot straight toward the ceiling in a solid pillar and then ran along the ceiling, extending at least six feet in every direction.

Thankfully, the pillar of fire wasn't constant, and I had time to come to my senses and shut the water off. Still, I endured two more of those bursting explosions before throwing a lid on the pot and ending the ordeal.

After it was over, I had no hope of covering the mess up. Droplets of wax covered the cabinets and blackened streaks ran across the ceiling. To this day, I am amazed that my parents didn't kill me.

Regardless, two things became clear. First, I got the distinct impression that God did *not* want me making any wax statues — perhaps it would have been too close to an idol — and second, I came away with a very clear respect for fire.

When fire rages, no one can stand in its way without being burned, and those burns are painful.

When the Holy Spirit is raging, when a spiritual revival is in full swing, there are no effective forces that can stop Him. That great and tremendous change the Spirit wreaks upon a society can be very scary for the one facing it beforehand. We don't like change, and many times change hurts.

For the Spirit to change us for the better, to renew us, He must burn within us like a purifying fire — and fires, even spiritual ones, can be painful.

The drier a place is, the faster and hotter it will burn. One way to stop most fires, of course, is with water. Soaking trees or houses in water is the only way to keep them from burning.

In other words, since water is a symbol for life, *the Spirit does not burn where He finds life (water) already exists.* There is no need for revival when life already exists.

We'll discuss more aspects of fire in the coming sections.

Lesson: *When we're feeling cold, far from God's love, let us remember the stories of old of His faithfulness.*

Forest Fires

*"For then there will be great tribulation, such as has not been
since the beginning of the world until this time,
no, nor ever shall be." (Matthew 24:21)*

Forest fires are a different animal from a campfire. They are not dried logs being tossed onto a controlled fire pit, but uncontrollable infernos that burn through vast swaths of whole, living trees, fed by oxygen and strengthened and directed by the wind. Forest fires can move at a slow, smoldering pace, or they can tear through a forest at unbelievable velocities. The speed of the fire is again controlled by the strength of the wind and the availability of dry material for burning.

In an article called *"How Plants Use Fire (And Are Used By It),"* by Stephen J. Pyne, the author explains that forests are by no means *destroyed* by a forest fire. The forest fire actually provokes many beginnings of new life.

> *Larch bear dense bark capable of withstanding surface fires. Ponderosa pine shed lower branches as they mature, shielding sensitive needles from scorching fires below. African aloes and Brazilian proteas surround buds with moist tissues capable of absorbing heat.*
>
> *Some plants use the heat to their advantage. Scrub oak and chamise, an evergreen shrub, resprout from roots or branches after fire has incinerated their outer limbs. If fire destroys their branches, many eucalypts will throw out new branches by sprouting from their trunks. After flames destroy their trunks, mallee, low-growing, shrubby eucalypts, send out vigorous shoots from special nutrient-storage organs found in their roots. Australian grass trees push out new leaves and even bloom—and may only bloom—after a scouring fire.*

Other plants opportunistically seize a site temporarily purged by fire to promote their own reproduction. Cape lilies lie dormant until flames brush away the covering over them, then blossom almost overnight. Lodgepole pine and jack pine rely on the pulse of flame through their crowns to melt away the waxy bond that holds their cones closed; their seeds then fall to fresh ash below, where they can take root without much competition. Sequoia seedlings flourish best on deep-burned sites free of grasses and other rivals.[4]

In 2004, researchers discovered that smoke from burning some plants actually promotes germination in other plants by inducing the production of a compound called orange butenolide.[5]

Forest fires are actually beneficial and even necessary for life in the forest to continue.

What is not immediately clear is whether forest fires represent a persecution of believers or a revival among believers. Instinct would lead us to lean toward the revival interpretation, since we know from Scripture that fire is a symbol of the activity of the Holy Spirit. The symbolic flames which appeared over the Apostles' heads as they were filled with the Holy Spirit at Pentecost, the first of all revivals, is strong evidence to support this interpretation.

However, forest fires are very destructive, in spite of their benefits. I know of no spiritual revival among God's people that has resulted in the destruction of believers. Revivals destroy the world's systems, transforming society from death to life, but they do not destroy believers. Revivals are *only* beneficial to believers.

The key to the interpretation of the symbolism here lies in further examination of forest fires. What is their function in Creation? Why do they happen?

---

[4] Stephen J. Pyne, *How Plants Use Fire (And Are Used By It)*, http://www.pbs.org/wgbh/nova/fire/plants.html (accessed on Dec. 4th, 2013).

First, forest fires are needed for forest renewal. In the past, U. S. Forest Services worked very hard to prevent forest fires of any kind. A problem arose, however, when it was realized that while these radical fire prevention methods preserved older trees, too few new trees were sprouting up. Forest fires are a natural part of the forest's life cycle that gives younger trees the chance to take root.

Forest fires occur when a forest is very dry, i.e. there hasn't been any rain for a while, and especially when there's a lot of dry brush, which burns very hot and very fast.

When a forest fire passes through, it swiftly incinerates all the brush and rubbish. While some large trees do die, most will survive and bud again the following spring, fresh, renewed, cleansed, and stronger. Many trees and plants have survival mechanisms built into them, which allow them to survive these forest fires. Some of these mechanisms are not in the plants themselves, but in their seeds. So, while the plant itself may perish, its seed remains to take root later.

However, if there is no fire in a particular forest for a *long* period of time, brush and other dry materials build up to the point that when a fire does finally occur, it is catastrophic rather than beneficial. When the quantity of brush grows too great, a fire will burn so hot that it kills *everything*, even the larger trees.

In this scenario, all trees and plants, along with their seeds, are consumed. Even more unfortunate is that such extreme fires also change the chemical composition of the soil, turning it into a harder clay-like substance that prevents anything from growing back for a long time.

If forest fires were a symbol of revival, they could not result in a sterile, barren landscape.

Therefore, the best symbolic interpretation for forest fires is that of persecution. Persecution is a necessary struggle that God's people must pass through regularly. Persecution renews God's people as a fire renews a forest.

---

[5] Flematti GR, Ghisalberti EL, Dixon KW, Trengove RD. A compound from smoke that promotes seed germination. *Science*. 2004;305(5686):977. doi:10.1126/science.1099944.

It's painful and it's scary. We cannot pass through it without being scarred, burnt in some way, yet those who survive are renewed and strengthened. Persecution (forest fire) clears the way for new growth in the Kingdom.

A classic example of this type of forest fire is the early church and the Roman Empire. The Roman Empire repeatedly and regularly persecuted Christians which consistently resulted in the weaker Christians (brush) being burnt away, allowing for many new Christians to spring up in their place, many of whom grew into stronger believers (new trees), strengthening the forest. It was this repeated and regular persecution that provoked the church to grow so rapidly that within a few centuries the entire Roman Empire was Christian.[6]

However, when God's people in one part of the Kingdom go for a long time with no persecution (no fire), the brush begins to build up. Brush is a symbol for weaker Christians, just as trees are symbols for strong believers. Lack of persecution allows these shallow-rooted, weaker Christians to flourish and build up. If this goes on too long, this part of the Kingdom becomes very vulnerable to a much hotter persecution that can completely eradicate believers from a given part of the Kingdom for a time.

Perhaps this is what happened to Japan? You'd be hard-pressed to know it today, but once upon a time, Japan was home to a large number of Japanese Christians. In the 17th century, some estimate as much as 50% of the Japanese population was Christian. The church in Japan then was growing at a tremendous rate due to the efforts of Catholic missionaries, but there is evidence that the Japanese church of four hundred

---

[6] Constantine did *declare* all of Rome to be Christian and compelled pagan Romans to give up the traditional roman gods. *However*, before he did that, Rome was likely around 50% Christian already. Saying Rome became Christian is similar to saying the United States is a Christian nation. It's not today, and it never was 100%, although it clearly was a "Christian nation," even just a generation ago. This is the same as saying Israel is a Jewish state. It *is* a Jewish state, but it's not 100%. There are Arab Christians, and even among those who have physical Jewish heritage, there is a large percent that are essentially secular atheists.

years ago was perhaps very "brush-heavy," i.e. a lot of worldly believers, fewer "trees."

A tremendous persecution broke out in the early 1600's. The emperor of Japan banned Christianity and ordered all Christians executed who would not convert back to the religion of their fathers.

Many scholars rank this Japanese persecution as the worst persecution in the history of the church (Think: *Worst forest fire of all time)*. He forced all Christians to walk over a symbol of a cross on the floor and spit upon it. If they refused, they were killed.[7]

Christianity in Japan has never recovered from this persecution, and to this day it is a very difficult mission field. Its soil has become a hard, clay-like substance, chemically altered by the severity of the former fire.

It's interesting to note that for the past forty years, the United States has worked very hard to prevent forest fires. Similarly, we have not experienced much spiritual persecution and we strive to avoid hardship of any kind as a people. We want life to be easy.

Forest fires do not have to symbolize persecution alone, they could also stand for hardship in general, as hardship among God's people produces similar results to persecution, though not quite as dramatic. Without hardship, God's people grow used to comfort and they grow fat and weak.

On the other hand, God's people in China experience regular persecution and hardship. American Christians, at times, have prayed with Chinese Christians for an end to the persecution. The response of one well-known Chinese church leader, Brother Yun, is typical of most Chinese pastors experiencing persecution, saying, *"Don't* pray for the persecution to stop! We shouldn't pray for a lighter load to carry, but a stronger back to endure!"[8]

---

[7] http://en.wikipedia.org/wiki/Fumi-e (accessed Sept. 25, 2013), and *Christianity in Japan*,
http://www.sbceo.k12.ca.us/~vms/carlton/Japan/Japanpersecution.html (accessed Sept. 25, 2013).
[8] Marcus Yoars, *Are We Praying for the Wrong Thing*,
http://www.charismamag.com/blogs/yoars-truly/17035-are-we-praying-for-the-wrong-thing (accessed Sept. 20, 2013).

I think they have the right attitude. *(I wonder if China allows forest fires to burn naturally...)*

Forest fires are regional, never covering the entirety of all land.
Persecution is also regional, never covering the entire earth at once (so far). Just as a fire moves from place to place as it burns, so does persecution move about the Kingdom from country to country, popping up here, coming to an end there. The only time in history when persecution will take place across the entire globe at once is during the end times as described in prophecy. Interestingly, during that time there will also be an unusual number of fires throughout the earth and eventually God will destroy the entire earth with fire.

Many Christians who are killed through persecution leave behind the seeds of their faith in others who sprout up after them, just like those plants whose seeds survive the fire. It has been said that the blood of martyrs is the seed of the church.

It was recently discovered that when certain cloud formations pass over a regional wildfire, the heat from the fire causes a change in the cloud's structure, which sucks significant amounts of sooty particles high up into the stratosphere. These concentrations of sooty particles can increase absorption of incoming solar radiation during winter months by as much as 15%.
So, forest fires keep the earth warmer during the winter months. In other words, persecution keeps the Kingdom filled with more love for one another while Christ is not with us (winter, night).

Lastly, we must note that oxygen, wind, and fire are the fuels, directors, and causes of forest fires, and all three are either symbols for the Holy Spirit or the activity of the Holy Spirit. **This would indicate that it is God Himself who fuels and directs persecution.**
That last statement may come as a shock to some readers, but was it not God who hardened Pharaoh's heart? Was it not God who caused the Canaanites, the Philistines, the Assyrians, and then the Babylonians to rise up against His people in order to persecute them? Was it not God

who put Jesus on the cross to die for our sins? Though these persecutions involve suffering, were they not what was best for God's people at that time? Yes, God is sovereign, yet loving, and we can trust Him that He always has an amazing plan and reasons for why He does what He does. Forest fires are for the health of the forest.

Understanding this, I reevaluate the symbolic flames that appeared over the heads of the disciples at Pentecost. When Jesus was baptized, the Holy Spirit descended upon Him in the form of a dove, a symbol of peace and renewal. Yet, when the Spirit came upon the disciples, the form was tongues of fire directed by a rushing wind. Perhaps this pictured to them the persecution they were about to endure.

Lesson: *May we pray for stronger backs to endure.*

TYPES OF PLANTS

Evergreens

Evergreens are the kings of the trees.

Any list detailing the tallest, widest, largest, or oldest trees will have conifers (which are evergreens) in the top four positions. Redwoods, cedars, pines, firs, cypress, and sequoias are all evergreens.

Evergreens not only grow taller than deciduous trees, they grow faster too. They're hardier, and their roots grow deepest into the soil.

When a strong storm blows through, it's not uncommon to see a heavy oak or maple toppled over because their roots could not hold firm in the rain-saturated soil. But you won't see that with an evergreen.

Pine trees have extremely long tap roots which anchor the tree so solidly in the ground storms cannot knock them over. When you see a fallen pine, it's been broken in the middle. I've seen pine trees snapped in half by tornadoes, but I've never seen one ripped out of the ground.

Evergreens never lose their color, not even in the coldest of winter. As the presence of the sun lessens at the end of the year, evergreens hold onto their needles long after the deciduous trees have become naked skeletons.

It's harder to kill an evergreen with a lack of light or warmth.

Drought is another story. Without water, an evergreen will not fare any better than any other kind of tree. However, because evergreens put down such deep roots, they reach farther down into the water table and will outlast all other trees in a drought also.

Evergreens, in general, require less nourishment from the soil than deciduous trees because they don't have to replenish their needles every season as deciduous trees do their leaves.

Evergreens represent the strongest and firmest of believers.
These believers grow faster than most and they sink their roots deep into the Body of Christ. A severe storm (judgment of God) can break them if it's too strong, but it will not uproot them from their faith in Him.

Evergreen believers can weather a deprivation of the presence of the Lord (sun) better than other believers. Through most hardship, their rugged appearance will remain the same. They won't be denuded in the struggle, but will wait patiently until He returns (spring). They won't lose their "needles."

Now, I know a lot of people think evergreens are pretty — I just don't happen to be one of them.

I love the vivid, vibrant greens of fresh deciduous trees in the spring. The dark olive needles of the evergreen don't do anything for me. It's a majestic color, for sure, especially in the dead of winter, but it isn't as beautiful as the younger, brighter greens.

This can be true of the firmest of believers as well. They aren't necessarily ugly, nor are they especially beautiful. They simply persist amidst hardship, stretching their arms toward Heaven in worship.

In 1521, Martin Luther was called to the city of Worms to defend his teaching on salvation by faith alone before the Emperor Charles V and a host of church officials. He was to renounce what he'd taught and written or be condemned. Johann Eck, the representative of those in authority, challenged Luther several times to recant. In the face of excommunication or death, Luther replied that he could only retract if convinced of his error through Scripture. He refused to waver, and finished with "I cannot and will not recant anything...May God help me. Amen."[9]

That is the perfect picture of an evergreen believer.

Evergreens are majestic.

They tower over all other trees, able to see the "big picture" of the arboreal kingdom.

God chose a majestic evergreen (Cedar) to be the construction material of His temple in Jerusalem. The wood of an evergreen tree is an excellent building material because of the speed at which it grows in comparison with hardwoods like oak, and because it is more malleable than that of a hardwood tree. Evergreens are made of what is called "softwood."

Softwoods, like Pine, are the most preferred building materials for general construction. Though not as solid as oak, it is still a very strong type of wood, yet allows for some flexibility. It can be cut and re-formed easier than hardwood. The reason softwoods are lighter and more flexible is because they are more porous.

The high porosity of softwoods allows water (God's power) to seep in, creating the flexibility.

Men like Martin Luther, John Calvin, and John Wesley were Evergreen Christians. Whole denominations, i.e. great houses, were built around their life work. They were men who, once the seed was germinated, grew very fast spiritually. They sunk their roots deep into the truths of God's Kingdom. They stood out, tall and in full view, among the forests of the Kingdom. They withstood storms without being uprooted, yet they maintained a certain flexibility that allowed them to move with the Spirit. This flexibility came from being spiritually porous, able to absorb the life God gives well.

Few would describe the lives of these men as "beautiful." A more apt description would be stately or majestic. They served as excellent building blocks for the church.

---

[9] *Luther's Two Narratives of His Hearings Before the Diet of Worms,* http://law2.umkc.edu/faculty/projects/ftrials/luther/lutherbyluther.html#secondnarrative (accessed Sept. 20, 2013).

Softwoods rot faster than hardwoods.

While the life work of these men was used to build entire denominations, we can see today these denominations are beginning to suffer decay. They are not lasting. This does nothing to impugn the character or quality of these great men of God, it is simply a reality of the type of "wood" they were. Oak lasts longer, but you could never build anything large with it because it is so prohibitively expensive. It doesn't grow fast enough.

The men of God already mentioned are by no means the only Evergreen Christians in the church, nor are Evergreen Christians limited to great preachers or teachers who began large denominations. Those men are just names we all recognize. There are Evergreen Christians in every congregation that is part of the Body, and their work is the stuff with which we frame our churches.

The seeds of evergreens are always contained in a conical pod (i.e. pine cones).

If you've ever walked around your backyard in bare feet, you know that pine cones will pierce the bottom of your foot more sharply than hazelnuts or acorns.

Thus, the testimonies (seed) of strong evergreen believers may come to the hearer in a less pleasant, abrasive form than the testimonies of other believers, but the unpleasant seeds of evergreen believers are no less productive.

In fact, pine cones seem to outperform the seeds of all other trees in reproduction capability. Perhaps their very prickliness prevents scavenger animals from snatching them away for consumption like they would an acorn. In the same way, a pleasant testimony to a non-believer seems to be snatched away by the enemy much more easily than a strong exhortation from a firm believer.

Exhortation penetrates deep in spite of its prickliness.

Lesson: *Stand firm, imitate the evergreen.*

Deciduous

"For our light affliction, which is but for a moment, is working for us a
far more exceeding and eternal weight of glory."
(2 Corinthians 4:17)

The difference between evergreen and deciduous trees is...
drum roll please...deciduous trees lose their leaves in winter!
Ta da!

Actually, no real surprise there, but what does it mean?

Of course, trees lose their leaves in winter because the days are shorter. There's generally less daylight and it's cooler out. We've discussed the meaning of light and heat, but our interpretation of deciduous trees in particular will obviously depend much on the meaning of winter.

So, what does winter represent?

We haven't really deciphered the seasons yet — we will later in the book, in much further detail — but let's go ahead and touch on them now.

We begin each year in the dead of winter, which is followed by a new birth in spring. Then comes the heat of summer, a beautiful, cooler autumn, and then finally, we return to dead, cold winter once more.

Many would say this symbolizes the stages of life: Spring being a child, summer, an adult, fall, the elderly, and winter, death. This interpretation is common and has been understood for thousands of years.

Others would see in the seasons a symbol for the life cycle of a church, an organization, a family, a business, or even a country.

Some see the ministry of Christ being symbolized over and over again with one spring being the beginning of His ministry and the following spring His resurrection.

So, which of these views is accurate?

What's clear is the seasons represent some kind of life cycle. A repeating pattern of new life maturing and then fading away. Which life cycle? For now, we'll leave it at that.

The seasons represent life cycles.

The fact that this life cycle applies to so many things teaches us something about God and His Kingdom.

God is not static, nor is His Kingdom.

Now, some readers think I just said "God changes." On the contrary, God does not change. Yet, He isn't static either. His person, His nature, His essence never change, but His movements and actions do. His Kingdom is *dynamic*, ebbing and flowing like the tides and the seasons.

No church, no family, no organization, no person can stay in the same place spiritually. Everything is constantly changing, either growing into the fullness of summer, or fading into dormant winter. This does not prove that a person only has one chance at "summer" in their life spiritually. On the contrary, perhaps a person will go through multiple spiritual life cycles of growth and dormancy during their life. What is clear is that we're always changing one way or the other.

God is dynamic, not static. He does not change, but He changes others.

So, back to our discussion of deciduous trees. We all experience spiritual "winters" in our lives, times when we struggle to discern God's truth or feel His love.

No tree grows any taller or wider in winter, not evergreens, not deciduous. Neither does *any* believer grow spiritually when they receive a diminished amount of His truth and love.

Yet, evergreen believers continue to bear fruit in these times. *Deciduous believers cease bearing fruit as long as the winter lasts.*

Evergreen believers, men like Billy Graham and Martin Luther, continue to "photosynthesize," to purify the air, to exhale God's Spirit for all to partake, even amidst struggles, these "winter times." Deciduous believers, on the other hand, stop transforming the atmosphere around them during struggles. They go dormant, waiting for spring.

Evergreen believers are *not* better than deciduous believers. God simply made them to work differently. He loves every believer.

Deciduous believers are not weak believers.

In fact, *hardwood trees are all deciduous trees*. The oak tree is a case in point. Deciduous believers can be very strong and firm and even prominent members of God's Kingdom. They simply go dormant during spiritual winters.

There are all kinds of deciduous trees, from fruit trees to weeping willows to oaks and maples, and they all have different characteristics. This pictures the wide variety of personality traits, talents, and spiritual gifting among the Body of Christ.

Many deciduous trees flower while they are still *leafless*, right at the beginning of spring.

This is comparable to many new believers!

A new, young believer looks especially beautiful in the joy of their newfound faith. They still bear the glow of a recent encounter with Christ, yet they lack the maturity (leaves) to actually conduct spiritual photosynthesis. Which, of course, will change as they mature spiritually.

Interestingly, a lot of these trees pollinate during this time. Have you ever noticed how new believers are so excited about their new faith that they will bring a number of their family or friends to Christ right after their own conversion? Remembering that we are not necessarily limited to one spiritual spring in our lifetime, doesn't it make sense that our most evangelistic period would be in the time when we are being renewed by God and we're excited about our new growth?

In the autumn, when days shorten and light decreases, deciduous trees cease their photosynthesis, which ends the production of chlorophyll. (For those of you rusty in high school biology, chlorophyll is the pigment that makes a tree look green.)

Trees don't *turn* yellow and orange in the fall, they actually just lose their green, revealing other colors that *were always there*.

Those yellow and orange pigments that transform trees into beautiful, colored canvases in autumn are always present in the leaves.

It is the absence of the dominant pigment chlorophyll that allows the other colors to be seen toward the end of the year.

So, as a believer is in an autumn period spiritually, their true colors shine through for all to see.

The most beautiful trees in the fall, in my opinion, are those that turn red and purple. Unlike yellow and orange, the red and purple pigments are colors that are *not* always present in the leaves. Those colors are actually sugars trapped in the leaves during late summer.

These red and purple trees represent those believers who have matured especially well, and during the height of their maturity (late summer) they develop a very real sweetness of spirit that becomes most visible (and most beautiful) in their autumn. I have known believers like this — men and women of God that just exude the love and peace of Christ as if it's second nature.

The man who married my wife and I, Roy Cooper, is a man of God like that. He was the director of the seminary I attended and has been a missionary for a number of decades. Both he and his wife, Dirce, never fail to have the largest of smiles on their faces whenever they greet you. The kind of smiles that are so big, so sincere and warm, you know they're genuinely glad to see you. They have a heart for the lost and a spirit of service like few others, and my wife and I have always greatly admired them.

They are like those gorgeous red maples that make autumn so beautiful.

It is also true that in years where there has been a drought during the summer, the fall is usually short-lived and not nearly as beautiful as those years when there's been abundant rain. In drier years, trees turn brown much more quickly. The prettier colors are more muted and last less. Sometimes, a tree will go straight to brown.

Similarly, believers that have not been immersed sufficiently in the Life that God offers (water) over time will show an uglier, browner autumn. Not much to look at.

Lesson: *Immerse yourself in the Life that God offers. Your maturity, or lack thereof, will be revealed in the end.*

Fruit / Seed

"...For a tree is known by its fruit."
(Matthew 12:33b)

All trees produce seeds. A seed is a symbol for our testimony, whether it be the truth we speak, the good we do, or the love we show. These testimonies fall into the soil of the Kingdom, and from them, new believers are born and grow.

Our seed, which is our testimony, corresponds exactly to our essence, our nature and character. Just as an oak tree can only produce another oak tree and an apple seed produces an apple tree, so can we only produce believers after our own kind. (Genesis 1:12). If we are full of knowledge of Scripture, but not generous with money, we will produce disciples who are knowledgeable, but stingy. If we are gifted with generosity, but morally lax, we will produce disciples who are also generous, but loose with morals.

Jesus said that a good tree bears good fruit. He cursed the fig tree that did not bear fruit. Understanding this, we must be careful when declaring what an unfruitful believer looks like.

(Paul does this very well when listing various parts of the fruit of the Spirit - Galatians 5:22-23.)

We typically assume that a believer who is not making disciples is unfruitful, but making disciples is a command of Christ, not part of the fruit of the Spirit. They could actually be a fruitful believer whose seeds are simply falling on barren soil. Barren soil is obviously not the fault of the tree that has managed to grow in it.

No, the sign of an unfruitful tree is that it *does not make seeds*. Again, these seeds represent testimony. Therefore, the unfruitful believer is one who does not testify of the glory of God through speaking truth, working good, or loving others.

Lesson: *Judge a person's testimony, not their accomplishments or lack thereof.*

Fruit Trees

*"But the fruit of the Spirit is love, joy, peace, longsuffering,
kindness, goodness, faithfulness, gentleness, self-control.
Against such there is no law." (Galatians 5:22-23)*

Fruit trees are the most loved of all trees.
In my mind, the phrase "fruit tree" sparks homey images of
orderly orchards filled with rows of apple, orange, and peach
trees, juicy treats hanging from their branches, ripe for the picking.

Other trees, that is to say *most* trees, bear dry seeds. There's nothing
sweet about these seeds, yet they remain full of substance and they grow
into new trees just fine.

The seeds of fruit trees, however, are encapsulated within a sweet
fruit. When the fruit falls the ground, the fruit's flesh surrounding the
seed acts as a fertilizer, providing everything the seed needs to take root
and flourish. Also, many fruits have multiple seeds within a single fruit,
further ensuring its success.

This difference in seeds is the same with believers. All faithful
believers give testimony to God. All such testimonies are potentially
effective for the sowing of new believers. Some testimonies fall on
barren soil. Some testimonies are "dry." Such believers are not
necessarily "beloved" by others, but their testimony is nonetheless
effective for growth.

Other believers produce testimonies that are "sweet" tasting. These
are fruit tree believers.

Most Christians have known believers who are a sheer pleasure and
joy to be around. We feel refreshed just by being in their company.
These fruit tree believers seem to make new disciples with greater
facility and they make them often.

Non-fruit tree believers can be stodgier. We don't necessarily *desire*
to be in their presence, but when we are, we still find plenty of
nourishment. This kind of believer is more comparable to the oak,
maple, and pine trees of the world.

However, the seeds of a fruit tree believer, those Christians that seem to ooze the love of Christ through their smile, are more effective in barren soil since the sweet flesh of the fruit (love) that encapsulates the seed will act as a fertilizer in an otherwise hardened soil.

In the church I attended right after college, there was a wonderful, older Christian woman named Mrs. Stansell. Since most of the congregation was college-aged, her grandmotherly heart was especially welcome and she was one of the most beloved people in our church. God's love just seemed to pour through her. Her sweetness made her a pleasure to be around. She always made you feel at home and made herself available to many of the young women in the church for mentoring.

The neighborhood our church was in could easily be described as barren soil. It was a very difficult area. Still, Mrs. Stansell was a "fruit tree" Christian. Of all the older members who attempted discipleship, she produced the most fruit. Her strong, sweet spirit was the reason.

Being southern, I would have to imagine she is a peach tree.

Vines

"I am the vine, you are the branches.
He who abides in Me, and I in him, bears much fruit;
for without Me you can do nothing." (John 15:5)

Vines stand out from others in a number of ways.
They travel to regions where no plant has gone before.
Vines maintain their main root structure in fertile soil, but then they are capable of extending themselves long distances over non-fertile substances. They can grow over rocks and asphalt, up walls and trees, and over pretty much anything they encounter (within reason). They continue to reach out, growing across the impermeable surface, until they stumble across another patch of fertile ground. Once they reach that, they sink their roots into it and send out another shoot.

Because of this tendency, **vines do not invest a lot of energy in a support structure**. They rely on the harder surfaces they're traversing to support them, and instead invest their energy in extending their shoots as far as possible to get to fertile soil.

These vines bask in the sunlight, absorbing it through all their leaves equally, whether over soil or asphalt, but their main source of water is back at the roots in the soil.

Vines obviously point toward missionary activity, but the symbolism should probably be applied to all evangelists just as well.

Evangelists typically maintain their roots in their home church (fertile ground) while they go out into the world (impermeable ground). Evangelists can travel a long way, even around the world, as long as they feel connected to their church back home. Without that vital connection, evangelists seem to "dry up," so to speak, becoming ineffective. The home church is the source of life (water) to the evangelist until they are able to plant some roots in fertile soil closer to where they've relocated.

At all times, however, they have full access to God's truth, goodness, and love (sunlight and heat), no matter where they go.

Successful evangelists have a tendency to not invest a lot of energy in "support structure" as they travel. They stay connected to their home church (roots), but many times will rely on people in the world for helping meet some of their support needs, i.e. housing, vehicles, food, etc. until they successfully plant a new church. *"Provide neither gold nor silver nor copper in your money belts, nor bag for your journey, nor two tunics, nor sandals, nor staffs; for a worker is worthy of his food."*[10]

Jesus is the Great Vine.

He is the Master Evangelist. I believe His analogy regarding the vine in John 15 is referring to His role in evangelism, in fulfilling the Great Commission. Evangelism for Jesus, however, is not just "bringing people to Christ," but making disciples, making the entire Kingdom fertile.

---

[10] Matthew 10:9-10

The lesson there is that no missionary nor evangelistic activity can bear fruit if it's not done while abiding in Christ. Jesus said it very clearly. Nobody can bear fruit unless they are grafted into the vine. Being rooted in Christ is a must to successfully bring people to Christ, or to bear spiritual fruit of any kind.

Lesson: *Abide in Christ.*

Bushes

Bushes are shorter than trees.

I know, that had to be the revelation of the century for you.

Regardless, though they're shorter, bushes have just as wide a variety of species as trees. There are flowering bushes, bushes that only bear berries, and still others that do nothing but grow leaves. There are deciduous shrubs and evergreen shrubs. Small shrubs, big shrubs, fast and slow growing shrubs, prickly shrubs, and even talking shrubs... well, okay no talking shrubs, but you get the point.

Really, the main difference between bushes and trees is only their height.

Height is not a symbol for spiritual maturity. Age would be the correct symbol for spiritual maturity, and age is completely unrelated to height in plants. For example, olive trees don't necessarily grow very tall, but they are known to live for more than two thousand years.

Height is a symbol for prominence.

Trees, especially tall trees, are believers who are *prominent* in the Kingdom.

Initially, all trees and bushes grow skyward, but once bushes reach a certain maximum height, their height won't noticeably change after that. Trees grow taller, faster, and for a longer period of time than bushes.

In the same way, dedicated believers universally grow in prominence within the church as they mature in their early years. Tree believers are those leaders in the church who continue to grow even more visible as they mature further. Bush believers are those dedicated believers who remain fairly invisible to the Body as a whole as they mature and serve. **They are no less dedicated, they are simply not designed to shine in the limelight.**

On the whole, bushes produce a lot more fruit (berries and things) than taller trees.

Even fruit trees tend to be shorter in general than other trees. *It could be said that leaders within the church lead, while the rest of the believers produce the flowers and sweet fruit of the Kingdom.*

Bushes, like trees, have mechanisms that will allow them to survive most forest fires (persecution).

Don't be mistaken — though not in prominent view, bush believers are *mature believers*, and should *not* be confused with "grassy brush."

Once the forest fire passes, most bushes will re-bud and grow again.

Lesson: *Learn to respect those mature believers who are not in leadership positions.*

Grass

"As they departed, Jesus began to say to the multitudes concerning John: 'What did you go out into the wilderness to see? A reed shaken by the wind?'" (Matthew 11:7)

In light of what we've learned so far, it seems impossible to avoid identifying grass as symbolizing weak or superficial believers.

We're not talking about what technically classifies as grass, which could include such plants as corn, wheat, and bamboo, but that which the average person thinks of as being grass, i.e. the grass of the field and your lawn.

Quick observation reveals that blades of grass have nowhere near the structure or stability of trees and bushes.

You know that friend you thought you could lean on like a firm tree, only to be unexpectedly disappointed? I've had my share of those. Friends who I've repeatedly jumped up and sacrificed for, serving them when they needed me. Yet, when I most needed them, when I expected to be able to lean on them for a change, they didn't show up (even when they said they would), and usually with the flimsiest of excuses.

It literally felt like I had tried to lean on them, but they had bent underneath my hand.

Grass is not firm.

It bends in the wind.

Also, grass is very short compared with neighboring shrubs or trees.

These two characteristics match what we know of superficial believers. They bend easily under pressure and are usually not prominent (not tall) in the church. Weak believers sit on the bench, they don't try to lead youth groups or cook meals for the homeless. They warm the pews. They don't step out in amazing faith.

Grasses' roots are shallow.

They penetrate the earth much less deeply than trees or bushes. Their roots are superficial.

The same goes with "grass believers." Their roots don't sink very deep in the Kingdom.

Truly, a number of verses in the Bible identify grass with that which is weak, temporary, or of low quality. Psalm 103:15, Isaiah 40:7, and Matthew 6:30 are a few examples.

20% of the land surface on this planet is covered by grasses.[11]

This would seem to indicate that only around 20% of the believers in the Kingdom would be "grass believers."

---

[11] Nancy A. Eckhardt, *Grass Genome Evolution,* http://www.ncbi.nlm.nih.gov/pmc/articles/PMC2254914/ (accessed Sept. 20, 2013).

I must confess, I perceived the percentage of superficial believers in the church to be much higher than that, but perhaps it's just a case of the bad apples standing out more visibly among the good ones. If so, this is very reassuring.

Either way, God is the only one who truly knows the hearts of men and how many of his children are firmly rooted versus being like the grass of the field.

Surprisingly, though, grass is a pretty hardy thing.

Step on a swatch of grass and it tamps down, only to spring back up after a few minutes or hours. Its resilience allows it to survive trampling under the feet of large animals without being crushed. The same lack of firmness that bends before the wind allows it to withstand much abuse.

In comparison, step on a bush and watch it snap. Mature trees do, however, have the strength to withstand all kinds of abuse.

Contrary to common belief, this resiliency is true of superficial believers as well. We tend to believe that a superficial believer will flee at the slightest difficulty in a church, but is this really true? Take a look at your favorite scandal-ridden televangelist church. Typically, such churches are large churches and are they not obviously filled with mostly superficial believers? If such shallow believers are not the primary component of those congregations, then how else do you explain such large attendances in spite of the church's severe sickness?

Those who regularly attend those churches survive all kinds of "trampling." They endure setback after setback in their personal lives, all the while being told that if they're poor or sick it's because they don't have enough faith. They see their leaders get caught in adultery or carted off to prison. Abuse after abuse, and yet they keep coming. If their church closes, they'll move on to another just as bad.

Eventually, with enough abuse, even grass succumbs and dies, but grass will certainly hold up longer than your average bush.

Now, these grass believers are *not* the same things as weak believers who are weak just because they are young. Weakness born of superficiality is very different from weakness due to immaturity, just as a blade of grass is very different from a pine sapling. There is a fundamental difference in the nature of a weak, superficial believer and a weak, young believer. The weak, young believer cannot withstand the abuse that a grass believer can. He or she will snap under abuse just like a tree sapling. Give them a few years of growth, however, and the only way to cut them down will be with an axe.

Note: Christ's parable of the sower is not referring to grass seed, but crop seed (i.e. wheat, etc.). The seed that falls among thorns in that parable grows up but is choked out, the point being it never produces fruit because of the cares of the world. This speaks to how potentially fruitful believers can get choked out by the world, not to the idea of superficial believers per se.

Grass, of course, gets along just find amongst thorns. As do superficial believers among the cares of the world.

Three things choke out or kill grass: A lack of water, being over-shadowed by trees, and forest fires.

Grass thrives in prairie land where some water is available, but not enough to support larger trees. Cut the water supply too much, however, and even grass can't grow. You'll get a desert.

So it is with superficial believers. They don't thrive in an environment where life in God is fully flowing (a forest) — they are not comfortable in a church that's alive in God's power.

They want to be in an environment where it's okay to be lukewarm. Still, the life that flows from God (water) must be present to some degree or even they cannot survive.

While superficial believers *can* live on reduced amounts of truth (lower quantities of sunlight), they don't do well when overshadowed by strong believers (trees) on all sides. It's not their ideal environment.

The surest way to kill grass is a forest fire.

Grasses do not survive a fire the same way trees or bushes can. They are completely burnt up.

This is further confirmation that forest fires symbolize persecution, as persecution is the absolute surest way to purge the church of all lukewarm believers.

Historically, persecutions have always achieved this "purifying" effect on the church, revealing who is true and who was just giving lip service to a commitment to Christ. When soldiers knock at the door, superficial believers turn tail and run.

Regardless, though grass burns up — its seeds do not. They lie dormant within the soil, ready to spring back to life once the fire has passed. So it is in the Kingdom. Persecutions clean up the church, but only for a time. Once the hardships have passed and it's safe to call oneself a Christian again, the grass will slowly bloom once more.

Lesson: *Work to be firm in the faith and deepen your roots. Avoid superficial believers.*

Flowers

"If then God so clothes the grass, which today is in the field and tomorrow is thrown into the oven, how much more will He clothe you, O you of little faith?" (Luke 12:28)

Flowers are beautiful.

Which means they represent believers in the Kingdom who appear especially beautiful (spiritually speaking).

Flowers come in many different forms: flowering trees, bushes, vines, and grasses. This means we'll find these "beautiful" believers among all types of Christians, from mature, prominent leaders (trees), to missionaries and evangelists (vines), and even among superficial believers (grass).

By beauty, we do not mean physical beauty. We mean spiritual beauty. And by spiritual beauty, we do not mean spiritually healthy. We have already interpreted various types of plants of being symbolic of those believers who are "healthy."

Flowers are symbolic of being spiritually attractive.

To be spiritually attractive is when a believer, by the nature of their personality, spirit, or countenance, is a person who is pleasing to be around. This is the kind of believer everybody admires, speaks highly of, and wants to hang out with. They attract others to themselves.

Spiritual attractiveness can be an indicator of a believer's underlying spiritual health, or it can just as equally mask spiritual superficiality. In other words, just because a believer is charismatic or a pleasure to be around, or even physically attractive, does not necessarily mean they are someone to emulate, or that they are spiritually mature. We need to look beneath the flower and examine the structure of the plant.

All fruit trees are flowering trees.

Previously, we saw that fruit trees are "sweet believers," those that ooze the love of Christ. Fruit tree believers are some of the best kinds of believers. They're firm in their faith (a tree), beautiful in spirit (flowers), shower others in love as they make disciples (much sweet fruit), and they're especially effective in otherwise barren soil.

Not all trees have flowers, but all do reproduce, bearing seeds.

In the same way, not all Christians are charismatic or spiritually attractive, but all Christians reproduce, making disciples one way or the other. Just as all plants produce seed, so do all Christians reproduce, whether they want to or not. Their seed bears fruit after their own kind, whatever that might be.

The purpose of flowers is reproduction. In spite of the previous observation, that all Christians reproduce, being spiritually attractive ensures a much greater fertility rate. Being spiritually attractive means that a larger number of people will flock around the "flower believer," ensuring a faster discipling rate, regardless of the type of discipler.

A quick review of many of our experiences verifies this. We've all known spiritually *healthy*, charismatic Christians and spiritually *unhealthy,* charismatic Christians.

Both kinds have large numbers of believers who want to be like them simply because they're attracted to them.

God also adorns the grass of the field with flowers.

This is what typically comes to mind when we think of flowers. Daisies, marigolds, tulips.

These flowers represent spiritually attractive, *superficial* believers. Yes, superficial believers can be attractive and they will reproduce after their own kind.

Many of these flowering grasses are annuals, meaning they grow, bloom, and die all within one year's time. They leave seeds that can bloom the following year, but the life span of any one particular annual plant is very brief.

Just so, many superficial believers, though very effective in reproducing themselves in other disciples, may last a very short time themselves before drying up. Their disciples will follow suit.

Now, some readers may be objecting here, saying that superficial believers don't make disciples; that disciple-making is the mark of a mature Christian.

Yet, as we interact with one another, each one of us leaves their mark on every person we contact. We all have a close ring of associates on whom our mark is especially present. Superficial believers are leaving their marks everywhere they go — they're just not doing it on purpose like a mature believer would.

And they won't be producing disciples that imitate Christ.

Lesson: *Don't mistake charisma for spiritual maturity.*

Crops

"But others fell on good ground and yielded a crop:
some a hundredfold, some sixty, some thirty.
He who has ears to hear, let him hear!" (Matthew 13:8-9)

Jesus used crops as symbols in a number of his parables, and since most of the readers of this book are likely familiar with the lessons He drew from them, I doubt we have much to add here.

In the parable of the sower, Jesus tells the story of a farmer sowing seeds in a field. The seed is the Word of God and it lands upon different types of soil, which represent the hearts of different types of people.

This matches and confirms our interpretation of soil representing people in the Kingdom, or their hearts, to be more specific.

The path is hardened by people treading upon it. The Word of God does not penetrate hardened hearts, hearts that have been hardened by being walked on. The seed is snatched away and does not take root.

In order for the seed to take root, the ground must be tilled, it must be broken up. This is why God "breaks" people. He brings them into trying circumstances where they lose all possibility of self-reliance. This brokenness forces them to cry out to God in their need. Now that circumstances have tilled their hearts, the soil is loosened and they can receive the Word of God and produce a harvest of fruit.

Without that tilling, the hardened individual is impenetrable.

The interpretation of the rocky soil is that the seed cannot take root among so many obstacles (rocks in the soil), and in the face of the true, powerful image of Christ (the sun) beaming down upon them, they wilt and produce no fruit. Tribulation comes and the person is faced with imitating Christ in purity and self-sacrifice in the midst of that struggle and because of the poor quality of the soil of their heart (filled with rocky obstacles), they fail.

If we amplify our interpretation using our understanding of stones, this would represent someone who has a lot of truth (rocks) in their heart, but not much room for fellowship. Or another way to look at it would be truths that are not broken down for consumption, grand truths that are not applied for practical living in fellowship with others. So, it could be said a deeper fellowship is what sustains us through tribulation. (We'll see that principle repeated in more symbolism later).

Jesus says the thorns represent the cares, riches, and deceit of the world, which sap the soil of its productivity. Thorns suck up all the nutrients and water from the soil and choke out good plants that would otherwise produce fruit. In the same way, the cares of the world, having one's heart in the world and being concerned with it, sucks the thoughts and life from a person's heart so they have nothing left for God to own. They are choked by the cares of the world and produce no harvest.

The good soil represents a good heart. The fruit, which is the harvest, is the fruit of the Holy Spirit shown in the life of a believer. It is also the fruit of good works produced by the power and presence of the Holy Spirit, and it is the fruit of making disciples through the power of God.

The lesson here is that since we have no control over the growth process in plants, thus we *also* have no control over the spiritual growth process in people, yet we *can* influence certain factors to aid growth. We can till and break up the soil. This is the preparation of the soil. We prepare the soil of non-believer's hearts by exposing them to the power of God, which acts like a plow, over time.

We can fertilize the soil, again peppering our own hearts and the hearts of others with the nutritious truths of God.

We can water the soil, putting people in touch with God's power, with the life that only He gives, allowing them to live.

We can remove stones from the soil. We search our hearts and look for the hardened places, asking God to remove the obstacles so His Word can take better root.

We can rip out the weeds and thorns, remove the cares of the world from our hearts so we are focused and dedicated to producing fruit for God.

We can do all those things, but we cannot make anything grow.

God loves to see harvest, to see fruit in our lives. He has tasked us with the responsibility of creating a good soil in our hearts for the seed, but He is the One who makes it grow.

Lesson: *Prepare your heart like you would prepare soil for fertility.*

Sea Plants

"And if a son of peace is there, your peace will rest on it; if not, it will return to you."
(Luke 10:6)

Sea plants, sea plants, sea plants.
Have you ever contemplated sea plants before now?
I bet you haven't.

Yet, if we're going to have a thorough examination of nature's symbolism, we can't neglect them.

If we've identified the ocean as the world, and plants as believers in Christ, then how in the world (pun intended) do we explain sea plants?

They can only be Christians who live in the world. If that's true, then are they missionaries or carnal Christians?

First, let's define what sea plants actually are. Many of the "plants" we think of as living in the sea, are not really plants at all. Algae is not considered a plant; it's too simple in its structures. Seaweeds are a type of algae, and so are also not true "plants." Sea sponges are not plants either. Believe it or not, they are part of the animal family. So, for the sake of clarity, we will refer to sea grasses as being the plants that live in the sea.

Sea grasses can only live in the very upper levels of the ocean, called the *photic zone*, where enough light gets through for photosynthesis to take place. In fact, 90% of all marine life lives in the narrow photic zone.

Though we imagine the oceans teeming with life, the truth is, once you get out of the photic zone, you'd be hard-pressed to find much alive.

In the same way, we imagine the godless "world" as teeming with life and fun. That's where life is, we think. It can't be just what we see here in the Kingdom.

Yet, just as marine life can't survive in the ocean without sunlight, so can no one truly live in the world without receiving at least a minimal amount of the truth and goodness that flows from Christ. His light is so powerful, it can spiritually sustain a person though it be 99% distorted and diffused by the world. 1% is enough for life to survive.

Yes, just like land-based plants, these sea plants receive light, breathe in carbon dioxide, and breathe out oxygen. Sea grasses are a big part of what pumps oxygen back into the ocean water, allowing fish and other marine life to breathe.

That is our first clue as to their identity.

Sea grasses provide several beneficial services to us. They have been called "ecosystem engineers" because they transform the environment around them, making it much more hospitable to fish and other marine life. They create "fishing grounds," which makes it possible for humans in boats to target their fishing efforts on focused areas and get bigger catches.

They protect the coasts from erosion by waves and tidal forces.

These sea grasses also show an extraordinary ability to adapt rapidly to changing environmental conditions.

So, who does that description fit best?

These sea plants would be Christians who live in world, are tuned in to the truth of God (sunlight), and transform the culture around them making it hospitable to spiritual life. They breathe God's truth into the world around them (oxygen). They help protect God's Kingdom from erosion by the world (coastal protection), and they are highly adaptive to cultural change around them, quickly adjusting to new situations or needs.

These are believers living in a hostile environment.

Take Pakistan as an example. In non-Christian or even hostile nations like Pakistan, you will find scattered throughout the country isolated individuals who heard about Christ at one point and received Him as Lord and Savior, but are not part of any larger body of believers, or who have hearts already prepared by God to receive Christ, but have not yet heard His name.

Missionaries run across this kind of person all the time. They call them a "person of peace." These are people who God has prepared beforehand to receive the message of the gospel and act on it, serving as a catalyst to facilitate a rapid expansion of the Kingdom in their community.

Sea grasses cannot be seen from land, nor can these "people of peace" be seen from the Kingdom. You can only find them once you dive into the world, and there they maintain a low profile.

Just as a "sea tree" would be quickly snapped in half by powerful ocean currents or storms, so would a prominent Christian leader in Pakistan quickly be snapped in half by the government or community at large.

On the contrary, a person of peace in Pakistan is highly sensitive and adaptive to changing currents and circumstances within his community. His flexibility and low prominence allows for his continued survival.

Yet, these people of peace act as salt and light in their communities, though they be few in number. Their presence preserves and provides for the non-believers in their communities to receive some spiritual nourishment (oxygen).

Their presence also "tames" their culture, preventing it from "eroding" the Kingdom. Bluntly said, it is the calming, civilized presence of these people that keeps Pakistan from descending into a full-blown aggressor against the United States. Think this is overstating the case?

I personally happen to know of a very prominent and powerful Muslim politician in Pakistan who was, until very recently, receiving weekly Bible studies from several Pakistani Christians. This Muslim leader is very influential and, even if he never changes faiths or allegiances, his spiritual demeanor has been significantly impacted and softened by these Christian studies given by believers living in a hostile environment. The influenced and softened politician will be a less aggressive and oppressive leader.

This is not an isolated case. We just can't see these sea grass Christians because we're not living in their community.

Now, previously, we negatively interpreted land grasses as being superficial Christians. Yet here, we're admiring sea grasses as men and women of peace living in a hostile environment. Why the difference?

In the Kingdom (on land), a believer theoretically has the freedom to become a wide variety of plants (ignoring God's role in determining DNA). In a free society like the United States, a believer has no excuse for a lack of spiritual maturity or strength, and being too flexible is a negative, signifying a lack of dependability and faithfulness. They have ample access to God's truth for growth and are part of large bodies of believers, which allows them to sink their roots deep.

In the world, in a country like Pakistan, being flexible and maintaining a low profile is the only recipe for survival. There, flexibility is no indication of being wishy-washy. Rather it shows resiliency, dedication, and creativity. They do not have easy access to God's truth, nor to a large body of believers to take root in, so they are not too blame for a lack of growth or deep roots.

Lesson: *Do not judge our brothers and sisters living in hostile environments. Respect them, love them, and help them.*

Rock-Eating Plants

"But He said to them, 'I have food to eat of which you do not know.'"
(John 4:32)

There are some very hardy plants that can root themselves in small pools of water among fresh lava rocks and grow without touching any soil. Unlike other plants, these guys are specially equipped to eat away at rock directly and break it down.

Only the hardiest of Christians (rock-eating plants) can take nourishment directly from the rock-hard truths of God. There are those hardy Christians that seem to defy nature and take root within the stones. They are able to feed where others are not, and they actually help accelerate the process of breaking down the bigger truths for other Christians. They help create the soil where there was none before.

Perhaps they could even be called church planters.

Lesson: *God is very creative, and He does unusual things.*

REVIEW

Land	=	God's Kingdom
Boulder	=	Jesus Christ
Stones	=	Truths
Soil	=	Body of Christ
Trees	=	Individual Believers
Forest Fires	=	Persecution of Believers
Evergreens	=	Mature & Constant Believers
Deciduous	=	Mature & Cyclical Believers
Fruit/Seed	=	Testimonies
Fruit Trees	=	Mature, Loving Believers
Vines	=	Missionaries
Bushes	=	Mature Believers (Less Prominent)
Grass	=	Superficial Believers
Flowers	=	Spiritual Attractiveness
Sea Plants	=	Believers Living in a Hostile Environment

BIOMES:

Churches

CLIMATES

Q uick! Name every kind of terrain you can think of on Earth. Deserts, forest, arctic, jungle, swamp, tundra, prairies... What causes the differences between them? If you think about it, all the different biomes and climates around the globe are created by variations in the amount of light, heat, or water available.

In the same way, as we shall see, differences in the quality or quantity of believers in different parts of God's Kingdom are due to variations in the availability of God's truth, love, or power.

Deserts

"Behold, I will do a new thing, Now it shall spring forth; Shall you not know it? I will even make a road in the wilderness, and rivers in the desert." (Isaiah 43:19)

S unlight and heat are not hard to come by in the desert, but water is. Without water, vegetation and animals are guaranteed to be few, if any at all. A place can have all the light and heat you could ever want, but without water, the land will be barren.

In the same way, parts of God's kingdom can be inundated with truth (light), His people can be overflowing with a love and passion for the lost (warmth), but if God is not moving, if He has not released His animating force (water) in the land, nothing will happen. There will be no new believers, there will be no new life, for men cannot create life from their own power.

The question then becomes, *can God make water flow in the desert?* Absolutely. Look at the wanderings of Israel as they were led by Moses, how God brought forth water from the rock. This event pictured

Christ (the rock) being the only source of God's power and life (water) to His people in the wilderness of their struggle.

I used to attend a desert church. I remember the way we all exerted tremendous effort (repeatedly) to reach out to our community. I remember the neighborhood festivals we hosted, the special activities we planned and put on. We went door-to-door evangelizing, praying, inviting people to visit our church. We spent Saturdays cutting people's lawns and doing other yard work for free to demonstrate selfless service. We hosted a dinner for a local Muslim group, we built a neighborhood volleyball court and invited neighbors to play, and we gave everything to God in prayer. We tried small groups, social projects, and everything else you can imagine in between, yet our results were negligible.

Well, I say our results were negligible since we never saw much in the way of new "converts" or attendees, but out of 200 members, we sent approximately 30 to 40 into ministry full-time, and many of the rest became solid believers, strongly equipped. Our frustration at the time was great, but looking back, I'd say God was strengthening all of us until He was ready to spread us out across the Kingdom.

Some may say that we just didn't have the right culture, or the right leaders, or the right evangelism techniques, but the truth is we were not lacking in dedication or a willingness to try anything new. There was little stodgy adherence to tradition, and in general, we thoroughly believed in God for the work, but He simply chose not to move in the way we wanted.

In my opinion, many churches in America find themselves in this situation currently, yet they are unaware of the fact they're in a desert.

They have truth coming out their ears. Access to God's Word has never been more prevalent in America.

The members feel a strong burden for the lost, and they exhaust themselves with programs, trying to save them, but very few new believers result, and certainly no movement of God occurs. The frustration of these churches is great, for they have "understanding" and they care about the lost, but nothing happens in spite of their effort.

With a lot of work, by carting in water, they can plant and cause to survive a few trees, but they cannot make a desert valley bloom without a river.

God must move in His power, or the land will remain barren.

This is a practical lesson that we can take from the symbol that is the desert. If you find your church is barren in spite of much effort, turn to prayer and rely on God to supply the life. Pray that God will make the water gush forth from the rock. He is the only one who can send the life necessary to make His Kingdom bloom.

Deserts are hotter than other environments because there is no moisture to cool things off.

In a desert church, our love for the lost (heat) becomes an oppressive frustration because God's failure to move in power makes it impossible for us to quench our thirst to reach them. We find ourselves sweating much more quickly as we struggle to reach the lost in our own power.

When God does move, though, reaching the lost almost becomes easy. We don't sweat as much and we aren't thirsty.

Lesson: *A church can be doing everything right, but will not see results if God has chosen not to move. His decision to not move is not necessarily reflective of the obedience of the members. Therefore, do not judge your own church or another's based on results, but on the state of the members' hearts.*

Desert Rain

"To cause it to rain on a land where there is no one,
A wilderness in which there is no man"
(Job 38:26)

As crazy as it sounds, it does occasionally rain in the desert. These rare rains often arrive in the form of severe, yet short-lasting storms. Being so sandy and having been without water for so long, desert soil isn't able to retain rainwater well. The fallen water soon disappears, evaporating too quickly for plants to take root.

In the spiritual realm, in our "desert" churches, God *will* bring the occasional rain into the collective spiritual life of those desert believers.

Experience shows that an unexpected movement of God in a church that is not used to such things does not usually handle it very well. Many members will often react negatively to what they are seeing, fearing the sudden shake up of their traditions. They aren't able to retain the life poured out among them.

Lesson: *Welcome God's shake-ups and work to hold onto the life He is providing.*

Desert Life

"The beast of the field will honor Me, The jackals and the ostriches,
Because I give waters in the wilderness and rivers in the desert,
To give drink to My people, My chosen." (Isaiah 43:20)

Most deserts are not truly barren. While a couple like the Sahara are seemingly devoid of life, most deserts have complete ecosystems consisting of both plants and animals.

Still, such wildlife is absolutely sparse when compared with that of a forest, and all the life in a desert, both plants and animals, are water "retainers," organisms capable of either retaining water for extended periods of time, or living continually on smaller amounts of water than most.

In the same way, *desert churches are not dead.* There is plenty of life to be found.

Desert believers are capable of living much longer on the things God has done in the past, or they are able to get greater joy than most from smaller movements by Him. They are hardier believers to be admired for their fortitude.

It's easy to live next to the current powerful movements of God. It's much harder to maintain your faith in the desert.

Also, many desert plants have deep taproots that descend deep, searching for water until they reach the water table.

In the same way, many desert believers find themselves having to dig deep in order to access the life that flows from God. Their deep, spiritual "taproots" are what enable them to survive, and even thrive, when no life is visible.

Lesson: *When God is not moving, dig deep.*

Oases

"The parched ground shall become a pool,
And the thirsty land springs of water" (Isaiah 35:7)

An oasis is a fresh water spring found in the middle of a dry desert. Trees and other plant life may surround an oasis, but that will be the extent of their impact on the desert.

One spring is not enough to water the whole desert.

Creatures living in the desert will know exactly where this spring is, and they'll remain close enough to it to drink whenever needed.

In spiritually deserted regions of the Kingdom, among all the churches where God is not moving, you will find a few scattered churches here and there where God *is* moving.

These churches are spiritual "oases." They are a refuge for men and women of God desperately thirsty for the life that flows from Him. Some believers (palm trees) will flourish in and around these churches and plant themselves there, and new believers will grow as well (new plant life).

Other believers (desert creatures) will visit such a church from time to time in order to get refreshed by the spiritual life in it, and then they will move off into the barren land again.

Lesson: *Even in the middle of a desert, God is moving somewhere.*

How to Make a Desert

"I will lay waste the mountains and hills, And dry up all their vegetation...And I will dry up the pools." (Isaiah 42:15)

Most people believe deserts are made by extreme heat beating down upon a region.

This is not true.

Heat doesn't produce deserts, deserts produce heat. There is quite a bit of evidence suggesting that the Sahara may have once been a lush, forested region.

No, deserts form because of a lack of plant life. Vegetation retains water which cools the air around it. Vegetation also releases moisture back into the air, further impacting humidity and eventually provoking rain.

Deserts are formed when trees and other plant life die or are cut down by humans. Trees pull water deep from the soil and water table with their roots, and release it through their leaves into the air.

As the density of vegetation decreases, so does rainfall. As that happens, heat increases, and the level of moisture further decreases. The increase in heat and dryness makes it harder for the soil to retain water, and what rain does fall evaporates more quickly. This cycle continues until what once was green has become nothing but an ocean of sand and dust.

The easiest way to create a spiritual desert is to cut down the strong believers (trees).

If a portion of the Kingdom experiences a decrease in the number of strong believers, God's activity in that portion of the Kingdom decreases (i.e. less water) since God primarily moves through believers. When a region is denuded of firm, mature believers, there is no one to tap deep into the Life that God offers and draw that life up for others to partake.

Also, trees root the soil down and hamper wind erosion. Without mature believers holding the soil of the Kingdom in place, too much is eroded and blown around freely.

Lesson: *Encourage the growth of strong believers in your church.*

A Blooming Desert?

"The wilderness and the wasteland shall be glad for them,
And the desert shall rejoice and blossom as the rose;
It shall blossom abundantly and rejoice,
Even with joy and singing." (Isaiah 35:1-2a)

Is it possible to make the desert bloom again?
Yes.
In the mid-1800's, Mark Twain took a tour of the land of Palestine (modern day Israel). He reported nothing but desert sand and a few sporadic Palestinians in sixty miles of travel. Others traveling in the region around the same time give similar reports of utter desolation, a land barren of life and people.

Today, Israel has become much greener, to the point it is the number one supplier of citrus fruits to much of Europe. I myself have visited, and I can report that there are now areas so lush they could even be compared to rain forest.

When Jews first began returning to Palestine in the early 1900's, the average annual rainfall slowly began to increase each year. Israel today is a very different place than it was 150 years ago. Since the time of Mark Twain, rainfall in Israel has increased 450% and over 300 million trees have been planted!

This increase of rainfall, this blooming of Israel, is actually a fulfillment of prophecy.

"So they will say, 'This land that was desolate has become like the garden of Eden; and the wasted, desolate, and ruined cities are now fortified and inhabited.'" (Ezekiel 36:35)

Obviously, after so many centuries of nothing, God has begun moving in Israel again. This is symbolized by the increase in rain (God's life-giving movement in power), and is literally seen in the immigration of millions of Jews to Israel once more, which is simultaneously symbolized by the planting of millions of trees (believers).

There is a scientific explanation for this increase in rainfall, though it in no way negates the fulfillment of prophecy. As Jews began returning to the land, they began planting trees. They planted orchards and began irrigating fields for farming. This purposeful increase in vegetation resulted in an increase in moisture in the atmosphere, which resulted in increasing amounts of rain.

This blooming of the desert is a reviving of the land (Kingdom of God), which can *only* represent spiritual revival.

To make the desert bloom, the soil must be fertile, seeds must be planted, and water must become available. Therefore, for a spiritual revival to ignite, God must have prepared the soil of men's hearts ahead of time to receive the seeds of truth. (This is the fertile soil.)

Seeds must be planted, i.e. testimonies of truth from believers must be planted. Fully mature believers (trees) may also be planted in order to jumpstart the revival.

Most importantly, however, God must move. A revival cannot occur without the movement of God Himself. Then, as new believers rise up, God begins to move more and more powerfully until the whole land is flourishing.

Irrigation would imply that men can somehow direct this animating force of God into a region of the desert of their choosing.

Perhaps God allows this.

Even so, *men cannot create the water.* Moses was not able to strike just any rock at random and cause water to flow out. He was only going to have success with that one specific rock God had indicated.

God must still *move*. He alone can make life flow through the Kingdom.

When He does move and life begins to flow, *if* He allows us to channel this animating force, we are still are somewhat limited in how far we can plant our fields from God's original movement. Just as farmers cannot extend their irrigation ditches endlessly from the original source of water, so we must stay near our original source of spiritual "water."

Still, as trees and other plants increase in number, rain increases, which is God's blessing upon the entire land. And as the rain increases, irrigation becomes less important.

So, perhaps God gives men the authority to choose the direction of the revival at the beginning. If so, their choice will later become irrelevant as the whole land is watered.

The key is whether the water flows at all. The key is whether God is moving.

Lesson: *If your ministry isn't flourishing, pray for rain.*

Arroyos

"For laying aside the commandment of God,
you hold the tradition of men..."
(Mark 7:8a)

Arroyos are dangerous. Not so dangerous you need to call your mama, but you certainly don't want to hang out in one.

An arroyo is a ditch or small canyon formed in the desert floor by fast-moving water. Arroyos have steep sides and vary from just a couple of feet to up to twenty or thirty feet deep.

If rain falls in the mountains or hills surrounding a desert, those mountains channel that rain into a temporary, concentrated river that rushes out onto the desert floor.

This sudden gush of water over time digs a channel in the floor of the desert that can extend for miles.

Lots of people have drowned in arroyos, caught by sudden flash floods. It's not uncommon for powerful walls of water to rush through these mini-canyons, even when the sky overhead is clear, not a cloud to be seen. A hard rain in mountains as far away as thirty miles can produce these killer flash floods.

Imagine you're strolling along the bottom of a small desert canyon in peace. Suddenly, you find yourself facing a twenty-foot high, roaring, churning wall of water that's tearing and smashing everything in its path. Then, the rushing water diminishes almost as quickly as it arrived. Within minutes, it's evaporated and the only signs of its passing are the inert, crushed forms of those who got in its way.

The danger of being caught in a flash flood like that is heightened by the relatively harmless appearance of the arroyo to the unsuspecting passerby.

It looks dry; it's in the middle of the desert. No clouds. Hey, where did that thirty foot wall of water come from?

Arroyos pose a second danger to desert dwellers. Generally, they can't be seen from a distance. Being so narrow, and the desert floor so flat, the driver of a car or a rider on a horse often only sees an arroyo once they're right on top of it, and by then, it may be too late to stop. While cars today typically stick to paved highways and roads, historically, many riders on horses fell into these hidden chasms.

At first, the symbolism behind an arroyo can be difficult to discern. It's a feature of the desert (dry, inactive portion of God's Kingdom). It's formed when water (God's animating power) falls somewhere else. That initial flow of water digs a channel that can be very deep. The flow of water in this channel is so rare that it cannot be depended upon for life, as one could a river in other parts of the Kingdom. If you dwell in this giant rut, you will be crushed by the water (God's activity) rather than revitalized by it. These ruts in the ground cannot be seen very easily, especially from the wrong angle, but are very visible when observed up close.

Arroyos are symbols for the traditions of men.

A tradition can be a rut. It's a path that is initially cut into the kingdom by the activity of God, but as the surrounding landscape dries up, it becomes a place of danger rather than vitality.

A Lutheran minister once shared with me that Martin Luther attributed his success in launching the Reformation to the worship music they used rather than his own teaching. Indeed, across Europe, many reformers came before Luther and taught the same things he taught, some of them more charismatically, some less.

So what was Luther's secret? He took many of the most popular, local bar tunes and put Christian words to them. God used this innovative music to reach the German culture, and even the rest of Europe, in amazing ways. God moved powerfully through this new way, and this is comparable to a river.

As the spiritual landscape in Europe began to dry up, however, Christians hung onto these songs with dear affection, remembering the power and influence they'd once held. Many of these songs are now some of our most well-known, traditional hymns. Today, they do very little as far as producing new believers, though they are emotionally powerful and do contain great truths. (In the desert, there's plenty of light (truth), but God is not moving.)

As centuries passed, new music was adapted. Christians have repeatedly put Christian words to whatever was considered a "contemporary" sounding melody from their era. These songs each had a great impact during their time, but once again, after a while, they also ceased to be part of God's movement in the Kingdom and joined the growing corpus of our traditional hymns.

Today, in many of our churches, we sing simple, contemporary choruses. This contemporary worship has been a breath of fresh air, a tool of God that inspires many to worship Him anew in Spirit and in truth. Our modern worship is currently being used by Him to produce new life.

Someday, however, He will choose a new method. When the spiritual landscape begins to dry up, we will turn our current contemporary worship choruses into tradition, hanging on to them for dear life, trying to make other Christians cherish and remember the impact they once had.

Tradition does not require sincerity. It allows the insincere worshiper to participate because their affection could originate in nothing more than a fond remembrance of family or youth rather than a passion for God.

New movements of God, however, discourage the insincere from participating. Since the would-be worshiper has no connection with the new song itself, or with a new habit, the only reason for a passionate response is a true passion for God.

God moves among sincere worshipers.

Another example is the tradition of circumcision. In the beginning, circumcision was a commandment of God and one of the primary ways in which God acted in His kingdom. He stamped His followers with this rite that marked their bodies for life. Believers chose to endure circumcision as an act of faith, choosing to follow God and commit their lives to Him.

However, as Israel became spiritually "dry," this act of faith began to become nothing more than a ritual, a tradition, performed by insincere followers of God. They went through the motions, but their hearts were no longer engaged with God's through the rite.

The Pharisees did not hang onto this tradition with weak fingers. They grasped it so tightly they became blinded to the new way in which God was moving in His Kingdom. They refused to move out of their tradition (arroyo), and were eventually crushed by the wall of water that struck them.

God is powerful. He can move gently in a providing, vitalizing way (like a river or rain), or He can move powerfully in judgment (like a flash flood in an arroyo). The Pharisees, who refused to step out of their "arroyo" and believe the words of their Messiah, remained in Jerusalem until 70 AD when the Romans attacked. Their fate is well-known.

The most interesting aspect of a tradition is this: We don't always spot them easily.

When we are traveling through or living in a portion of God's Kingdom which is currently barren, a river flowing through that desert is easy to spot, because it will always be surrounded by flourishing trees.

An arroyo, on the other hand, cannot be easily seen and a traveler is wise to move through this section of the land at a slow pace, or they could fall into the trap of this "tradition" before they know what's happened.

In the life of our home church, many times we'll do things a certain way, and think that is the right way, the only way, and we fail to realize that we are just doing things that way because of tradition. It is easy to fall into the trap of hanging onto that tradition, even to our own peril or the peril of our church.

Bottom line, arroyos are fascinating to look at and study, as are the traditions of the church. *But don't hang out in one*, and be sure you know where they are before you start moving too fast.

Lesson: *You can enjoy a tradition, but don't dwell in it.*

Sandstorms

"The Lord will change the rain of your land to powder and dust; from the heaven it shall come down on you until you are destroyed."
(Deuteronomy 28:24)

The low roar of the approaching wind is second only to the terrifying wall of sand that stretches to the sky, relentlessly advancing like an army of wind-blown ants. Frantically, you scratch a depression in the desert floor, hunkering as low as you can as waves of grit begin their assault on your body, enveloping your senses with a suffocating embrace, ripping at your skin with ragged fingers.

The sand clogs your nostrils and trickles into your ears. It's all you can do to keep your eyes covered and hold your shirt across your mouth just so you can keep breathing. You will most likely survive, but getting to the other side of this storm will not be pleasant.

Thankfully, sandstorms aren't common to every desert. For example, they generally don't afflict the Western United States. Of course, the Dust Bowl years of the 1930's were a different story. Due to a combination of severe drought and generations of poor farming practices, dust storms did become commonplace in the mid-western U.S. for a time. Still, those conditions have been rectified, and the dust storms have not returned.

Today, the large majority of sandstorms occur in the Sahara Desert, the Middle East, and parts of China (and of those, most are in the Sahara). These storms only form in sections of the desert that are *completely* dry and almost devoid of life.

Sandstorms are created by strong winds that scoop up enormous amounts of dust as they blow through.

Three things result: 1. Soil and nutrients are picked up, 2. They are redeposited in another place, and 3. In the process, for those living there, life becomes unbearable until the storm passes.

Sandstorms in the Sahara blow away large amounts of nutrients from the soil in northern Africa, rendering it ever less fertile, and the range of this movement of dust is unbelievably far. Significant portions of this dust cross the entire Atlantic Ocean and reach as far as South America, continually making that region even more fertile.

We have firmly established that wind symbolizes the movement of the Holy Spirit.

Remembering the parables of Jesus, we identify the sandy soil with people in whom the Word of God has not taken root. The desert is the section of God's Kingdom that is spiritually dry, denied God's living movement.

So, sandstorms represent times when the Holy Spirit blows through these deserted regions of the Kingdom, moving believers around and re-depositing them elsewhere.

Some of these believers just land back in the desert again. Others fall into the world (the ocean). Others get blown into new parts of the

Kingdom (like South America) where God *is* moving (flowing water) and seeds of truth can now take root. For those people that land in well-watered regions, they are no longer part of a sandy soil, but are now partaking in a fertile land.

There are times when the Spirit of God blows through the driest of churches, stirring up believers who could grow or be of service elsewhere. When the Spirit moves for this reason, these believers, tired of being thirsty, find themselves suddenly moved en masse to find a new church.

Some of them land in other churches that are just as dry as the one they came from. Some fall away and land in the world.

Others find their way to fertile churches full of life where they will finally bloom and receive the Word.

Throughout the ordeal, those members of the original "dry" church who are not stirred up and remain in place, find living in their church unbearable until the storm has passed and the movement of people has ceased.

At times, the ripping apart of their church may feel like it will never end.

The recent events surrounding the ELCA (Evangelical Lutheran Church in America) are a good example of this. This permissive protestant denomination, which has rejected the Bible as God's authoritative Word, recently voted to allow unrepentant homosexuals to serve as clergy.

Interestingly, on the day this denomination's leaders were gathered in Minneapolis in conference to vote, God spoke.

At 2:00 PM, the *very minute* the denomination was scheduled to vote on this decision, a strong and unexpected tornado swept through downtown Minneapolis, causing significant damage to both the convention hall and the church where the vote was taking place.

Just moments before, the skies had been clear.

The tornado swung down out of nowhere, struck the *only two buildings* involved in the conference, and damaged little else in the city.[12] The vote was delayed, but unfortunately, the denomination ignored God's clear warning and passed the measure a few hours later by a *one-vote* majority.

Immediately following that, a mass exodus of Christians from this denomination ensued, and continues to this day. They are being moved by the Spirit to seek new churches.

The ELCA is a spiritual desert. God is not moving in that denomination. The people who are leaving are seeking the true life that God offers. They are thirsty.

Some of them will end up in churches just as dry as the one they came from, but we rejoice to know that many will end up in healthy, vibrant churches. In the meantime, those clergy who voted to approve this measure are hiding, pinching shut their mouths, noses, and eyes until the sandstorm is over and they can breathe again.

Lesson: *God manages His Kingdom.*

---

[12] John Piper, *The Tornado, the Lutherans, and Homosexuality*, http://www.desiringgod.org/blog/posts/the-tornado-the-lutherans-and-homosexuality (accessed Sept. 20, 2013).

Than Tibbetts, *Tornadoes Cause Damage Across Twin Cities Area*, Minnesota Public Radio, http://minnesota.publicradio.org/display/web/2009/08/19/minneapolis-tornado (accessed Sept. 20, 2013).

Forest & Jungle

"Break forth into singing, you mountains, O forest, and every tree in it!
For the LORD has redeemed Jacob, And glorified Himself in Israel."
(Isaiah 44:23b)

If trees represent strong, mature believers, then it only follows that a forest will represent large groupings of these believers in certain areas of the Kingdom.

The next time you find yourself near some woods, take a moment to go stand silently in the midst of them and listen. It's not the quiet place you might assume.

A forest is like a church and the constant chatter of cicadas is reminiscent of the chattering of believers within a church family, discussing everything from soccer practices, to the pastor's sermon, to predestination vs. free will. This chattering is a sound of life.

Next, you'll notice melodious songbirds trilling in worship of their creator, like soloists adoring in praise from the stage.

Wind rustles through the leaves, moving them just as gently as the Spirit moves believers within the Body.

From time to time, you'll hear the crack of a dead branch snapping off from high in the canopy and landing with a dull thud below. With no apparent cause in sight, this tree trimming reminds us of the way in which God prunes His children every now and then for their own health.

Occasionally, a giant tree groans as it begins a slow crash to the ground, slicing branches off the surrounding trees as it falls and destroying any plant life on the forest floor beneath it.

For such a large tree to fall, however, there must have already been significant rot within, and such corruption is usually not visible until after the fall. This is like a prominent pastor or other leader within the church who is caught in some grievous sin and falls.

A spiritually healthy leader will not be susceptible to the fall. Pastors only give into sin when they've already experienced significant corruption from the inside out, having allowed envy, lust, or other sins to fully take root in the flesh of their heart. Only after that has occurred are these heart-hosted sins culminated by a physical act. Unfortunately, such internal corruption is not usually visible to those on the outside until the fall occurs.

On their way down, the pastor's fall may "prune" other strong believers in the church. The fall of the pastor serves as a warning, pushing the one pruned into a place of stronger spiritual health. Even as the leader falls, God still uses the leader to lead others, though it be a negative example.

Yet, those weaker Christians who were growing in the shadow of this pastor will not be pruned. These are the immature believers who still lack discernment and understanding, who are like the smaller plant life on the forest floor. They are crushed.

Sometimes, a tree falling in the forest will be stopped halfway down, caught in the fork of another tree. This happens in the church too. A strong believer near the fallen leader will deflect the blow to those weaker brothers and sisters below, preserving them. This believer has also come to the aid of the leader, preventing the sinful nature (gravity) from pulling the leader all the way down. Regardless, the leader's ministry is nevertheless broken. His trunk has snapped and he can no longer conduct spiritual photosynthesis or bear testimony (seed).

Forests are not still; they are not silent. They are vibrant biospheres, full of wide varieties of life.

Just like a church.

And while every forest on earth has characteristics that distinguish it from all the other forests on earth (just as all churches are different from each other), there are three basic kinds of forests. They are: Rain forests, which occupy the tropical regions surrounding the equator, deciduous forests, which are the temperate forests we are most familiar with in the United States, and boreal forests, which occupy the more northern, subarctic regions of the planet.

Lesson: *To appreciate the vibrancy of the Church, stand in the forest and listen.*

Rain Forest

"Then David danced before the Lord with all his might; and David was wearing a linen ephod. So David and all the house of Israel brought up the ark of the Lord with shouting and with the sound of the trumpet."
(2 Samuel 6:1-15)

Rain forests are lively places teeming with activity and sound and full of the smell of fresh rain. Yet, in many ways, they are strange when compared with the forests here in North America. At least they are to me, and probably will be to you as well once we get into what makes them so different.

A number of unusual and unexpected characteristics stand out about rain forests. Even more interesting, as I pulled the undeniable symbolism from these biological facts and began laying out a picture of the kind of church they describe, it became apparent that the church model described is typical of the kind of churches one finds in many tropical regions of the world, i.e. Latin American and African churches. This amazing correlation between geography and symbolism astounds, but then, what else should we expect from God?

Students of Christian mission work know that culture determines much about the internal structure and life of a church. We're not talking about doctrine, but about *how* we teach doctrine. The differences don't impact whether or not we worship, but how we worship. A church in Indonesia will look nothing like a church in Metropolitan Atlanta.

While some readers may view the distinguishing characteristics of "rain forest churches" in a negative light, it should be noted that much of the differences are simply due to cultural differences. Because of our culture, the United States does not generally produce "rain forest churches," so they seem foreign to us. In fact, they *are* foreign to us.

God's symbolism for the internal life structure of a rain forest church is neither necessarily positive nor negative. It's simply a description.

For brevity's sake, I will henceforth refer to rain forest churches as being Latin American churches. The rain forest church description, however, well describes the church in many tropical regions of the world, i.e. Central Africa, the Philippines, etc.

My wife is a *latina* from Costa Rica, and I had the privilege of living in that beautiful land for several years, so I'm well aware of the cultural differences with the United States, especially in the church.

Also, the reader should take all statements regarding Latin American churches as broad generalities. There are, of course, going to be a few exceptions to every statement. As usual, though, exceptions often prove the rule.

Rain forests have three major growth layers: The canopy layer, the understory layer, and the forest floor.

The large majority of trees in a rain forest are very tall.

This is the canopy layer. The canopy layer absorbs 93% of the sunlight. Only 5% of the sunlight reaches the understory layer and a measly 2% reaches the forest floor.

Latin American churches are notorious for being pastor-centered. In contrast with North American churches where a spirit of democracy abounds, the pastors in Latin American churches will decide most issues by themselves. They are usually *the* major, prominent, mature Christian visible to the congregation. They are also usually surrounded by a few key leaders in their congregation, which pictures the understory level of trees in the rain forest. These understory leaders are prominent as well, but are severely overshadowed by the pastor.

In Latin American churches, there is typically a great divide between the biblical knowledge of the pastor and the lay people. Hispanic pastors are often very studied and know the Bible well. They have access to all kinds of study tools and resources. They have a great access to truth (sunlight), while, *in general,* their congregants' knowledge of Scripture is often much poorer.

This corresponds to the 93% of sunlight being absorbed by the canopy layer while only 2% reaches the forest floor.

Astoundingly, 50% of all plant species in the rain forest are rooted *in the tree canopy*, not in the forest floor.

This is one of the most unique features of a rain forest and this happens because the canopy layer is where the sunlight is.

These plants are called Epiphytic plants. They are smaller plants *that attach their roots to the trunks of larger trees* so they can live high enough to receive sunlight. Instead of the soil, their roots pull minerals and water from runoff on the tree trunks during the daily rains.

These Epiphytic plants are easily recognizable in the Latin American church. They are believers who are not rooted in the larger Body of Christ (soil), but in their pastor (the tree). Rooting themselves in their pastor allows them full access to truth (sunlight) since their pastor will freely share with those he is actively discipling.

Of those members in a Latin American congregation who are actively "photosynthesizing," a majority of them will be this kind of "Epiphytic" believer, either rooted superficially in the pastor, or in the understory leaders directly beneath him.

On the other hand, in this kind of church, believers who root themselves in the general Body of Christ (soil) instead of their pastor, will find that the pastor's form (the shape and nature of the tree) actually prevents them from receiving much of the truth of God. His neglect prevents them from perceiving God's truths well.

In a rain forest with a strong canopy layer, there is very limited undergrowth.

Where dominant pastors abound in the rain forest church, the growth of less prominent believers underneath them is severely limited.

The lack of undergrowth means that old-growth rain forests are easier to walk through and navigate. However, if the upper canopy layer is removed or thinned, i.e. larger trees are cut down, an immediate and chaotic explosion of tangled growth bursts forth from the forest floor.

Numerous vines, shrubs, and small trees scramble to thrive in the newly revealed sunlight. We refer to this jumbled mess of vegetation as jungle, which is different from old-growth rain forest. This jungle eventually gives way to rain forest once more as one or several trees grow tall enough to plug the hole and block the sunlight again, eclipsing the others.

This is also true of Latin American churches. Suddenly remove the strong pastor and immediate chaos ensues, with numerous believers rising up simultaneously in competition until one grows tall enough to restore order to the church.

In comparison with the temperate, deciduous forests of the Unites States, rain forests appear wild and chaotic.

To the American observer, life in a Hispanic church can seem messy and disorderly in contrast to the ordered nature of their church back home. However, this style is not wrong, just different.

Surprisingly, the soil in most rain forests is relatively *infertile*.

I was truly surprised to discover this truth. Rain forests seem like they would be the most fertile places on earth. Seriously, 45% - 70% of the world's species are indigenous to rain forests, so how can rain forests not be fertile?

Well, rain forests *are* fertile, but the fertility is not in the soil. Again, most of the sunlight and minerals are only available in the upper levels of the canopies. Even the lizards, snakes, and insects live primarily in those levels because of this.

And again, this is symbolic of how discipleship is done in Latin American churches. It is one-dimensional, from top to bottom. Very little discipleship occurs amongst the lay people of a congregation, outside the influence of a leader. There is no side-to-side discipleship, just up-down discipleship. Believers who root themselves in the lay people (soil) will struggle.

Another reason fertile soil does not develop is because of high levels of bacteria.

Humus, which is fertile soil derived from broken-down plant matter, doesn't build up in a rain forest because of rapid bacterial decay.

We will discuss bacteria later, but it is certainly true that in Latin American churches, lay people rarely spend time studying the history of the church (fallen leaves and trees), testimonies of those who have gone before that can serve as powerful object lessons for believers today. Life lessons are rapidly lost to decay.

Rain forests are wet!

Receiving upwards of seven feet of rain per year, they are the wettest places on land. Rains come daily and rivers gush through their gullies. Water is something never lacking in a rain forest.

Whatever else may be said about rain forest churches, there is no shortage of God's energizing life force, His power. Latin American churches are full of life. Worship and prayer pour out of their bodies.

When I lived in Central America, I remember being struck by the passion and joy infused into worship each Sunday. At churches that would not be considered charismatic by any means, believers sang at the tops of their lungs with hands raised and danced from overwhelming emotion. It always reminded me of the way David danced for joy as they brought the Ark up to Jerusalem.

While the average American Christian might view life in the rain forest church as being chaotic or disorganized, we are at the same time forced to confess to abundant levels of vibrancy in the Latin American church.

The prevalence of water in the rain forest is symbolic of how powerfully God is moving in the midst of rain forest churches, showering them in revival with the Life that is in Him.

Rain forests have been called the World's Largest Pharmacy.

This is due to the large number of natural medicines found there. Is it a coincidence that reports of God's miraculous healing are much more prevalent in rain forest churches than in North America?

Question: *Do you judge churches from other cultures for the wrong reasons?*

Deciduous/Temperate Forest

"These were more fair-minded than those in Thessalonica, in that they received the word with all readiness, and searched the Scriptures daily to find out whether these things were so."
(Acts 17:11)

Temperate forests are much more familiar to those of us living in North America. These forests are lush and green and vibrant for most of the year. Then, during winter, they fade into a cold, bare gray. They sport a varying mix of evergreen and deciduous trees, although the deciduous trees usually dominate the mixture by a large margin.

Temperate forests differ from rain forests in a number of significant ways.

Rain forests have two clearly distinct tree-height levels, whereas temperate forests are much more evenly distributed, i.e. tree heights are varied and unpredictable.

Temperate forests simply *look* more democratic. Trees are evenly spaced apart; you won't find a chaotic scramble for sunlight among the saplings. The forest floor is orderly, with clear paths for a traveler to follow.

Taller trees do absorb and block a good bit of the sunlight, but much of the light remains available at the forest floor level for growth of all kinds. Small saplings, medium-sized maples, large evergreens, bushes, and even wispy grasses are all able to tap into enough light, water, and fertile soil to grow healthily.

Temperate forests picture many North American churches. We tend to be much more philosophically egalitarian in our view of other Christians. We generally don't recognize separate classes of Christians. We view ourselves as all being equally important before God as brothers and sisters in Christ. We don't crowd each other; we respect the space of other believers around us. We are orderly, just like a deciduous forest.

Temperate forests receive more than enough rain and river flow to support lots of life.

In a "temperate church," God does move powerfully (water flow), just not quite as much as He does in a rain forest church.

In a rain forest, the main variable is rain.

Rain forests have two seasons: rainy and dry. A rain forest can see six months of heavy rain each and every day only to be followed by six months of dry. During the dry season, when the rain stops, rain forest trees slow their growth down.

This means when God moves in power in a rain forest church, believers grow. In the seasons when He withholds His power, the growth of those believers slows down or even stops. The only factor affecting growth of believers in a rain forest church is the level of God's movement in power.

On the other hand, the seasons of a temperate forest are impacted by the passage of time and circumstance. As time passes, trees go dormant, or grow, in relation to changes in the availability of light, warmth, and water.

While there are months of the year that are rainier than others, rain is generally available all year long. For example, in Georgia, you'll get heavy rains in February, April, July, and October, and sometimes November or December. Rains fall throughout the year, yet trees still slow their growth down during winter, regardless of how much water they have.

I have witnessed this firsthand. Latin American believers get very excited about miraculous healings and other powerful movements of God. And, coincidentally, such things seem to happen with a lot higher frequency in Latin American churches. These movements of God, this evidence of His power and activity seems to have a tremendous impact on the building of faith among Latin American believers. This godly rain makes them grow.

North American believers, on the other hand, don't get all that excited about a miraculous healing. Tell them about someone who was spontaneously healed of cancer after prayer and most of the time you'll get a smile and a "That's nice." It's almost like they don't quite believe it, like it would have happened anyway and the prayer was just coincidence. Unless the healing happens to them or someone they love — then they perceive God's love for them and *that* does excite them.

Hearing third party accounts of healings does not seem to do much for building the faith of a North American believer. But a believer who finds a job after getting laid off, or a couple who receives some unexpected money for a vacation they didn't think they were going to get to take, these will sense that God has provided for them in His love, and they will grow in their faith.

Rain forest believers *expect* those smaller miracles — they are much more impressed with God's movement in power. Yet it's almost like temperate believers cannot handle those larger miracles, their growth is stimulated by smaller flows of water combined with a reappearance of heat.

The main variable in a temperate forest is heat.
More of it in the summer, less in the winter.

Heat represents God's love, which means in North American churches, our seasons, our life cycles are impacted more by how much of God's love we receive.

Now, God doesn't stop loving. Just as the sun's position in the solar system is constant, so is God's love constant; it does not change. Receiving love, however, is a two way street. Just because God offers His love does not mean that we are open to receive it.

In the northern and southern hemispheres, the annual seasons change along with the earth's tilt. As our hemisphere tilts toward the sun, the earth retains more heat and summer begins. As the earth tilts away, winter sets in.

It is our *perception* of God's love, our nearness to Him, that changes, not God's love itself.

The lack of heat in winter ties in to the lessening of available sunlight. It's this lowered sunlight that results in less heat.

Thus, as we tilt away from God, we are bathed in less of His truth. As we step out of His truth, our ignorance blinds us to His love and we aren't as capable of receiving it. When we are not abiding in His truth or love, our spiritual growth stops.

Truly, there are times in our lives when everything seems to be going right, when all is new and fresh. When we feel like God is smiling at us, like He's right there with us, blessing us. When we are happy and renewed. Those are our spring times.

But, there are always those *other* times. Those days when you cut your finger, your car gets a flat, the dinner burns in the stove, and the baby is sick with colic. Everybody under the sun is demanding your time, but nobody appreciates what you're already giving, the IRS sent you a letter saying they're going to audit you next week, and you just found out your dog needs to be put to sleep.

Those are our winters. Those are the times when God and His love (warmth) feel far away, like He doesn't care, like we've been left out in the cold.

In times like those, our leaves fall to the ground. We appear to lose our spiritual maturity in the face of affliction and we cease redeeming the world through spiritual photosynthesis. (We don't truly lose our maturity, just the outward visibility of it for a period.)

Who has the time or strength to minister to the world when our own is falling apart? How many of us can redeem others when it doesn't even feel like God is with *us*? Not many.

Yet, evergreen trees are of a different sort. They somehow hold on to their visible maturity in the face of hardship. They're made of different stuff from the rest of us deciduous believers. When the winds of trouble and affliction blow chilling frustration into their path, evergreen believers hold fast, ministering and redeeming the world anyway, while the rest of us deciduous believers have to wait until spring to recover.

All believers are on this cyclical spiritual journey that passes from seasons of fresh joy, to deep maturity, to reflective wisdom, to enduring hardship, and then back to joy again.

Soil in temperate forests is highly fertile, unlike rain forests, and there are very few Epiphytic plants to speak of.

In contrast to the rain forest, plant life in a temperate forest is rooted in the soil. This should be interpreted to mean that in "temperate churches," the primary method of discipleship is side-to-side, not top-to bottom like in a rain forest church.

Which, in fact, is true in most American churches. In order to receive discipleship and tap into God's power, North American believers generally root themselves in the larger body of believers (soil), rather than binding themselves to some strong leader figure.

Here it is not the pastor who primarily disciples, it is every believer within the church family sharpening one another.

Again, this is not a validation of one form over the other — God is simply describing both through the symbolism incorporated in the different kinds of forests.

Question: *Can you perceive God's love in difficult times?*

Boreal/Evergreen Forest

"That is why, for Christ's sake, I delight in weaknesses, in insults, in hardships, in persecutions, in difficulties. For when I am weak, then I am strong." (2 Corinthians 12:10)

Boreal forests primarily consist of evergreen trees. These forests, which are also called *Taiga*, always lie in the colder regions of the earth. In North America, boreal forests cover most of the land of Canada, roughly between the border with the United States and the Arctic Circle.

Most of Russia is also covered in boreal forest.

In addition to the larger percentage of evergreen trees, the primary distinguishing features of a boreal forest are the almost complete lack of undergrowth and the relative infertility of the soil.

Boreal forests are always in the cold.
This represents churches that are continually under hardship. "Coincidentally," the Russian church has almost continuously been under hardship whether it be through oppression by the Czars or the Soviets, or just because of the hostile climate and corrupt, authoritarian culture.

The result is a church built around a few prominent leader types who are strong, mature believers and not much else. These strong believers are usually evergreen believers, able to continue to teach, disciple, and bear fruit amidst a hostile culture and oppressive government. They are also able to thrive on much lower doses of God's love (warmth).

Large temperature swings in a boreal forest are normal between summer and winter, with winter often lasting up to 9 months of the year.
In a boreal church, the hardships may last three times as long as the times of joy and growth, but they are endured.

Boreal forests have very low rainfall.
This is tempered by a lower evaporation rate.
Translated, this would mean God moves less in a boreal church than in other types of churches, yet when He does, His previous movement in power is remembered and sustains spiritual life longer.

Because of the cold climate, the soil remains infertile.
Leaves don't decompose well in the lower temperatures and pine needles drip an *acid* into the soil, creating a special type of soil called Spodosol.

Pastors from churches in Russia and Eastern Europe that have endured lengthy hardships do tend to have personalities a bit on the abrasive side, even acidic, if you will.

So, the picture painted by a boreal forest is of a church with a strong pastor that has an abrasive personality in the middle of a country covered in hardship, where God's love is not perceived (less warmth), truth is less available (less sunlight), and God does not move in power as often (less rain).

Is it any wonder the general body of Christ in such a church would be relatively infertile?

In fact, the forest floor in Taiga is covered in mosses, lichens, and weak grasses, and not much else.

Because the soil is so thin in a boreal forest, the trees tend to have shallow roots. Also, these *taiga* trees alter their biochemistry to "harden" themselves against the severe freezing winters.

So, in a boreal church, you will find a number of rugged, tough, prominent, mature believers who are individualist in their thinking. Their roots in the body are shallow. Fellowship will be lacking and there will be few weak or superficial Christians due to the hardships facing the church and believers in general.

Geographically speaking, boreal forests are the largest biome in the world.

When considering density of life, however, rain forests and temperate forests win hands down, with rain forests dominating a contest between those two.

Of course, Russia, Canada, and Alaska (the homes of boreal forests) represent a huge section of the landmass of the world. When considering density of believers, however, these countries fall way short of the United States, Latin America, Australia, and Africa.

Question: *Do you judge austere, authoritarian churches without having walked in their members' shoes?*

Arctic Regions & Snow Caps

"From whose womb comes the ice?
And the frost of heaven, who gives it birth?"
(Job 38:29)

Like deserts, the frozen realms of the earth are inhospitable to life. Survival in these ice-covered landscapes is tough. Of course, the difference is that a desert has plenty of light and heat, but no water, while the icecaps have plenty of water and light, but no heat.

Vegetation abounds in the temperate, cooler parts of the planet, but regions covered in ice year round are *completely* devoid of plant life. Vegetation can survive normal winters with little problem, even long winters, but not when ice is an ever-present reality. There *has* to be a melt at some point for a plant to grow.

The polar regions are frozen deserts.

These snowy regions represent portions of the Kingdom in which God's animating force is frozen for lack of love. These are churches where the Love of God is not experienced. This lack of love "freezes" the movement of God until a day when love (warmth) returns.

God's people are the vehicle for God's love to be expressed to others. When a church is dry, there is an urgent need for God to move. When a church is cold, it's a people problem.

A desert church is waiting on God, and the people must rely on Him in prayer for change.

An arctic church must repent of their apathy and cold hearts, surrendering their hearts to God so that He may flow through them in warm love toward others.

It should be noted that light (God's truth) is available to all areas of the earth without regard to other factors. It is heat and water that vary.

Ice-covered land represents the *unloving* church.

The Arctic has comparatively low precipitation.

This precipitation mostly comes in the form of snow. True snow-falls in the arctic, then, are relatively *infrequent*. Strong winds will blow through and kick up the snow already on the ground, which can create an illusion of continuous snowfall.

This symbolizes that God is willing to move in this unloving church, but His power is frozen until the church becomes loving. He withholds more power, more movement until the situation changes. This is pictured in the low precipitation.

The Holy Spirit blows through the unloving church, lifting up God's frozen power for the arctic believers to behold so they can be reminded that God is waiting to move.

This stirring up confuses these believers though. They see the reminders of how God wants to move and confuse it with His actual movement, believing that He is acting. They become blinded to truth by the snow.

For example, the unloving church is thrilled to see its benches filled to overflowing on Christmas Eve and Easter, believing they are seeing God moving. In fact, God the Spirit *has* moved. He's blown these attendees into the church in order to show the unloving church what God wants to do, that He wants to reach these people, but the unloving church thinks He has already moved and brought these people to them for good.

Yet, the next week, the pews are empty again.

Lesson: *Love others if you want to see God move.*

Mountains & Valleys

"Yea, though I walk through the valley of the shadow of death,
I will fear no evil; for You are with me;
Your rod and Your staff, they comfort me." (Psalm 23:4)

I don't know about you, but it often feels to me that when everything seems to finally be running smoothly in my life, I can be sure a challenge is about to come my way. Nothing ever seems to go perfectly for more than a few days before something breaks.

Sure, a lot of this could be psychological, our poor perception focusing on the 20% that is wrong instead of the 80% that is right. Yet, I do think there is an underlying reality to this cycle.

Mountains and valleys represent the highs and lows of our lives.

Valleys represent our times of trouble, times of suffering and difficulty. A valley is easy to walk down into. In fact, a person walking down into a valley will often have to strain against gravity to keep their descent from becoming an uncontrolled free fall.

So it is with difficulty.

In the blink of an eye, we find ourselves falling into a time of trouble. Suffering knows our address and you don't have to beg him to come knocking. We strain against the sinful nature (gravity) to keep from falling into trouble, many times to no avail.

Sometimes, a valley is just in our path through no fault of our own.

To get to the other side we have to pass through tribulation. And once we're down in it, we find that walking up and out the other side is much harder than was the descent down.

Mountains represent the peaks in our lives, the times we're on top of the world. Those moments after we've fought and overcome challenges. When we've struggled with all our might to work our way out of the valley and ascend that slope until we reach the peak.

If we overcome a great obstacle or challenge in life, we're as exhilarated as the mountain climber who has fought his way to the summit.

There's a wonderful sense of having conquered something significant, of having entered into a great battle and overcome.

We'd be remiss not to point out the force that makes climbing mountains so difficult is the same force that makes falling into a valley so easy — the force of gravity.

As previously deciphered, the law of gravity is a symbol for our sinful nature. It is our sinful nature that sucks us down into trouble so easily, and we must struggle against our very own sinful nature in order to overcome and win.

The higher the mountain, the rockier it becomes.

As you ascend, vegetation grows sparser, thinner, and shorter until there's nothing but rock left. And at very high elevations, mountaintops become permanently encased in snow.

Oxygen is much thinner on mountain peaks (though still present).

Also, these rocky crags are always devoid of water. No rivers or streams run down from a summit.

Instead, rivers spring up from the clefts between mountains, or maybe partway up the slope, but never from the very top. Of course, from there these rivers rush down into the valleys.

On the other hand, valleys are lush places, filled with life. They are warmer than the mountain peak. The oxygen is thicker, more breathable. And you'll almost always find some kind of creek, stream, or river flowing through a valley.

Have you ever wondered why your life seems to be filled
with so much more trouble than success?

It's because God did not intend for us to live in moments of success. Like the mountain peak, moments of success are not habitable.

He *does* want us to overcome, to climb the mountains in our lives. When we succeed, we should bask in those moments of success, breathing deep the fresh air as it invigorates us.

Yet, we do well to remember we cannot build our house on the peak. We must descend back into the valley. The valley is our home. Or maybe a little ways up the slope, but never on the peak.

The oxygen is thinner at the top.

God (oxygen) is not as present with us in our moments of success as He is in our suffering. When we struggle, He's right there by our side to breathe His life into us.

When we have conquered, He is proud, but simply looks on, smiling, not supplying us in the same way.

This is pictured in Jesus' parable of the Pharisee and the Tax Collector who go to the Temple to pray. The Pharisee is proud of himself; the Tax Collector broken and humble. Jesus made it clear that God will be more available to the broken man.

Success and overcoming are not bad things. In Scripture, God constantly exhorts us to both. Yet, the benefit of overcoming is not in reaching the peak, but in the strength we gain through our struggle against the law of gravity as we fight our way to the top. That moment after we have conquered, when we can look down upon the rest of the world from that peak, is a moment to be enjoyed, but it cannot last.

Valleys are lush with vegetation and flowing water.

It's during the times of struggle that life truly blossoms and we can tap into the flow of God's power. Success is a reward, but it does not bloom. Suffering births life within us.

But if we stay in the valleys, we will grow fat and lazy. Unable to overcome the force of gravity and unable to leave. We must work to overcome our sinful nature in order to stay spiritually fit. On the other hand, if we try and reside on the mountain tops, we will not survive. There's nothing to eat or drink up there, nor much to breathe.

Topsoil is thickest in the valley.

Soil symbolizes the Body of Christ, so this means at any given moment, you will find the majority of the Body of Christ down in the valleys of life, under affliction from something.

For a time, as you ascend the mountain, you can depend on fellowship with other believers who are simultaneously working to overcome gravity, but the soil thins as you get higher. There will come a time when the soil will end and you'll be walking on bare rock. As we hike to the summit of our mountain, we'll reach a point in our struggle when other believers can no longer help us. Then, we must depend fully on Christ, the rock.

God's best is found in moving from valley to mountain to valley to mountain and on and on.

The ideal is a journey from the ocean (the world) to the continental divide, the highest point on land (God's Kingdom).

As you travel further inland, the average elevation of each successive valley and mountain becomes higher. Eventually, the valley floors you cross will be higher up than some of the hills you climbed earlier in your journey when still close to the coast.

This is the path of spiritual maturity. We move forward through times of affliction, struggling against our sinful nature until we overcome. As we mature, our moments of struggle start to look more like our early spiritual successes in height. And as we get closer to that continental divide, we draw closer to God (the sky).

Mountaintops are cold and lonely.

"It's lonely at the top," as the saying goes, refers to the fruits of success. It *is* lonely on the top of a mountain.

We should take great joy in the successes of our spiritual lives, but we'll find ourselves alone up there as most of the other believers we know will still be in the valley below.

It's colder up there. You will not feel nearly as much love (warmth), especially God's love, in your moments of success as you will in times of trouble. This does not mean He has stopped loving us, just that we cannot perceive it as well up there. When we're on top of the world, we don't reach out in need.

There is no difference, however, in the amount of light available on a mountaintop versus a valley. God's truth and goodness are equally available in all parts of our journey.

If there's ever any difference, it is that mountains sometimes cast great shadows over valleys, blocking the sun through part of the day. This pictures how success, whether it be the success of others, our past successes, or our dreams of future success can block the truth of God's presence with us in the times of suffering. Sometimes, previous success, or expectations of the perfect, successful life, make us think God has abandoned us when we find ourselves struggling.

This is not true of course, and thus distant success blocks truth in the struggle, just as mountains can overshadow the valley.

Yet, during present success, on the mountaintop, we can see clearer than ever how God has provided.

Lesson: *Struggle out of the valley, help others as you go up, depend on Christ in your success and as you descend back down again.*

Plains & Grasslands

"Because 'all flesh is as grass, and all the glory of man as the flower of the grass. The grass withers, and its flower falls away.'"
(1 Peter 1:24)

Experts are mostly speculating when they guess at how grasslands originally formed. It's believed that some prairies were formed treeless, while others are man-made, i.e. farmers of antiquity cleared the trees and they've never returned.

Prairies are flat.

While it's true that there are flat places on Earth that are forested, such regions are usually well-watered. Plains and grasslands are more *arid* than forested terrain.

Personally, I love the open beauty of a prairie. I could stare for hours watching the wind ripple its endless lengths.

Long swaths of tall grasses bowing, waving gently before a breeze, stalks rasping lightly as they dance — it's a sight that soothes the soul.

Yet, if I'm honest, the view does get a little boring after a while. Nothing like the wide variety of animal and plant life that fill forests. There's always something new to see in a forest, something happening.

Grasslands aren't inactive by any means, but overall, they're just rows of grass followed by more of the same.

Prairies do receive rain, just less of it.

Prairies and grasslands also have fewer creeks and rivers traversing them, partially due to the lesser rainfall.

However, where creeks or rivers *are* found in a prairie, you'll usually see trees lining the banks. Think Eastern Oklahoma.

These grasslands represent areas of the Kingdom that are filled with a *few* strong believers (trees) and a lot of weaker believers (grass). The lack of valleys and mountains is symbolic of the lack of either success or suffering in their spiritual lives. Their spiritual lives are "flat."

So, is there a lack of strong believers in grassland churches because the weaker believers have never been challenged by valleys or mountains, or does God limit the valleys and mountains to protect the weaker believers who cannot handle it? Perhaps both are true.

The diminished availability of water means God is not moving as powerfully as He does in other parts of the Kingdom, though He does still move here. The prairie is not a desert.

Does God move less because of the weakness of the believers, or are the believers weaker because God moves less?

Wherever God does choose to move powerfully (river) within the spiritual grassland, you will find stronger believers (trees) nearby, so the second option would seem to be the answer. Additional proof is that the second option makes man dependent on God, while the first option makes God dependent on man.

Therefore, the truth is that plains represent regions in the Kingdom that are filled with weaker believers because God moves in a reduced capacity. Man is dependent on God.

The existence of flat, woodsy areas proves this interpretation further. Such forested regions are still flat, yet they support numerous trees solely because of greater rainfall.

So, if we believe that rain symbolizes the Life God gives, then the dominance of weaker grasses in prairies is due to His decision to not give as much Life to that part of the Kingdom.

In a valley, in the midst of our suffering, the life God offers is *always* flowing, and there forests abound.

In a flat church, He may choose to not pour out His power, and the result is a grassland church, a church filled with mostly weak believers.

God uses challenges to build us up, yet in cases where there are few challenges and the spiritual landscape is flat, God may choose to intervene and build us up anyway (trees by the creek). Or He may leave a church in its weakness.

Grasslands represent the lukewarm church.

Lesson: *Live in a church where God is clearly moving.*

Side Note:

Some may take exception to the previous section(s), not accepting that God would withhold Himself, or His life, from any believers or any portion of His Kingdom. If you find yourself objecting in such a way, you should be specific as to what exactly your objection is.

To deny that God's Kingdom has a variety of spiritual terrains, is to deny the obvious reality that the worldwide Body of Christ has all kinds of believers, some hot, some cold, some lukewarm.

God's Kingdom is clearly not uniform.

However, it is most likely that you object to the idea of God deciding to not make "water" available equally. You may believe that anybody can choose to follow God at any time. Truthfully, to believe such a thing is to say that God's role in our salvation is minimal. This belief relegates His role to merely responding to what we choose. This smacks too much of Deism to be biblical.

Jesus clearly teaches that the Spirit moves where He will (John 3:8). That we cannot know where He's going, where He's coming from, or even why He's going there. Scripture also says that man cannot respond to God without the Spirit calling him, opening his eyes (John 6:44, 1 Cor. 12:3, John 3:27).

God is in control, not us.

Swamps

" 'But I tell you truly, many widows were in Israel in the days of
Elijah...but to none of them was Elijah sent except to Zarephath, in the
region of Sidon...and many lepers were in Israel in the time of Elisha the
prophet, and none of them was cleansed except Naaman the Syrian.'
So all those in the synagogue, when they heard these things,
were filled with wrath..." (Luke 4:25 - 28)

What exactly is a swamp?

Swamps are flat lowlands flooded by large amounts of pent-up water. The barrier to this water's draining is a blockage tall enough to flood the region under a couple feet of water, but short enough that the water escapes before a full-fledged lake is created.

Swamps are not hospitable to *people*, though you'll find all types of vegetation there, from marsh grasses to large, gnarled trees. They're bio-diverse places, but only certain types of plants can thrive in such an environment, i.e. ones that can't live without a *lot* of water.

While some lovers of nature see an odd, ethereal beauty in swamps, the truth is most people's first impression is of a spooky or scary place.

You won't find strong oaks or maples flourishing in a swamp, just gnarled, twisted trees and other bizarre plant life. Nor will you find an apple or peach orchard, or many other fruit trees to speak of.

Swamp grass is tall.

Which only serves to conceal creatures like alligators and snakes. Speaking of those guys, alligators and snakes are a large part of the reason we're afraid to randomly wade through that murky water. Still, even without them, there remains a certain uneasiness the sight of a swamp provokes in our spirits.

Strolling through swamp water can be a dangerous endeavor.

At the very least, a walking stick is a must. It's difficult to see where you're putting your feet. Unexpected holes deeper than a man's height can make for a nasty surprise.

Swamp water is not drinkable.

You can't drink it without filtering out the dirt and debris. Swamp water does flow, but it's a slow process, which makes it a prime candidate for bacterial growth, just like stagnant water. There's great potential for getting sick even after filtering. It's safer, not to mention more pleasant, to drink from a river.

Swamps are not arable land.

You can't plant crops or other productive plants unless you first drain the swamp. In previous centuries, farmers would drain swamps wherever they found them, turning them into productive farmland. *Once a swamp is drained, the exposed soil is very fertile.*

So, swamps are parts of the Kingdom where God is moving, but His movement is being held back. There's plenty of light, heat, and water, but the water (God's activity) is not being allowed to flow out into the rest of the Kingdom and the world.

These are churches that receive and receive from God, but refuse to go out into the world and share the Good News with others.

This is the "fat" church.

The church that partakes and partakes until its cup overflows, but won't let the blessings flow outside of its walls, is in disobedience to God. Churches where this is happening have life, but the believers (trees) within such a church are usually "gnarled" and spiritually "ugly."

These churches are usually self-oriented, self-focused, and seem intimidating and uninviting to non-believers. Non-Christians visiting such a church may feel out of their element, unwelcome, and even a little bit fearful of the church's members — exactly the same feelings I get when I'm in a swamp.

"Fat" churches usually are filled with prominent, knowledgeable believers. Believers who consistently take in God's Word, but don't actively serve to expand the Kingdom will develop stunted, gnarled, and otherwise unusual personalities. These are the gnarled trees.

Snakes live in virtually every environment on earth, but there is an overabundance of them in a swamp. Also, an even more dangerous animal inhabits these places: the alligator. These animals represent those who pose a danger to others walking through. Fat church believers must take care of where they step lest they get bit.

Whether or not alligators and snakes represent non-believers pretending to be otherwise, or believers who just stink at following Christ, is a discussion for later. For now, note that alligators and snakes are not creatures who seek out victims, but if they feel threatened, they will not hesitate to attack, and the result will often be fatal to the human. These "animals" are usually hidden under the water or by swamp grass.

This is also true of the "fat" church. The "snakes" and "alligators" hide out in the activity of what God is doing (water) or their presence is masked by the multitude of weaker believers in the church (grass).

How do you know when you've encountered a spiritual snake or alligator? Well, you step in the wrong place and get bit, that's how.

Because the swamp church does not allow the life that God gives to flow out, it becomes brackish and prone to cause illness. Just as the manna God gave Israel in the desert began to rot if not consumed in the day it was given, so is the life God gives designed to be used in the day it is given and not stored up.

Partaking in the life of a "swamp church" will make a believer spiritually sick. They can become legalistic, overzealous, eccentric, greedy, ungracious, strangely withdrawn, or just plain weird.

I recommend if you find yourself in a "swamp" church to either get out or drain it. It is not a place where the harvest of God can be planted.

If you do manage to drain it, however — *if* you can manage to impact the culture of a church so much that it changes its ways and begins ministering to those outside its body — you may find yourself in the middle of some very fertile soil indeed.

Lesson: *Work to change a church that refuses to minister outside its walls, or leave it behind.*

"...but its swamps and marshes will not be healed; they will be given over to salt." (Ezekiel 47:11)

Beaches & Coastlines

"Then Jesus said to them, 'Follow Me,
and I will make you become fishers of men.'" (Mark 1:17)

"Do not love the world or the things in the world. If anyone loves the
world, the love of the Father is not in him." (1 John 2:15)

Spiritual coastlines are those places where the Kingdom meets the world.

Fishermen regularly sail out from the coasts, trawling the waters, casting their nets into the seas to see what they might catch.

They are symbolic of missionaries who travel in the world casting their spiritual net, which is the Good News of the Kingdom, seeing what hearts they might catch. They are fishers of men, made so by Christ.

Beaches, on the other hand, are of a slightly different nature from your generic coastline.

Beaches are fun! Good food, good moods, and good times all around. (Sometimes too much so.)

Many of us flock to the beach for a week or two of summer fun each year.

This is symbolic of Christians taking a short break from the rigors of the spiritual life of the inner parts of the Kingdom to frolic in the world (ocean waves).

Spiritually, a lot of us periodically relax in this way, and God, in His mercy, overlooks it.

There *are* those beach goers, however, who decide to make a lifestyle out of the beach. The first time that salty air hits their nostrils and that ocean breeze blows across their skin, they're captivated and decide *Hey, I'm going to live at the beach.*

They represent those Christians who permanently reside near the world, centering their lives around its waters. They are worldly Christians.

(Disclaimer: This is not an attack on people who live near the physical beach. If you like the beach and live there, great! It's a beautiful place. In this book, we deal only with symbolism. We are not making judgments on where people choose to live.)

Worldly Christians live near the world because it seems like a beautiful place to be.

Living at the beach is an easy-going lifestyle.

Slow-paced, relaxed, not uptight at all.

Worldly Christians are that way about spiritual things. *Relax, mon.* There's no urgency to spread the gospel, it will get done in its due time.

A worldly Christian is also very relaxed about obedience to God's will. If they even recognize He *has* a will for them that needs to be obeyed, they believe His requirements are minor. They would describe Christians who take their faith seriously as "uptight" or "radical."

It's no coincidence then that beach towns and port cities, historically and today, tend to be dens of sin and worldliness. Sailors, pirates, whalers, and casinos. Choose any port in the world, and you will find a higher level of crime and depravity there than in other inland cities within that same country.

Years ago, I undertook an investigative mission for an acquaintance. A lady from a church local to me had a prodigal sister who had dropped off the map in Costa Rica. She knew about my connections with Costa Rica, so she asked if I could make some inquiries in the town of Jaco the next time I visited. Jaco is a small beach community there and the last known location of her sister.

We actually did find some people in Jaco who knew the missing woman and gave us information on how to find her. They gave us a fairly detailed picture of some of the morally bankrupt things she and her boyfriend had been involved in, and I remember my mouth almost falling open in shock at the description of the regular activities going on at one of the local bars. Such things are not fit to mention here, but suffice it to say that it's worse than you would even be able to guess.

On the surface, this small beach community seems quaint and wholesome like any small town in America. Yet, beneath the surface, sickness is festering unseen. This phenomenon is not unique to Jaco, but is true of many coastal towns. Maybe it's something in the salty air?

Regardless, vacationers, those who visit for a few weeks, don't even know such places exist, nor do they fall into such depravity. They simply enjoy the beach and maybe get a little wild once in a while. It's the permanent residents that succumb.

Worldly Christians face several dangers.

First and foremost, they must be careful around the world (ocean). They must remain very, very close to shore. If they swim out too deep, too far, they'll find themselves so far from the Kingdom they won't have the strength to get back and they'll drown.

Sharks and undertows are unexpected risks, dangers that can sweep away and destroy even those who are doing nothing more than just wading. Which means those worldly Christians who only flirt with the world, even just a little bit, can still be destroyed by its dangers.

Even those who live at the beach but never get in the water still face the possibility of being hit with a hurricane or a tsunami. If a Christian lives near the world and never moves inland (i.e. maturing as they walk over spiritual hills and valleys in the Kingdom) they are at risk of being washed away by God's judgment with all the other worldly Christians who are playing in the world's waves, even if they've never stepped into the water themselves.

Lesson: *Move inland. Seek God and His Kingdom.*

REVIEW	
Deserts	= Lifeless Church
Arroyos	= Traditions of Men
Rain Forest	= Dynamic/Pastor-centered Church
Deciduous Forest	= Fertile/Democratic Church
Boreal Forest	= Austere Church
Arctic Regions	= Loveless Church
Plains	= Lukewarm Church
Swamps	= Fat Church
Beach	= Worldly Church
Mountains	= Times of Success
Valleys	= Times of Trouble

WEATHER & DISASTERS:

Spiritual Cycles & Judgments

SEASONS

Seasons represent life cycles.
They can picture the entire life cycle of an individual, a church, a family, an organization, a business, or even a country. They can also symbolize repeated, mini-life cycles within the spiritual life of a believer.

The most glaring lesson for us from the existence of seasons is that there's nothing on earth that does not have a birth, a life span, and a death. We know this about people, but it applies to everything else too. No matter how much we may treasure our country, the United States is not eternal. At some point, it will come to an end.

No matter how much we love our home church, it also has a life cycle and will someday end.

Only God is constant and never-ending.

Spring

Spring is the beginning of new life.
It sings of tulips blooming carpets of rich red, crystalline brooks bubbling clear, and fresh buds sprouting green on each and every tree. Can't you hear the birds chirping the first notes of their morning melody?

A little girl in a white cotton dress has clipped daisies tucked behind her ear as she runs through a field, giggling. A young couple rests on a blanket under an old oak, enjoying an afternoon picnic and romantic conversation.

Spring is a beautiful, energizing time.

It's pretty easy to see how seasons might apply to the physical life cycle of a person, so we'll focus our attention on the spiritual life cycle.

Spring represents the birth of a new believer, the very beginning of their walk with Christ.

In the freshness of their encounter with their Lord, there is great joy. All is alive and beautiful as it never was before. New believers are full of energy, excited about sharing their faith. Their faith is clear, bathed in simple, crisp understanding.

Before, God's power in their life was frozen like snow.

In the winter of their confusion and ignorance of God, they could not perceive God's love and lived in extreme cold. Now that they know Him, they perceive His love and are warmed. His love for them did not change, but in winter, they had leaned away from God just as the earth leans away from the sun.

Now that they have new life in Christ, they have begun the maturing process and begin to lean into God. With new and increased light (truth) in their lives, and new warmth (God's love), the snows melt. God's power is now flowing in their life.

Spring is a time for new growth, for fast growth.

Trees and plants that were dormant in the winter suddenly reignite the growing process in earnest. The majority of the width of a tree ring is produced in spring and early summer.

Many new believers do this as well. Their sudden spiritual awakening out of a wintry dormancy launches them into an impassioned study of the Bible. They'll join every small group they can find in search of spiritual food, seek God in prayer and dive into the Word with a vengeance. Their advance from being a babe in Christ to an adolescent in Christ is usually a quick process, relatively speaking of course.

One qualification: We're speaking of tree believers here, not grasses. Grass believers spring up in spring, they grow a foot or so, and that's about the extent of their growth before they die.

Spring is the time when annual flowers bloom.

Annual flower believers are similar to grass believers in that after coming to Christ they never grow very much, they don't set deep roots, and they only last for one season. However, in their spring when they first come to Christ, they look especially beautiful and full of joy. These believers fool others with their initial sudden beauty into thinking they are destined to become something spectacular within the church. But, it's not to be.

It does no good to bemoan their weakness and temporary nature though. Do we mourn when a tulip blooms because we know it won't last, or do we enjoy the tulip's color while it's there?

Don't fret if you meet an "annual" believer. Enjoy the joy and vibrancy of their new faith while it's there.

Spring is a time for planting.

The planting season has dual symbolism. On one level, this represents the Word of God (the seed) being planted within the prepared Body of Christ (plowed, fertilized soil) right at the end of the winter when the waters of God's power are ready to flow. The seed produces a new plant (the new believer) who grows into maturity over the course of their spiritual life until they are harvested in autumn.

On another level, the planting season symbolizes how the spring times of our lives, those times of refreshed newness in our walk with God, are the best times for us to evangelize and sow seed. When we are filled with a fresh, new passion for what God is doing in our lives, our testimonies are most ripe for planting. Then, as we enter the maturing phases of our own spiritual walk, we will observe the seeds we planted start to produce a harvest.

Spring is also a time of unstable weather.

The rapid change in temperature, the clash of cold winds with warm fronts, produces all kinds of storms and even tornados. A new believer experiences this too. As they are newly exposed to God's love (warmth), they find themselves confronted with a wide range of areas in their life that need repentance and transformation.

God's interaction with a new believer is a sudden exposure of His love combined with intermittent bouts of critical revelation when the new believer must make changes or face judgment like a flood or thunderstorm. It is a time of great turbulence.

As we've said several times already, spring does not just represent new belief. These seasonal cycles can be repeated many times within the spiritual life of any believer.

Imagine a believer, for example, who is undergoing a painful divorce, or a wrenching bankruptcy. They are not in spring, but winter.

These hardships produce not joyful growth, but a withdrawn hardening of the inner self. A follower of Christ in the middle of a divorce is not going to be filled with joy and feel compelled to evangelize others. On the contrary, they may simultaneously feel abandoned by God and unworthy to proclaim His name. They will often become a dormant Christian.

Yet, the great news is that with God, all seasons come to an end. As beautiful as spring is, an eternal spring would grow quite boring after a while. And we can take great comfort in knowing that our winters, the hardships of our lives, will all eventually come to an end as well, giving birth to new springs!

Lesson: *Wait for spring. Rejoice at its arrival.*

Summer

"He who gathers in summer is a wise son;
He who sleeps in harvest is a son who causes shame."
(Proverbs 10:5)

I'll never forget those awesome summers growing up as a kid. Who does? No school, running around barefoot over dirt paths and wading through clear streams and muddy ponds in search of elusive catfish and tadpoles. I remember getting to play outside till 10 o'clock because the sun hadn't gone down yet, and then after that we'd catch fireflies. Treehouses, neighborhood gangs, and adventure galore.

I remember other summers as a teenager studying abroad, and still others during college when I framed houses under a burning sun with hammer in hand and sweat pouring off my brow in rivulets.

Now, I spend them entertaining my kids.

How we spend our summers reveals our ever-changing growth.

Summer is a time of deepening maturity.

Just as the earth tilts closest to the sun in summer, so does a believer tilt closest to Christ in a spiritual summer. This is the "adult" phase of spiritual growth, when a follower of Christ is achieving their greatest likeness to Him, the greatest conformity to His image.

Summer growth is strong, but more evenly distributed than spring.

It does not consist of sudden shoots, new sprouts, or flowering blossoms, but a deep strengthening of the core of the plant under the heat of the sun.

As usual, light, heat, water, and air are what produce this growth, which, in order, represent God's truth, love, and power combined with respiration of the Holy Spirit. Yet, in the summer, God's love can become quite oppressive.

Wait a second — what did he just say?

Yes, the maturing process is the slow removal of impurity from our spiritual lives over time. It is the continual perfection of our rejection of rebellion against God and turning to obedience. This is no easy process. To squeeze out impurity requires pressure.

It is God's love for us that presses us to renounce our infirmities and become strong in obedience.

By pressure, I mean *pressure*. God does not sweetly ask us to change because He knows we would never respond with a joyful "Sure, why didn't you ask before?" No, He bears down on us. He refines us like a silversmith stirring a pot of silver over hot coals. Under this pressure, we are refined and matured, just as the heat of the sun bears down on the crops of the field.

"He will sit as a refiner and a purifier of silver; He will purify the sons of Levi, And purge them as gold and silver, That they may offer to the LORD An offering in righteousness." (Malachi 3:3)

One caveat: A plant denied *water* under the heat of the sun will soon wither.

If God is not moving in His power to restore life to us (water) during this process, we will wilt spiritually. So, as you find yourself being refined by God, make sure you are rooted in a moist field, a body of believers where God is moving.

Summer is also a time for recreation and enjoyment.

The heat can make it difficult to work. At times, we'll take respite in the shade. It's the most popular season for a vacation at the beach. These vacations, however, don't fill the entire summer, just a week or two. Normal work occupies the rest of the days.

In the same way, during the heated maturing process of a believer's summer, they may seek temporary respite in a vacation from their spiritual work. Going to the beach symbolizes hanging out near the world, not living in the world, but frolicking in its waves.

I've taken brief spiritual vacations before. In times when you feel most pressed spiritually, you seek temporary respite from the heat. You say, "Okay, I've been faithful for a long time, I've led Bible studies,

I've given sacrificially to the church, to missions, to this ministry and that. I've served in a million different ways. Frankly, I need a break."

We all need sabbaticals, extended periods of rest so we stay fresh and don't get burnt out in our service.

Some take driving vacations across the country to breathe in the beauty of God's creation. This pictures a believer stepping out of ministry for a time to rest and meditate on God and His Kingdom.

Beach vacations would be like saying 'I've had enough Bible study, I'm going to sit on the couch and watch TV for a full week straight.' This could appear like a relapse into worldly ways, but Christians who see their brother or sister in Christ acting this way should probably not panic unless the behavior continues for an extended period of time, or worsens.

It's only bad if a believer decides to renounce "work" and "live at the beach" permanently.

(The above in no way means it's somehow wrong to take your family to the beach for vacation. Again, it's symbolism, people.)

Summertime has more consistent weather.

The tornados and floods of spring have passed and the hurricanes and rains of autumn have not yet begun. While nightly thunderstorms are common, many times they just remain distant rumblings in the sky rather than nearby torrents.

Symbolically, this is because in summer, believers are most conformed to Christ and they are actively being transformed and grown by God. As we'll see in a later section, strong storms and natural disasters are symbols of judgment, but our most glaring impurities were removed during the growth of spring and so, in summer, God's actual intervening judgment is less frequently needed.

However, during this phase, He does consistently warn of potential judgment through the distant rumblings in the Heavens. These rumblings refresh our healthy fear of God and remind us of the consequences of remaining immature.

Lesson: *When under pressure, seek to conform yourself more to the image of Christ.*

Autumn

"Be glad, O people of Zion, rejoice in the LORD your God,
for he has given you the autumn rains in righteousness."
(Joel 2:23a, NIV)

The young boy slowly lifts his head, a wide grin plastered across his face. He narrows his vision and focuses on the target. Then, he launches himself forward in a rush of pumping arms and legs and leaps high into the air, arcing, falling, and finally crashing into an explosion of dry leaves that had been piled high by his father.

Don't you love autumn?

As an author, I can assure you that autumn is the absolute best time for writing. The cool air, frequent rains, the gradual shutting down of nature — they come together to provoke a reflective spirit.

Autumn represents the golden years in a believer's spiritual life, a season that's almost as beautiful as spring.

In autumn, God's refining process is wrapping up and spiritual growth is slowing down.

It's time for the harvest. This is the period in our spiritual growth when we look and see the fruit of what we've sown during the previous years. Our fruit will be in proportion to our growth.

The effort to remain close to the image of Christ during this time wanes. We're tired and the effort to maintain that closeness is too great. So, as we tilt away from Christ (We don't leave Him, we just temporarily tilt away), the warmth of His perceived love lessens. We start to get colder.

The pressure of summer is lifted and so now the harvest becomes the main evidence of His love for us. It is a visible evidence of His past work in us, of the past presence of warmth and Love.

In the autumn, as the climate cools, trees cease to photosynthesize and their true colors, their other pigments, show through.

In the same way, believers in this phase of spiritual growth, as they slowly tilt away from Christ, cease to spiritually "photosynthesize." They cease to redeem the world as they once did during their spring and summer phases.

When photosynthesis ceases, the vibrant greens of life disappear. Instead, the reds, oranges, purples, browns, and yellows shine through in the leaves.

Since leaves are a sign of maturity, it is in this phase of a believer's spiritual life that their true colors shine through, and the beauty of those colors will depend on the type of health they had during the previous seasons.

If a tree is dehydrated, then during the fall its leaves will go straight from green to brown, revealing the tree to be dry. Lengthy rainfalls in previous months, on the other hand, are what create the most spectacular autumn displays to behold.

So, believers that previously abided in the life that God gives (water), look beautiful in this autumn season. Those who did not, don't.

The color of leaves is similar to the fruit of the harvest in revealing the health of all previous growth.

Autumn is a melancholic season, a time for quiet reflection and appreciation of beauty.

The Christian in their spiritual golden years has a similar feeling as they reflect back on life spent so far, how they've lived, how they've sought God, and appreciating the fruit of any harvest they may have reaped.

In a spiritual autumn, the pressure of summer is relieved. We are freed up to look back on what we've accomplished. This contemplation is bittersweet. We miss the time of strong growth, but we don't want to return to the pressure of the heat. This provokes a sweet melancholy.

This melancholy can be worse and even approach depression levels if we did not do well in spring or summer and have nothing but rotten fruit to show for our time.

Autumn is a time of winter approaching.

The hardships of winter are on their way. Trees, during the latter parts of fall, begin producing the harder, narrow portions of their tree rings. They harden themselves in the face of the coming winter.

Believers also, as they perceive approaching hardship or a seeming lessening of God's love, hunker down and unconsciously harden themselves in their hearts against what may be coming.

It is this hardening process that gives the tree its strength, and it also is what gives the believer their strength. Without this hardening, both would be completely soft and much more easily broken.

Lesson: *Reflect and learn from past life experiences.*

Winter

"He says to the snow, 'Fall on the earth'"
(Job 37:6a)

Winter is a time of hardship and dormancy.
Spiritual winter is the time when a believer is tilted farthest away from Christ, and the coldest of those days is symbolic of a time of pure hardship. Just as the cold comes because the earth is tilted away from the sun, so does God bring hardship in response to a believer's tilt away from Christ in order to bring them back.

Both winter and summer are hard seasons. However, the sources of our struggle are different in each. In winter, we struggle with hardship that makes us feel unloved, but has a purpose of driving us back to Christ. In summer, we feel pressured, not unloved, and struggle with our lack of conformity to the image of Christ that has become more evident because we are closer to Him.

In spiritual winter, the believer perceives less of God's love (less warmth), and he or she may possibly even believe this is because God has moved farther away from them rather than the other way around. At some point, in the fullness of their difficulty, the believer realizes the only way to get warm again is to fully seek God once more.

Then, they tilt back toward Him and spring ensues.

During wintertime, God's power is frozen.

Water (His power) is still given, but in a potential form, an un-released form. This shows His willingness to move in the life of a believer, but not until that believer has begun to tilt back toward the image of Christ. As a believer conforms their life to Christ, God's power is released in the Kingdom and free to flow.

Before and during winter, animals engage in some of their most unusual activities.

Some animals like bears and squirrels store up food, get fat, and hibernate. Others migrate to territories away from the winterized coun-tryside. And still others stay active, but resist the wintertime by losing the color in their fur, which allows them to blend in with the snow to avoid predators.

In the same way, as Christians see hardship or difficult times approaching their section of the Kingdom, their church, or their family, they have different reactions. Some Christians dig into the Word, storing up on food from it and getting themselves fat so they can hibernate through the difficult times.

Other Christians migrate away. They abandon the afflicted territory for however long the difficulty lasts and will return once it's over.

And still others blend in. In the face of less exposure to God's truth and love, they lose their "colors." They appear bland and no longer stand out from the landscape around them.

This might seem unusual, but imagine a church suffering, where the entire church was under some sort of affliction. A joyful, peppy Christian entering that environment would get chewed up just as surely as a colorful rabbit will get taken out by a fox amidst white snow. Afflicted people, believers or not, are in pain and they don't appreciate a cheerful person dancing around.

By winter, deciduous trees lose all their leaves.

Leaves are a sign of maturity, and in a time of cold hardship, a believer may seem to lose their maturity. If a believer is going through a divorce or a bankruptcy, they must have lost their spiritual maturity, right?

No, we cannot judge a believer during hardship by the apparent lack of maturity (leaves) or fruit. The true maturity of a tree lies within its core, its trunk, the leaves are merely a visible sign of that maturity to others.

Evergreen believers are the only ones who are capable of showing maturity in the face of hardship, but even they don't produce full fruit (pine cones) during those times.

Fruit is not constantly born — it's harvested in its appointed time.

It has been noted by psychologists that people in the Northern Hemisphere who endure very long winters can suffer from something called *Seasonal Affective Disorder*, which is basically a mild to moderate depression caused by lowered sunlight exposure.

Spiritually, this translates to believers becoming spiritually depressed while suffering under a long, extended hardship, and receiving lessened amounts of God's truth during that time.

Thankfully, there is always the promise of the resurrection pictured in the symbol of the coming spring. From the death of Christ to His glorious Resurrection, from our own physical deaths to our resurrection into the eternal life God has promised us, spring always follows winter.

Regardless of the hardship we're facing, even if it's the end of our own life, let us remember that spring is just around the corner.

Lesson: *Looking forward to spring, endure.*

WEATHER

Sunshine

"Truly the light is sweet,
And it is pleasant for the eyes to behold the sun"
(Ecclesiastes 11:7)

The warm glow of sunshine on your skin just feels good. A sunny day brings joy to the spirit and energy to the soul. It restores health to the prisoner who's been locked in isolation.

Sunny days symbolize the good times in our lives, when everything is great, when God's truth is obvious and clear. We have no doubts, no questions, because we have no problems. On sunny days, we are immersed in His truth and accept it easily. And when we're bathed in His truth, we feel the warmth of His love. We see the light and are warmed.

However, since water is symbolic of God's power, it becomes clear to us that He does not move in power on sunny days. He moves within us — and we experience the most growth — *when we face problems* (rainy days). Those are the days when we exercise our faith muscles, when we learn to trust Him.

Lesson: *Enjoy the sunny days in your life.*

Rain (again)

"He shall come down like rain upon the grass before mowing,
Like showers that water the earth." (Psalms 72:6)

W e've already discussed many aspects of rain in previous sections of this book, but there are a couple left to mention in comparison with sunshine.

As sunny days represent good times in our lives, rainy days symbolize the tougher times.

As with most spiritual truths, the true nature of problems is counter-intuitive. We tend to view the disappointments and obstacles in our lives as bad things.

And, of course, they are.

Yet, across the world, whether it's a tropical rain forest, a temperate deciduous forest, grasslands, or swamp, every *fertile* land is well-watered by regular rains. When rains cease, the result is a desert. Rain inspires growth and life.

So it is with problems.

This is not a nice teaching, nor something any of us really wants to accept, but it is a clear, undeniable truth that spiritual growth really only occurs during trials and sufferings. You can't exercise without weights. Faith cannot grow if there is no need for faith. When problems loom, faith is required to see us through, and that faith grows as a result.

Yes, we all have problems. God, in His love, is the one who gives us these challenges, so we can live and grow.

But He is pained by the process. That's why rain looks like tears.

Lesson: *Embrace rainy days and grow.*

Storms

*"So pursue them with Your tempest, And frighten them with Your storm.
Fill their faces with shame, That they may seek Your name, O LORD."*
(Psalm 83:15 -16)

A thunderstorm evokes a much different emotional response than a gentle rain. Violent winds and loud, booming rolls of thunder provoke fear, timidity, trembling, and humility, not the bitter-sweet melancholy of a romantically grey day. Every time I hear a clap of thunder, the belief that I'm somehow hearing the angry voice of God is impossible to avoid, no matter how much I dismiss the idea as childish.

Thunderstorms are symbols of God's judgment.

The fearful feelings that run through us during them are *strong* evidence for this interpretation.

Thunderstorms bring rain, but the rain can seem more of a side effect than the main show. When you hear the rumbling thunder and the sizzle of lightning, you can't help but feel God has just spoken, and that He is striking in judgment.

On days when I have been particularly rebellious against God's will, or have allowed sinful thoughts to run uninhibited through my mind, and thunder suddenly bellows through the sky, my heart quakes in fear, and I quickly humble myself in repentance.

On the other hand, on those days when I feel mostly obedient, such thunder produces in me an awed, fearful respect for the power of God, but I don't tremble.

No matter what, my response is always a fearful respect, but how much I'm *afraid* depends on my current level of guilt.

Certainly, most ancient cultures saw judgment in thunderstorms. The idea that lightning bolts were judgmental strikes by some god was very common.

The dark nature of thunder clouds is further symbolism of the blackness of the judgment that comes, as opposed to the standard white clouds of a sunny sky that simply point to the purity and abundance of life in God.

During thunderstorms, the land is darkened.

This dimming is symbolic of the doubts we experience in the face of the *perceived* lack of goodness (lower light level) we feel from God while under His judgment. His truth and goodness toward us during judgment seem muted, yet it never becomes truly dark like nighttime — just dimmer.

During sun showers, the rain quickly evaporates and does not soak in. Darkened skies cool the land and allow the rain to remain.

These doubts and fears (dim light) are actually what allow us to better receive restored life (rain) from God as they force us, in our desperation, to our knees before Him, depending on Him, trusting Him. Those in need seek God more than those who aren't. A man who does not fear God is less humble, and humility is needed for God's power to nourish.

The dimmer light under darkened skies, our momentary doubts, allow God's life to better soak into us.

Thunder and lightning are almost always accompanied by heavy rain and wind.

Much more so than a normal rainstorm. This would seem to indicate that when God executes judgment, abundant life (rain) and strong movements of the Holy Spirit (wind) are the result.

This is actually true. Throughout the history of Israel, the United States, and the rest of the world, great spiritual revivals (sudden, sharp increases in spiritual life and movements of the Holy Spirit) usually occurred before, after, or simultaneously with serious trials and hardships.

As God's people prosper (sunny days), they always become complacent, resting in God's love (warmth) and all the power in their life (water) seems to evaporate. As their complacency grows, so does their level of sin. It is only God's judgment of His own people that historically has been able to restore them to life in such a situation.

Interestingly enough, sin can be symbolized by waste products and other filth on the earth. When there are many days without rain, filth and pollution begin to build up on every surface. A strong rain will wash that filth away, just as God's judgment washes away our sin and restores life to us.

We should ask how storms are formed.

Scientifically speaking, whenever a low pressure system in the atmosphere develops in the middle of a high pressure system, you get a storm. In other words, when hot air clashes with cold, and the temperature difference between the two air currents is significant, storms brew.

Remembering that warmth represents love, and cold would necessarily be hate, apathy, or anger, this should mean that God's judgment is born of a clash of love and anger.

The warm air currents involved in storm creation rise up from the ground, heated by the earth. On the other hand, at the same time, cold fronts are flowing down from higher up. This would seem to indicate that the anger is flowing down from God (definitely true in judgment), but that the love is flowing up from us.

Now, it should be noted that love cannot truly come from us, we are not capable of being a true source of love. Just as the earth does not produce warmth by itself, but merely retains or reflects the sun's warmth back up, so does a believer not produce love within themselves. They merely retain or reflect God's love.

But, why would God judge if love is indeed flowing up toward Him?

Isn't it true that God seems to judge His own people on a stricter basis than those who are strangers to Him? Look at Israel. Did He not use Babylon to judge Israel? God used a more wicked pagan nation to judge His people who were more righteous than Babylon.

Also, when God's people begin to stray and grow apathetic toward God, there is always that faithful remnant within that society or culture who maintain a strong love for God and those faithful always end up being persecuted by the nominal believers who are straying. Could it not be understood that the love (warmth) of these martyrs is rising up to God, intensifying the clash as His anger over the persecution descends?

Regardless, as snowstorms demonstrate, the "warm" air that rises up to create a storm does not really have to be warm by our standards, just warmer than the air descending. All that is necessary for a significant storm to develop is for there to be a significant difference in the temperatures of the descending and rising air currents.

In other words, whenever God's anger is sufficiently high, no real amount of love from the people on the ground is necessary for judgment to come. Whenever our view of the status of things differs significantly from God's view on the matter, a storm will result.

Lesson: *Fear God.*

Lightning

"Listen! Listen to the roar of his voice,
to the rumbling that comes from his mouth.
He unleashes his lightning beneath the whole heaven
and sends it to the ends of the earth."
(Job 37:2-3, NIV)

When I was a young boy, I believed lightning descended from the sky to strike the ground. Later, my school gleefully flipped my understanding on its head, explaining that lightning actually goes from the ground to the sky. I was told the electric discharge actually travels from the ground up to the sky, but then a flash of light returns from the sky to the ground along the same path, giving the impression it runs from top to bottom when it's really bottom to top.

However, the Discovery Channel recently straightened me out once and for all. (Not that many of their documentaries would be considered trustworthy, but they had a nice slow-motion video to accompany this particular unconventional teaching).[13] The video clearly shows the electric discharge, simultaneous with the flash, slowly descending, seeking out a path to the point of least resistance.

Many weak "step" charges can be seen forming in the sky as the charge descends, making the path look like the branches of an upside down tree. These step charges flicker in and out of existence as the main charge *decides* which way it is going to go *while descending.* Finally, when the charge gets close enough to an object, it strikes, releasing an enormous volume of current in a bright flash.

So, lighting definitely travels from the sky down to the ground, high school science classes notwithstanding.

And thank goodness for our symbolism, because it doesn't make

---

[13] http://www.youtube.com/watch?v=RLWIBrweSU8&feature=
player_embedded#t=35 (accessed Sept. 20, 2013).

much sense to say the Kingdom of God somehow strikes God in judgment and then He responds by sending truth (light) back down? No, God strikes His Kingdom from time to time in momentary judgment during storms.

Thunderstorms are symbols of God's *impending* judgment, lightning strikes are symbols for the actual strikes of judgment, no longer impending.

God judges His Kingdom through a release of power (electric discharge) and the judgment is accompanied by a momentary flash of light (truth).

While floods are symbols of a wide, general judgment of God upon a section of the Kingdom, lightning strikes are brief and specific. Floods are indiscriminate in what they destroy. They sweep away an entire landscape. A bolt of lightning is extremely powerful, but very targeted. It strikes in one spot for a brief second and then is gone, leaving whatever it hit a charred mess.

So, while a flood symbolizes God judging an entire church or country, a lightning strike represents God's judgment on an individual in the Kingdom.

This kind of a judgment is not mere chastisement. A person may survive a lightning strike, but most don't, and trees almost never do. They are blown apart.

A lightning strike seems to represent a moment when God has had enough of a believer. He's given fair warning. He's rolled in the dark thunderclouds and made His displeasure clear to all, eclipsing much of the light of Christ (sunlight). Eventually, He judges (lightning), and a flash of truth (lightning flash) illuminates the Kingdom for all who are watching. This flash of truth is a sudden reminder of the justice of God, of how His justice cannot sleep forever.

The accompanying thunder sounds so much like the voice of God, how could it be interpreted any other way? As He judges, He speaks, and powerfully. His voice rolls out like thunder through our souls, causing us to quake.

Lighting is one of the most common causes of forest fires.
We've already seen that forest fires symbolize persecution of the

church. This means that sometimes God's judgment of a few inspires a wider persecution of the church for the good of the entire church.

At first glance, lightning seems completely unpredictable. How can you defend against lighting if it's unpredictable? No one knows where it will strike next.

Unlike a flood that you can usually see coming and hopefully get out of the way, lightning seems unavoidable.

Isn't it just random?

Yet, there was another very interesting revelation in the slow-motion film developed by the Discovery Channel. In the video, as the lightning descends on its path, seeking a target, dozens of tiny electric "leader" charges can be seen *floating up* from each of the various objects standing on the ground.

I'd never seen anything like it before, and without a slow-motion, high definition camera, it truly wouldn't have been possible to know it was happening.

Moments before a lighting strike, these little leader charges, which look like thin lines of weak light, rise out of every tree, lamp post, and house as if stretching for the sky, reaching for it. It's these leader charges that finally determine where the lightning will strike. Whichever object on the ground has the tallest and strongest leader charge will attract the main electric discharge from the sky as it descends.

Since electricity is symbolic of power, and lightning is God's power in judgment, then these "leader" charges from objects on the ground represent the "power" of people reaching up toward God. In other words, it is their pride.

God opposes the proud.

Whoever rises up before God in the pride of their own power is inviting a lightning strike. He'll hit whoever is tallest, or the most prideful (strongest charge). And yes, lightning *does* strike in the same place twice.

So, if you want to avoid being hit by lighting, you get humble. You stay as low as possible. God never judges the humble.

Lesson: *Humble yourself before God.*

Snow

"Have you entered the treasury of snow,
or have you seen the treasury of hail?"
(Job 38:22)

Icy snow blankets a frozen landscape. Tree limbs bow beneath the pressure of heavily laden boughs. Peaceful curtains of chilly white drape in gentle slopes, lulling all into sleepy hibernation until warmth returns.

As night descends, blue moonlight caresses the snow-covered fields in soft, azure glows. All lies frozen until the thawing of spring, that inevitable season hoped for, yet secretly feared may never show.

If rain is the life-giving power God pours out upon the earth, that animating force He gives that transforms inanimate matter into living, then snow is that same force, but frozen. Frozen for a lack of warmth, which means a lack a love.

Land covered in snow can only represent the loveless church.

The loveless church does not show love to others, nor does it receive love from God. This is because Christian love shown to others is actually God's love channeled through us. We are only vessels.

The loveless church has no love being channeled through it, and as we saw in the section on winter, that is because those believers have moved away from Christ.

A snowy field's beauty inspires peace in one's spirit.

So, at first, this seems contradictory. How could a loveless church be at peace — *or beautiful?*

We would remember that frozen rain, which is snow, is basically symbolic of God giving His life to us, but in a frozen form. He is ready to move, to flow through the Kingdom, but only once love has returned. He is not withholding life as He does in a desert church, but is simply freezing that which He wishes to give until the climate is right once more.

Christ said that He did not come to bring peace to the world, but a sword. Clearly, when God is moving powerfully in a church, there is no peace. When God moves, an ordered upheaval of sorts always follows.

In fact, let's clarify. The peace a snowy landscape inspires is not really a harmonious peace among brothers, but a simple serenity of spirit that is distinct from the former. In the same way, God's pouring out of life into a church does cause minor conflict between brothers, which, as we've already discussed, is symbolic of water erosion. The primary upheaval in that case is an upsetting of one's heart and spirit. When God moves in power, He does not allow us to stay in our comfort zones.

The serene church is the one where God is waiting to move, but has not yet begun to do so because of a lack of love. You can't be at peace if God is moving.

We see many churches like this in our country today. Churches steeped in beautiful traditions and pageantry, churches where not much of significance seems to be happening, where God's activity is frozen, waiting, where brothers and sisters in Christ are in isolated hibernation from one another. All is at peace because nothing is happening.

A lot of theologically liberal churches seem to fit this model. They tend to talk a lot about social justice and loving one another, but when you really immerse yourself within their body, you discover a real lack of the dynamic brotherly love you'd find in your average God-fearing, Bible-believing church. The members of theologically liberal churches do their beautiful traditions week after week in serene isolation from one another and from real life.

Consider the source of the lack of warmth in a snowy field. It is because that section of the land has tilted away from the sun, and it receives less light than other warmer regions of the earth.

Liberal churches, having for the most part abandoned the Bible, have consequently moved farther away from Christ and from being conformed to His image. They receive less truth (sunlight) because they spend less time in the Bible. A lessening of exposure to Christ's truth (sunlight) results in less love (warmth) among believers.

Just as a man may momentarily emerge from his cabin to gaze at the beautiful winter wonderland layered in white only to retreat back into the warmth of his home so he does not freeze, so the members of liberal churches may gaze upon the church in which they reside and appreciate its serene beauty, but only for a moment. They do not engage in strong, warm fellowship with other members of their church. The climate may look serene, but it's actually very harsh for survival. They quickly retreat back into the security of their own homes.

Everyone living in a snow-covered region must virtually hide out in their homes for warmth until spring. In just such a way, members of liberal churches seek out the love (warmth) they need among their own immediate family members living in the same house rather than reaching out to other brothers and sisters in Christ in their church, since warm fellowship in that part of Kingdom is not available.

Winter snows diminish the senses.

Blizzards reduce visibility, preventing the viewer from seeing the landscape around them. Snow-covered ground can cause snow blindness and dampen acoustics, making it difficult to hear across longer distances.

In the same way, in *loveless* churches, believers are less able to perceive the rest of the Kingdom and what is wrong with their own church. As God releases His potential power upon their church (blizzard), the members of the church sense His presence among them, but the visibility is cut because of that very sense of His presence and they cannot see out into the rest of the Kingdom to perceive that things are different elsewhere.

Snow blindness is a temporary burning of the eye's cornea by the sun's UV rays reflecting off the snow on the ground.

Ironically, the truth of Christ (sunlight) reflects off of the potential power that God has released (snow) in order to illuminate the very problem, the lack of love, but this very process only blinds these Christians further, making it harder for them to perceive truth. They see that God has given life, but fail to realize there's a problem with the form. They see the presence of His power as evidence they are on the right track, but they don't realize He's not moving.

The only solution is to tilt back toward Christ, warming up the church so the water flows.

For example, the City of Atlanta is filled with older and more theologically liberal churches. Yet, among the church of Atlanta proper, only Passion City Church and a few others have truly stepped up to the plate to fight the scourge of child trafficking that has plagued Atlanta in recent years. While many liberal churches give lip service to fighting trafficking and other social ills on any given Sunday, Passion City Church's members have given their time and treasure (literally hundreds of thousands of dollars) to engage in the battle. They are serious about loving others in a sacrificial way and are to be commended.

The difference? The other churches don't respect God's truth (His Word), so they neglect it, but Passion City holds to the belief that God's Word is authoritative — thus they strive to lean into God and be transformed by Him.

The result of leaning into God is they are more loving. They are "warmer."

The members of the snowy churches nod their heads in agreement, but then go home to be with themselves. There's usually not a fellowship dinner after the service either.

These church members can hear each other clearly enough, but sound is dampened over longer distances. They aren't able to hear the exhortations and messages of believers in other parts of the Kingdom calling them to repentance, to seek God once more. Instead, these loveless Christians dismiss those voices as fanatics.

There is one way God does move powerfully through a loveless church: Through an avalanche.

A spiritual avalanche is when God's frozen power builds up in high places and suddenly descends with a vengeance onto homes and villages in the valleys beneath. It is a symbol for His intermittent judgments upon loveless churches.

Thankfully, in His mercy, avalanches are rare. Still, when it happens, trees, houses, churches, and everything else in the path are uprooted and smashed.

If God decides to move in judgment on a loveless church, individual believers, families, and whole churches can be removed permanently.

When a loveless church repents, when they move back to a passion for God's Word and prayer, and to conforming themselves to the image of Christ, the love of God will once more shine down upon their land, releasing the pent up power of God into fresh, living waters that irrigate the whole land.

The rivers of spring are contained within the potential of winter.

Lesson: *God may be waiting to move until love increases.*

Fog

"And He spoke a parable to them: 'Can the blind lead the blind? Will they not both fall into the ditch?'" (Luke 6:39)

"Therefore they could not believe, because Isaiah said again: 'He has blinded their eyes and hardened their hearts, Lest they should see with their eyes, Lest they should understand with their hearts and turn, So that I should heal them.'" (John 12:39-40)

My father was an army interpreter (Vietnamese) during the 1960's, so he attended the Defense Language Institute in Monterey, California before being shipped overseas. He used to tell me that some mornings, fog would roll into Monterey so thick that you could barely see your own hand in front of your face.

They literally would have to feel their way along the curbs with their feet to get to wherever they were going.

Fog makes it hard to see.

Water is a symbol of God's power, so fog represents God, with His power, by the Spirit, blinding people to His truth.

Fogs and mists are simply clouds that are near or touching the ground, mist being a lighter, thinner version of fog.

This means that when God blinds people, He doesn't always do it to the same degree. Some people He blinds completely. Others He allows to see part of the truth, but blinds them to other truths.

What creates fog?

Fog occurs when the difference between the current temperature and the current dew point is less than 4 degrees Fahrenheit. (I know, mumbo jumbo.)

In layman's terms, it means the greater the humidity, the higher the temperature at which fog will form. So, if the air is dry, fog would only form at very low temperatures. But, if the air is heavy with moisture, you may get fog at relatively higher temperatures, even in the 60's or 70's Fahrenheit.

Translate that to our spiritual symbolism template and it means that when God is more powerfully present (high humidity), He expects higher levels of conformity to His Son and higher levels of love (more warmth). When His expectations in this regard are not met, He may reduce visibility (cause spiritual blindness). **To phrase it another way, spiritual blindness is the result of disobedience in the face of God's powerful presence.**

Like the Pharisees in the presence of Jesus.

If there is lower humidity, i.e. God's power is less present, He tolerates less conformity, a little less love (lower temperature before fog forms) and less obedience.

Fog is a frequent phenomenon in valleys and on the coasts.

In other words, we are more prone to be spiritually blinded by spiritual fog when we are in the tough times of our lives (valleys) or living near to the world (coasts).

The coastal fog part isn't hard to understand. He's made His presence known through power, yet we stay near the world. Spiritual blindness comes as a result.

The valley is not as obvious, but when we're stuck down in the valley, stuck in the middle of a difficult time of our life, we can be temporarily blinded to certain truths of God, like the fact that He loves us.

Truth be told, it is also common for clouds to cover mountain peaks. And so are we susceptible to spiritual blindness when enthralled with our own success.

Where we don't typically see fogs is halfway up the slope, when we've already begun working our way out of the valley but have not yet reached the peak of success.

Fog waters the land.

After fog has dissipated, the land and everything on it lies coated with a fine layer of water from the mist.

Once God lifts spiritual blindness, the Kingdom is left watered for new life to spring up.

Dew

Dew usually occurs in the middle of the night or very early morning. It's the result of temperatures falling below the dew point. (The dew point changes relative to the humidity in the air.)

So, during the night, when Jesus (the sun) is not with us and the love of many has grown cold, wherever God's power is significantly present (humidity), He waters the Kingdom, restoring life to it in the face of reduced love.

DISASTERS

Earthquakes

"For nation will rise against nation, and kingdom against kingdom. And there will be famines, pestilences, and earthquakes in various places." (Matthew 24:7)

"You have made the earth tremble; You have broken it; Heal its breaches, for it is shaking." (Psalm 60:2)

My wife's family is terrified of earthquakes. I'm not, but then I didn't grow up in Costa Rica. Being on a major fault line, they get quakes and tremors all the time, and they've been through quakes bad enough to shift some places up six feet higher than they were moments before.

Anyone I've ever heard describe the experience says it's absolutely terrifying because the earth is giving way beneath your feet and there's nowhere to run.

Makes me appreciate the solid stability we enjoy every day and so often take for granted. What could we build if the ground were constantly shaking? How poor would we be?

Earthquakes are a sudden release of energy within the earth's crust. *Since land symbolizes the Kingdom, then earthquakes represent sudden, massive shake-ups of God's Kingdom.*

There are two causes of earthquakes: either tectonic plates in the Earth's crust grinding against one another, or volcanic activity.

The results of earthquakes are that they knock down buildings and other man-made structures. They change the lay of the land. They create mountains and valleys.

The collision of tectonic plates is symbolic of competing forces within the Kingdom grinding against one another.

In the Bible, earthquakes are associated with God's judgment.
The gospels say that a great earthquake occurred at the moment of Jesus' death on the cross. That particular quake symbolized God's judgment on the status quo of the Kingdom under the rule of the Pharisees and Sadducees. It symbolized the great collision between the tectonic plates of the rule of the Pharisees with the influence of the followers of Christ. The Kingdom quake that ensued changed the terrain of the Kingdom forever.

An earthquake's destruction of houses and other buildings pictures God's destruction of man-made traditions (man-made structures) to clear the land of hindrances.

At the end of days, as described in Revelation and other prophetic sections of the Bible, there will be a great number of earthquakes, some so massive they shake the entire world. At the end of days, God will repeatedly shake the Kingdom up again, destroying many of the unsound, unstable, man-made traditions littering the land in an effort to purify once more the terrain of the Kingdom in preparation for the coming of the Messiah.

Earthquakes are generally rare.
In the same way, Kingdom quakes don't happen that often. When they do, they are significant and memorable.

Pre-tremors and aftershocks are simply lesser echoes of the big collision.
For example, it could be said the beheading of John the Baptist was a pre-tremor to the crucifixion of Christ. And there were flare-ups of conflict and persecution between the Pharisees and the followers of Christ after the crucifixion, which would be the aftershocks.

Soil liquefaction is a phenomenon of strong earthquakes.
When earthquakes exert enough pressure on moist soil, the soil's consistency temporarily changes from a solid state to a liquid state.

This liquefaction of the soil is what causes most of the destruction of buildings during larger earthquakes. A heavy concrete foundation doesn't float very well and when the soil that supports it becomes as fluid as water, it sinks and the building collapses.

During the larger Kingdom quakes, the people of the Kingdom (soil) suddenly become very mobile, insecure in their position. They are no longer rooted firmly enough to support any previously held traditions. They will soon settle and firm up again once the quake has ended, but by then, the man-made structure has already toppled.

Soil liquefaction occurs where there is some water present in the soil. In other words, this strange behavior on the part of believers during a Kingdom quake occurs in regions where God is actively working (moist soil). In the desert, buildings may still fall during an earthquake due to shaking alone, but you won't get the double damage caused by the occasional soil liquefaction.

For example, during and after the ministry of Christ, the collision of God's tectonic plate through the work of the Spirit and Christ against the tectonic plate of the Pharisees exerted tremendous pressure on God's people in Israel. I imagine this was a time of great fluidity and insecurity for many of them, which can be seen in how quickly they shifted from praising "Hosannah" on Palm Sunday to crying "Crucify Him" a few days later. Then, a few months after that they were joining the apostles by the thousands.

When things settled down and firmed up again, many of the Pharisees' traditions lay broken in the streets.

Lesson: *Kingdom shake-ups are evidence of God moving.*

Landslides

*"Then they will begin to say to the mountains, 'Fall on us!'
and to the hills, 'Cover us!'" (Luke 23:30)*

*"Therefore we will not fear, even though the earth be removed,
And though the mountains be carried into the midst of the sea."
(Psalm 46:2)*

Landslides slip into existence suddenly, then quickly crescendo from a low rumble to a deafening roar as stone, rocks, and dirt plummet down mountain slopes into valleys below, stripping bare everything in their path.

The direct causes of landslides are either earthquakes or very heavy rains that fall within a brief period of time.

Landslides are symbolic of another kind of massive movement within the Kingdom.

Those that are caused by earthquakes have a symbolism identical to that of earthquakes alone, except that instead of just knocking down traditions, which could possibly be rebuilt, landslides are cases where man-made traditions are swept away and buried forever. Houses and businesses are covered deep.

To climb a spiritual mountain requires a struggle against the sinful nature, which by definition can only be done by more mature believers. Therefore, a landslide represents the sudden descent of more mature believers (mountain soil), truths (stones), and even Christ Himself (boulders) for the destruction of traditions (structures).

A picture of this can be seen in the Reformation of the church in Europe around the time of Martin Luther. Unlike the general shake-up of the Pharisees during their collision with Christ and the Apostles, the Reformation was more like a landslide than a general earthquake. The Reformation did not result in a general shake-up of the Catholic church, knocking down some traditions and leaving others.

Instead, men like Luther, Zwingli, Calvin, and other mature believers descended upon the Kingdom in a torrent of truth transforming whole regions of the Kingdom forever. They did not affect every region. Some areas remained wholly Catholic. But those areas they did affect were massively transformed. Traditions were not just damaged and altered, but buried or swept away. These regions switched from all Catholic to all Protestant. And everyone but Catholics recognize that Jesus was in the movement (And even many Catholics do recognize it).

Note: This interpretation does not mean that wherever a physical landslide occurs, there were traditions of men that God wished to destroy. Not at all. That is a misuse of the symbolism God incorporated into nature.

Landslides are not to be used to pass moral judgment on their physical victims, but should simply be interpreted for their symbolic value.

Earth's Core

"...and on this rock I will build My church, and the gates of Hades shall not prevail against it." (Matthew 16:18)

So, where exactly is hell? Okay, take a second and point toward it. Let me guess…you're pointing down.

That may seem childish or simplistic, but it is revealing that our natural instinct is to point down for hell and up for God. No, I'm not saying that hell is physically below us in the center of the earth, but the sky isn't actually God either, is it? It is simply a symbol of Him.

Most ancient cultures associated hell with the direction "down." That was believed to be the location of the lake of fire where people go after death. The Greek concept of Hades and the biblical hell are very similar. Volcanos get their name from Vulcan, the Roman god that ruled death and Hades.

Symbolically, there's really no other possible interpretation for the Earth's core. If the heavens represent God's Heaven, then logically, the opposite direction must lead to hell. In fact, if you were to dig down deep enough, you would find yourself facing an actual lake of fire.

Just as the land we live on completely contains the molten mantle, so does the Kingdom of God contain hell, exerting downward pressure upon it.

When one views a cross-section of the earth, the earth's crust seems so thin and weak compared with the massive mass of the fiery mantle.

At first glance, the church also seems flimsy against the forces of hell. Yet, just as Jesus promised, the gates of hell have never prevailed against her, nor shall they.

However, while the earth's crust seems to "contain" the mantle, this is not really an accurate view. It's the cooler temperatures of the sky and water above that keep the crust from disintegrating into magma. Every time magma bursts forth from its prison, air and water cool it off.

Much of the upper levels of the mantle are of the same composition as those rocks in the crust and are heavy in silica (sand). Since sand is a symbol for people, it can be seen that both hell and the Kingdom are populated by people. It is only God's presence and power (air & water) that redeem people from the fires of hell.

As much as magma would like to escape from its depths, the law of gravity firmly draws it downward.

Also, every region of mantle within the earth's core exerts pressure downward upon every other part of the core below it.

Lastly, the weight of the crust above the mantle, under the influence of gravity, exerts tremendous pressure down upon the core. The source of all this pressure is the law of gravity. We remember the law of gravity represents the sinful nature.

The lesson is this: People are irresistibly drawn down toward hell by their sinful nature. It is only God's presence and power that intervene in this inevitable process. The sinful nature of others who are unsaved (in the mantle) causes them to exert tremendous pressure upon other unsaved individuals, pressing them to stay within the grips of hell. Those who are hell-bound are determined not to go alone.

The Body of Christ is made up of believers who still have a sinful nature. These believers recognize the danger in which their sinful nature places them so they put pressure on hell, fighting its pull and containing it.

Let's be precise on that theological point. When we are born again in Christ and enter the Kingdom, we become a new creation and are liberated from our absolute slavery to sin, but we still possess sinful natures, which means left to our own devices, we will usually choose sin over obedience. After being justified in Christ, the Holy Spirit indwells us and supernaturally intervenes, allowing us to escape our own sinful nature through His power. Just as the air cools the earth's soil and prevents gravity from drawing it down into the depths of the mantle, so does God save believers from being drawn down into hell.

One day, when we finally receive our glorified bodies, we will finally be free of this sinful nature within us — able to fly.

The pressure exerted upon hell by the Kingdom causes the forces of hell to erupt (volcanos) from time to time in an attack upon the church, but these attacks are quickly stopped by the presence and power of God in His Kingdom.

Now, what of the great levels of heat that are characteristic of the earth's core?

We've identified heat as representing love, generally God's love. This leads to an interpretation of hell as being an expression of God's love. We could therefore say that hell is God applying the full extent of His love in an effort to purify and redeem the unredeemable.

Some scientists calculate that temperatures within the earth's core may approach temperatures that can be found on the surface of the sun. The sun represents Christ and temperatures on its surface would be equivalent to the fullness of His love, which obviously is astronomical in intensity.

We are fragile creatures. We cannot bear the fullness of any aspect of God. His full power would destroy us, but so would the fullness of His love. So, ironically, He protects us by exposing us to a lesser, limited amount of His love, enough to let us flourish, but not enough to overwhelm us with intensity. He protects us in this way because He loves us fully.

However, in hell, He unleashes the fullness of that love in order to burn the dross out from unbelievers.

The earth's core contains innumerable impurities. You might be under the impression that magma is uniform, all the same stuff, but in reality it's made up of all kinds of elements. The extreme temperatures and pressures cause the dross within the core to slowly descend further into the core, separated out from the lighter material, but the process is virtually eternal. Just like hell.

Lesson: *Resist the sinful nature. Immerse yourself in the presence and power of God.*

Volcanos

" 'Behold, I am against you, O destroying mountain,
Who destroys all the earth,' says the Lord.
'And I will stretch out My hand against you,
Roll you down from the rocks,
And make you a burnt mountain.'"
(Jeremiah 51:25)

"For we do not wrestle against flesh and blood, but against
principalities, against powers, against the rulers of the darkness of this
age, against spiritual hosts of wickedness in the heavenly places."
(Ephesians 6:12)

In 70 AD, Titus Flavius Vespasianus supervised his Roman armies as they utterly destroyed God's Temple and the City of Jerusalem. The Jewish people had rebelled, and his soldiers massacred thousands of them in angry vengeance and carted off tons of gold and other precious items back to Rome.

Nine years later, Titus became emperor of Rome after the death of his father. Many of his generals and higher officers, those same officers who had sacked Jerusalem, settled in several resort communities surrounding the Bay of Naples. The principal of these resort cities was called Pompeii and much of the lavish lifestyle enjoyed by these roman nobles was financed by the treasure taken from Jerusalem.

Pompeii was known for perversity and hedonism. Archaeologists have actually had to conceal many of the artifacts found in this city from the public's eye because of their offensive and over-the-top sexual nature.

Ancient graffiti was also uncovered. An unknown resident of Pompeii painted "Sodom and Gomorrah" in Latin on a city wall before its destruction.[14]

On August 24, 79AD, *one day after* the citizens of Pompeii celebrated Vulcanalia, a festival worshiping Vulcan, the god of the underworld, and two months after Titus had become emperor, Mt. Vesuvius exploded with wrath. Gases and rocks superheated to over 1,800 degrees Fahrenheit poured down the side of the volcano in a pyroclastic flow at some 450 miles per hour toward the fated city. The inhabitants were probably suffocated or scalded to death long before they were buried in the tons of ash that suddenly buried the city.

And so, Pompeii lay frozen in place for nearly two thousand years.

When Pompeii was rediscovered, archaeologists found men, women, children, and even dogs right where they had fallen. The ash had so well preserved their final moments that their expressions of terror could still be seen in their faces.

It seems obvious that the Mt. Vesuvius eruption was part of God's judgment on those responsible for the destruction of His people and His City. Symbolically, it's as if God used the forces of the underworld to execute judgment on those who worshiped the underworld.

Yet, Pompeii is the rare exception. Most volcanic eruptions are not judgments on a city or a people, but simply part of the natural order of things. So, the symbolism of all volcanos may go beyond a simple interpretation of judgment.

Following our interpretation of the molten core of the earth, **a volcano represents an attack by the forces of hell on the Kingdom of God**. Essentially, *spiritual warfare.*

The Bible tells us that evil spiritual forces do make attacks on God's people, and some of those attacks are stronger than others.

---

[14] Gil Shefler, *Pompeii's Destruction: Godly Retribution?* http://www.jpost.com/Israel/Pompeiis-destruction-Godly-retribution (accessed Sept. 20. 2013).

Note that in the entire history of the physical world, **no volcano has ever been successful in its molten attack upon land or water**. Superheated lava may persist momentarily, but air or water quickly cools it into hardened rock again. Not long after that, small plants will pop up in puddles of water, shooting their roots down into the hardened lava and beginning the process of breaking it up into fertile soil.

In the same way, no spiritual attack from hell will *ever* prevail against the Kingdom of Christ. God, through His presence and power (air & water), immediately begins cooling the attack and solidifying the "lava" into new fertile land for the Kingdom.

The hardiest of believers, those believers who are especially equipped for fellowship with hardened new believers (newly hardened lava), are the first to begin digging into this new part of Kingdom, setting their roots down, breaking it up. In very short time, these "hardened, new believers" are softened up for full fellowship with all believers (trees, bushes, etc.).

Soil derived from volcanic rock is especially fertile.

Some volcanos erupt suddenly, pressure having built up in the mantle by the earth's crust pressing down. Such a volcanic explosion can be a violent displacement of massive amounts of land and rock, combined with billowing, super-heated clouds of ash.

Other volcanos erupt with a slow, regular leak of lava and sulfur dioxide gas. This kind of eruption is not violent; it merely kills whatever vegetation might lie in the way.

These two types of eruptions represent the two kinds of battles in warfare. The history of physical warfare is full of examples of both types: Sudden, massive clashes and long, drawn-out sieges. Most likely, this distinction in the types of physical warfare carries over to spiritual warfare.

The sudden volcanic explosion would represent a one-time battle. In such a spiritual battle, just as a physical volcano blows huge amounts of rocks into the air and flattens trees, many believers would suddenly be ripped from fellowship, destroyed spiritually. Think Mount Saint Helens.

The spewing ash is grey, like death, symbolic of the deathly pallor of unbelievers who have yet to be born again into new life in Christ. These spiritually dead people are thrown into the Kingdom by this spiritual attack. Once there, the forces of the atmosphere (God the Father), water (God's power), and plants (believers) begin transforming this ash into the most fertile of soils, creating rich new fields in which life can take root.

Grey ash becomes rich soil.

Dead unbelievers find life in the Body of Christ.

What would this spiritual attack look like in our world? Perhaps it's another symbol for the persecution of God's people, like a forest fire. In fact, lava flows do often provoke forest fires. Volcanic explosions could be likened to the Roman persecutions of Christians, which were irregular, yet forceful in spite of their infrequency.

These sporadic persecutions were inspired by the enemy of Christ and swept away many believers from the physical world, releasing them to return home to Christ. Many unbelievers were left standing in the aftermath (ash), and through God's power and the work of other believers, many unbelievers found new life in Christ and became rich soil.

The other kind of volcanic eruption, the more regular kind (Think Hawaiian Islands) is representative of a slow, steady siege upon God's Kingdom. This could be compared to constant persecution, like the constant persecution by the communist Chinese government on the Chinese Church.

Wherever the lava flows, vegetation will be killed. These lava flows can actually provoke a full-fledged forest fire, which represents a spiritual attack fomenting persecution on the church.

However, because of the constant cooling effects of the sky and water, this lava creates new layers of land on top of the old, and wherever it contacts the sea, *brand new* land. After the lava stops and cools, vegetation is able to take root again.

China is a good example of this. Atheism and communism are both inspired by the enemy and thus the Chinese government's persecution of Chinese Christians is a massive, constant spiritual attack.

Yet, there is constant growth of the church in China. Whenever the government focuses its attention on a specific group of believers and persecutes, that particular church will suffer. Its growth will be hampered temporarily while the government's heavy hand is upon it, but as soon as it escapes the spotlight, that church will experience tremendous, reinvigorated growth. This is comparable to lava killing plants and trees that are later replaced by even more plants in the renewed, and even more fertile soil.

It is the sinful nature (gravity) of those doing the persecution that brings this "lava" down upon the believers.

Volcanos can create new islands in the middle of the ocean.

The continental coastlines around the world are fairly consistent. There will be some erosion here, some river delta growth there, but overall, the relative boundaries of the ocean with the continents do not change.

New island volcanos are the sole exception to this. In March of 2009, astounded spectators watched as an undersea volcano began spewing ash into the air from under water off the coast of Tonga. New land surface in the middle of the ocean was formed in a matter of days.

A volcanic eruption is the only way to create significant amounts of new land in the ocean. River deposits don't even come close.

The lesson here is that for God's Kingdom to be established in a new place in the world, for new territory to be taken for Christ, which is essentially forming an island in the middle of the ocean, spiritual battle will have to be engaged.

Pakistan has very few Christians. That country would definitely be considered part of the "ocean." If we wish to establish God's Kingdom there, if we wish to form an island in that part of the world, missionaries will have to undergo spiritual warfare. Just as plants cannot overcome lava through their own power, neither can believers overcome evil in spiritual warfare without the help of God. He is the One who acts to cool off the attack, creating the island. Then, the missionaries (hardy plants) are in place, ready to take root, fellowshipping with the new believers and making the soil more fertile.

Volcanos can create new mountains in the middle of a plain.

On February 20, 1943, Mexican farmer Dionisio Pulido was plowing his relatively flat cornfield when suddenly, a fissure in the ground cracked open and gas and stones began spewing out.[15] Within a week, a mountain five stories tall had formed. Within a year, it had grown to over 1,100 feet high, and when it finally stopped erupting eight years later, the volcano had attained an altitude of nearly 1,400 feet. Several villages were buried under the new volcano, and the landscape was forever changed.

Referring back to our previous interpretations, plains are symbolic of the lukewarm church. These are churches where there are no valleys or mountains, where nobody's trying to make the hard climb of spiritual growth from trouble to success. Lukewarm people are content to be flat.

A spiritual attack, i.e. spiritual or physical persecution, on such a church can radically transform it from a flat, lukewarm church into a church that, from necessity of being under fire from hell, learns to seek God and make the hard climb required by a growing relationship with Him.

The result of this "volcanic" attack is not the creation of a valley, but a mountain (success).

Three primary gases are released from volcanos: water vapor, carbon dioxide, and sulfur dioxide.

Sulfur dioxide is new. We haven't discussed that one before, mainly because we haven't seen it before. Of course, sulfur is associated with hell and brimstone, which is further confirmation of the symbolism behind a volcano.

If carbon dioxide is symbolic of the human spirit, because of the combination of carbon (human) and oxygen (spirit), then sulfur dioxide would be the spirit of hell. In other words, during a persecution of the church motivated by the forces of hell, a hellish spirit lies beneath the attack and is released, along with the selfish human spirit. An immediate result of such persecution is the death of many believers, which is

---

[15] Parícutin, http://en.wikipedia.org/wiki/Par%C3%ADcutin (accessed Sept. 20. 2013).

represented by the release of water vapor (life) rising toward the sky during a volcanic eruption.

Sometimes a small lake will form within a volcano's crater. These lakes are saturated with sulfur dioxide and are extremely acidic. *Some of these lakes can be twice as acidic as battery acid.*

In my wife's home country of Costa Rica, there is a popular tourist destination called Volcano Irazu. It has one of these eerie green lakes filling its dormant crater. I'll never forget the first time I visited, the guide explained that not long before a German tourist had crossed the barrier and tumbled down the hundreds of feet into the lake. The body had still not been recovered, and never would be.

Since fresh water is symbolic of *God's power* and ocean water is the world, these sulfur lakes must represent the power of hell.

Yet, two characteristics immediately stand out regarding these sulfur lakes: They are always small and they are destructive.

This means there is no wide-ranging power of hell within the Kingdom. It is contained within a small area within the volcano. If the sulfur lake were suddenly released down the slope, the flow would not be that great and only moderate, temporary destruction would occur in its path. Also, the water would quickly transform into fresh water as the sulfur leeched out.

Really, the only power these sulfur lakes have is the destructive power of their acid while contained in the crater, and that destruction is only a threat to those who might stumble and fall into it.

In other words, believers are only at risk after climbing a mountain in their walk with God. And not just any mountain, but a volcanic mountain. The walk up the volcano would symbolize overcoming in spiritual warfare (which is really a dependence by the believer on God's power in overcoming). Once at the top, the believer's peril would be a puffed-up pride inspired by the victory, somehow believing themselves to be responsible for it. This believer, blinded by their pride, can stumble over the lip of the crater and fall into the lake, where the enemy is waiting to burn them.

Interestingly, sulfur dioxide is mined from these lakes for the production of refined sugar and cosmetics. Everyone who's ever struggled with an addiction to chocolate, candy, or cake knows how deceptively evil refined sugar is to the waistline. And need it be said that cosmetics by definition create false beauty? So, this mining represents the spirit of hell being tapped to create false beauty in the world and make that which would otherwise be unhealthy to eat taste sweet.

Volcanic explosions are known to impact the climate of our planet in significant ways.

Ash ejected into the atmosphere reflects so much sunlight that average global temperatures can actually decrease by a degree or two. *In fact, one particular volcanic explosion by itself is known to have lowered temperatures around the entire globe for two entire years.*[16]

During spiritual conflict, when unregenerate non-believers are thrown into contact with believers (ash cloud), the result can be a *moderate* crisis of belief for the believer as they're suddenly exposed to many broken, unhealed lives. The believer sometimes questions God and His love for humanity in the face of such brokenness. Sunlight (truth) and warmth (God's love) are temporarily blocked by the ash.

This blockage is temporary, usually minor in nature, and soon to be overcome. It only drops the temperature a degree or so.

While the image of God (sky) may seem polluted by the deathly brokenness of humanity (ash), tarnishing our view of Him, He is not polluted, just as the sky cannot be stained. Broken humanity has merely sought Him, rests in Him temporarily, and then through His power (rain), they are washed into the Kingdom, transformed into fertile soil. We see this process as messy and ugly, but it is the process of redemption.

---

[16] Alexandra Witze, *The Volcano that Changed the World*, http://www.nature.com/news/2008/080411/full/news.2008.747.html (accessed Sept. 20, 2013).

Volcanic eruptions are often accompanied by earthquake tremors.

The explosion itself can cause tremors, or the opposite can happen, an earthquake can cause the eruption by opening a subterranean gap through which the magma flows. This means hellish spiritual attacks on the Kingdom (volcanos) can cause brotherly conflicts within the Kingdom (earthquakes). Or conversely, conflicts within the Kingdom can create openings for the enemy to mount an attack where such an opening did not previously exist.

Volcanos usually occur where tectonic plates are converging or diverging, but not where they are simply grinding past one another.

Converging means that one plate is pushing another plate down. Diverging means they are pulling apart.

This means that when two sections of the Kingdom, be it two churches, two believers, or two Christian nations, are simply bumping against one another as they move in two different directions, no opening for attack is created.

However, when one group of Christians tries to oppress or dominate another group of believers (converging) or when brothers and sisters in Christ move apart from one another in division, the enemy has room for attack.

Is it any wonder that Christ's longest prayer for His Bride (John 17) is that brothers and sisters in Christ would live in fellowship and love each other as He loved us?

Lightning can accompany volcanic eruptions when they spew great amounts of ash and gases into the atmosphere.

This lightning is symbolic of God executing judgment upon unregenerate men and women as they erupt from the spiritual attack into the Kingdom. The lost who rush into a church during a revival are often driven there because, in a sense, they are experiencing God's judgment in a minor or major way. Whether it's the serrating pain of a divorce, the frailty brought on by a deadly STD, or just getting put in jail, these micro judgments of God are designed to provoke repentance, and they do.

Volcanos destroy things.

In spite of the images of revival and redemption that follow God's overcoming the forces of evil, we do well to remember that people die in battles. Spiritual warfare does destroy.

The danger is not limited to a volcano's immediate environs either. Acid rain is produced by sulfur dioxide mixing with water in the atmosphere. When it falls, it can corrode metal and kill plants.

Thankfully, clean rain will soon follow and wash it away.

So, a spiritual attack on the Kingdom can contaminate life in that section of the Kingdom for a time, but God will soon wash that contamination away through a release of His power.

Lastly, a sky laden with volcanic ash can produce gorgeous sunsets exploding with color.

The sun represents Christ, and these sunsets are made by the sun reflecting off the ash as it leaves us. Therefore, these sunsets symbolically point to the beautiful, cultivated, but still empty field Jesus left for us to harvest.

The ash is unregenerate men and women. The beautiful sunset light is the truth that Christ taught as He left, shining upon them, revealing the wonderful, potential harvest in the field of the Kingdom. Right before He ascended, Jesus spoke of our main task, the Great Commission. He charged us with planting seeds, watering, and harvesting that field. To most, the lost of the world look devastatingly depressing. To the missionary, their potential is a beautiful opportunity.

And Jesus has the biggest missionary heart of all.

Lesson: *God protects the church. Seek Him during spiritual warfare.*

Tsunamis

"For certain men have crept in unnoticed...ungodly men, who turn the grace of our God into lewdness and deny the only Lord God and our Lord Jesus Christ...[they are] raging waves of the sea, foaming up their own shame..." (Jude 1:4;13b)

Only the young don't remember the massive tsunami in 2004 that slammed into Indonesia and many other nations bordering the Indian Ocean. The scenes of the aftermath were horrific. Over 200,000 people lost their lives.

Tsunamis, otherwise known as tidal waves, are birthed by major undersea earthquakes, landslides, or other oceanic movements of land that displace great amounts of water.

These enormous waves can grow to anywhere between 20 to over 100 feet high when they near shore.

However, while still out at sea, a tsunami's wavelength is stretched out over a great distance, perhaps as much as 100 miles. Which means that if you were on a boat in the middle of the ocean when the tsunami passed underneath, your boat would only rise a total of a few feet, and that would take around fifteen minutes to happen. In other words, at sea, a tsunami is virtually undetectable.

Yet, this stretched-out swell moves at 500 miles per hour, so when it reaches shallow water, it backs up on itself, creating a massive tidal wave that destroys everything near the shoreline.

If earthquakes on land represent movements within the Kingdom, then undersea earthquakes can only represent large movements within the world. These sudden shifts in the worldly landscape produce large "swells" that overwhelm the shores of the Kingdom.

A tsunami is the world moving suddenly and powerfully against the Kingdom. This is not a persecution of the whole church for being followers of Christ, but a sudden overwhelming of the edges of the church by the world.

An example of this would be internet pornography. The modern-day plague of online pornography is the result of movements within the world culture. What once was taboo even by the world's standards has now become commonplace and accepted as normal behavior. This shift in the world's morality is the earthquake.

The resulting spiritual tsunami is very hard to detect by unre-generated people living in the world. Just like a ship at sea is unable to notice the tsunami swell, so do those of the world not really notice such shifts in the morality around them. It always seems the same to them.

Yet, for those Christians near the spiritual shore, the coming tsunami will be devastating. There are many Christians who love to hang out at the figurative "beach." They want to frolic in the waves of the world, having a good old time, never really committing themselves fully to dwell in the land of the Kingdom. They do not want to go inland, to increase their altitude, to grow spiritually. No, they are content to stay at sea level. They want to have one foot in the Kingdom and the other in world.

Their fun is about to be shattered by the coming disaster.

Christians who frolic in the salt-water waves of the world are abiding there as if the world will give them life, but salt water kills if you drink it. And a believer who hangs out near the world is susceptible to coming tsunamis like internet pornography.

They can be suddenly swept away and destroyed because they refused to go inland and mature spiritually. Christians who do move inland and stay far away from the world are not susceptible in the same way.

Thankfully, while a tsunami's destruction is devastating and takes lives, the wave recedes quickly once it's passed. Worldly Christians will have been swept away, but the damage to the Kingdom (land) is temporary. Tsunamis never actually affect the shoreline of the land significantly. The world has no real power against the Kingdom. It just sweeps away worldly Christians.

In the moments right before a tsunami strikes, a strange phenomenon occurs called a "drawback." As the tsunami approaches, water near the shore drains backward, feeding the growing wave. An observer would suddenly see hundreds of feet of newly exposed ground and rock that had been submerged just moments before. This is a very curious happening to those who witness it, and many inevitably wander out to explore the new territory.

Right before the 2004 Indian Ocean tsunami, hundreds of people, if not thousands, walked out into the dry sea bed to see what was going on. Few of them survived the severe thrashing of the tsunami racing toward them at speeds faster than they could run.

"Drawback" would seem to imply that right before this sudden attack of the world upon the Kingdom, there would be a very brief false revival of sorts where worldly Christians (believers living near the world) would for a moment believe they were witnessing a receding of the world and an expansion of the Kingdom. Those worldly Christians who venture out into the midst of this false revival are even more assured of destruction by the world than the others.

I must admit, I have never experienced such a thing personally, so I have nothing to draw on to verify this interpretation of drawback. Regardless, the symbolism doesn't really lend itself to any other apparent interpretation, so I hypothesize that worldly Christians might in fact witness a small, false revival of sorts before being swept away by the world. Perhaps, on a small scale, this could be comparable to a worldly Christian who hangs out with a lot of non-Christian buddies and right before he's swept away by their ungodly habits and lifestyles, thinks he's making progress with them.

Mature believers should absolutely imitate Jesus by befriending, loving, and hanging out with tax collectors and prostitutes, but this may be risky for the immature, worldly, uncommitted believer.

Numerous cities around the world have tried to hinder potential tsunamis by building tall sea walls to block future, enormous waves. However, no sea wall constructed by man has ever successfully stopped a tsunami because the sea walls are always too short.

The only thing ever observed to actually diminish the destructive forces of a tsunami is a thick, well-rooted forest. Tree trunks do effectively diffuse the power of the wave.

In other words, worldly Christians try their best to build human constructs (sea walls) to protect themselves from the onslaughts of the world, but to no avail. They're destroyed anyway. The only thing that can successfully diffuse a sudden flooding wave from the world is a forest of mature believers.

Lesson: *Move further into the Kingdom, away from the world.*

Floods

"And behold, I Myself am bringing floodwaters on the earth, to destroy from under heaven all flesh in which is the breath of life; everything that is on the earth shall die." (Genesis 6:17)

Water represents the *active, energetic, transforming force of God at work in the world*. Normally, God releases His power upon the Kingdom in gentle ways like rain, streams and rivers for the purpose of creating vibrant life.

However, there are those instances when He pours out His power in overwhelming torrents upon the land and the result is destruction.

Floods are associated with the judgment of God, and honestly, how could they not be? While some floods result from oceanic storm surges or rapidly melting snows, the large majority of floods are simply caused by too much rain.

Rain comes from the sky (symbolic of God the Father), and clearly, only God controls the rain.

Floods are symbolic of a pouring out of God's power in judgment. They sweep away human structures (traditions) and cleanse the land (Kingdom).

We drown when the water rises so high that our access to air is blocked.

The water blocks our breathing.

When God moves in judgment through His power, access to His Spirit (oxygen) for those falling under His judgment becomes limited or even blocked completely. The result is spiritual drowning.

Obviously, God is capable of killing us both physically and spiritually, and when He does kill someone in either sense, He does it through His power.

His power applied to us in gentle ways sparks life, but we need access to His Spirit to continue to breathe.

Thankfully, physical floods are relatively rare in most places.

God's judgments on His Kingdom are similarly rare and limited thanks to His tremendous mercy. Yet, when He does move in judgment, the devastation is tremendous. Just as crops ready for the harvest can be ruined, so can a church's harvest be destroyed before ripening.

Trees are resilient in the face of floods.

If trees are shallowly-rooted and top-heavy like an oak, they can topple over in the super-saturated soil, or if they remain submerged for too long, they may suffocate, but overall, trees normally survive a flood without much problem. Other plants may survive too, but they don't possess anywhere near the hardiness of deeply-rooted trees.

Again, strong believers are like trees. They are resilient and can weather God's judgment upon His Kingdom for a time, but if it lasts too long, even they will perish.

Also, if a believer only has shallow roots in the Kingdom, the judgment can topple him or her. Deeply-rooted, mature believers will survive God's judgment on His people as long as God does not stretch out the duration of the judgment.

Floods temporarily contaminate the water supply.

In the same way, when God moves in judgment upon a church, the church feels contaminated. Members will no longer want to abide in the "life" of that local community of believers. Life there becomes undrinkable for a while.

If the water supply is contaminated, those who drink from it are likely to get sick. Disease runs rampant. This would be the equivalent of church members getting infected with bad teaching if they continue to abide in the life of a church under judgment. If they wish to remain healthy, they must get their "life" from outside that church.

Let's illustrate: Imagine a large church led by the stereotypical (in the very worst sense) televangelist pastor. He is a worldly man whose main concern is gaining material wealth and looking good rather than glorifying God. After years of his teaching, many of his parishioners have also come to believe that health and wealth follow strong faith. This pastor has taught them that all they have to do is say they want something and believe God will do it, and then God is obligated to give it to them.

Curiously, there are healings and passionate prayers and other signs of God's movement within the church. This river running through the church, a river of God's power, is just large enough for all to partake as they need, to find life in God if they drink from it.

Yet, one day, God suddenly moves in judgment upon this church for its worldliness, false teaching, and covetousness. He exposes to light the true nature of the corrupt pastor and tragic scandal flows into the church from the outside. This is the flood.

Numerous people were observing the church and on the verge of committing their lives to Christ because of this church's influence, but now they are disillusioned and wander away without having ripened. This is the ruination of the crop harvest.

Many believers within the church will leave, at least temporarily, due to the scandal. They will either search out different bodies of believers for fellowship or they will stay away from church altogether. The pastor would most likely step down from his position under pressure. Once the scandal has long passed, some of these believers will timidly return — others will stay away forever, having sunk roots in new churches. This is similar to what happened after Hurricane Katrina.

New Orleans was changed forever in the aftermath of that flood. Some of its former residents returned, but many stayed away forever, planting roots in new places.

During the flooding in New Orleans after Katrina, those who refused to seek higher ground faced a severely contaminated water supply.

So it would be for the believers who refuse to leave this scandal-ridden church. They will no longer have access to the pure life that flows from God, but will mistakenly drink from the contaminated church life that remains in the aftermath of such a scandal. And they will get sick.

Those brothers and sisters who move on to other healthier church families will find themselves doctrinally refreshed by pure teaching, uncontaminated by the "name-it and claim-it" false teaching of their old church.

But those who stay in the original church would likely dig further into the teachings they've always espoused, refusing to admit that those same teachings were a big part of the cause of the scandal now enveloping the church. Out of pride, they will continue to drink from this contaminated well, getting sicker and sicker, until they die spiritually or until God's cleansing power finishes washing away the contamination and healing returns to the church.

Of the prominent believers in the church, those whose roots don't go very deep in the Kingdom will topple over in the face of the movement of God's power and the Holy Spirit. Those who have sunk deep roots into the Kingdom will weather the storm better, but if the judgment lasts too long, even those believers will wilt and perish.

In our example, perhaps the scandalous pastor might refuse to resign, adamantly and pridefully defending and justifying himself and his actions. This would result in a strong continuation of God's judgment in the form of heightened and extended scandals. Even the strongest believers would perish in the midst of that after a time.

Many superficial believers, i.e. grass, will find themselves covered in "mud" when it's all said and done, though if the flood does not last too long many of these will also survive.

Floods re-fertilize the land.
They redistribute the soil, laying down new layers of silt on top of what had been before. The aftermath of a flood, the messy tangle of ruined vegetation and mud-covered objects has an appearance of death, but the flood has actually primed the land to spring forth new life.

God's judgment on a church is similar. While it temporarily contaminates the life within that church, the judgment has the same effect as pruning a bush. It restores health and cleanses the land.

Lesson: *God moving in your church does not mean He isn't about to judge it. Discern your church's spiritual health by its conformity to the Bible.*

Tornados

"Then the LORD answered Job out of the whirlwind..."
(Job 38:1)

To understand tornados, we must first understand what forms thunderstorms. Storm clouds are created as hot air bearing moisture rises toward the sky. This rising warm air clashes with cool air, which causes the water in the warm air to condense.

This removal of moisture from the warm air, releases energy that heats the warm air further, causing it to rise even higher, and the cycle continues as more moisture condenses.

A storm is born when this occurs at an accelerated rate.

The storm is symbolic of God's judgment, and the hot air rising represents love leaving the Kingdom. As love leaves the Kingdom, it carries God's power with it (God's power is more present with us when we are truly loving others).

This removal of love from the Kingdom clashes with the cold air of God's justice and stirs up a storm of His judgment.

In some of the strongest storms, wind shears may cause the rising hot air to spin very fast. This spinning air can eventually form a funnel. Under the right conditions, further updraft of hot air from the ground causes that spinning air to tilt downward, creating a tornadic funnel cloud.

So, whenever a part of the Body of Christ stops loving others as it should, God removes some of His power. He also begins preparing a storm of judgment for that section of the Kingdom, and if those believers do not repent, but continue to decrease their level of love, the potential judgment becomes actual judgment (active thunderstorm). In most cases, the judgments are individual in nature because, as we've already discussed, lightning strikes are very targeted.

Yet, if a significant wind shear event strikes a thundercloud horizontally, it sets the air within the cloud spinning. This is symbolic of the Holy Spirit moving to ratchet up the level and type of portending judgment. If believers persist in their disobedience to Christ's command to love one another in the face of such dark judgment, the result is a *communal* judgment rather than an individual one. This judgment is like the funnel cloud that destroys whole communities. Entire churches or other communities of believers can be wiped out.

This type of judgment will vary in strength. Some may be lighter, like an F-1 tornado and only result in minor damage. Others will be devastating like an F-5, which have been known to wipe entire towns off the map.

One very interesting characteristic of tornados is that they generally occur in areas with a flatter topography, like the Great Plains region of the United States. Plains represent lukewarm churches, so we can safely say that these most terrible of judgments on the Kingdom will usually be upon lukewarm churches, not the body as a whole.

This reminds us of Revelation 3:16 where Jesus says *"So then, because you are lukewarm, and neither cold nor hot, I will vomit you out of My mouth."*

Strong rainfall always accompanies destructive tornados. Dry whirlwinds, and other weak funnel-type clouds that don't occur in conjunction with storm clouds, may result in minor wind damage, but they are very different animals from a full-fledged tornado and they never utterly destroy like a tornado. Those lesser whirlwinds are more symbolic of simpler movements of the Holy Spirit moving parts of the Kingdom around.

The rainfall symbolizes God releasing His life-giving power back unto the earth simultaneously with the judgment. Even in judgment, God is merciful and He uses judgment to produce life.

Lesson: *Heat retention, continually loving one another, is a way to avoid judgment.*

Hurricanes

"...and on the earth distress of nations, with perplexity,
the sea and the waves roaring."
(Luke 21:25b)

Hurricanes are very similar to tornados in the way they form, i.e. hot air rising to clash with cold air, which results in a cyclonic movement of winds and clouds. However, there are four main differences between tornados and hurricanes.

The first difference is the source of the rising hot air. Tornado judgments are executed upon lukewarm churches because of a loss of love in the Kingdom. Hurricane judgments are formed because of a loss of love in the world (rising hot air from the ocean).

Second, hurricanes strike coastlines and beaches, not plains and prairies. So, these world-induced judgments strike worldly Christians as opposed to lukewarm Christians (There *is* a difference).

Third, hurricanes are much larger than tornados. They devastate large swaths of territory, completely indiscriminate in what they destroy, as opposed to the more targeted tornados. This symbolizes how God is more specific and merciful when He judges the Kingdom, but when He releases the world to participate in the judgment, there is no discrimination among targets.

Lastly, hurricanes bring with them a large storm surge. This is a powerful wall of ocean water that rises up ahead of the storm and floods coastal areas, sometimes bringing about even more destruction than the winds themselves.

This signifies how worldly Christians are swept away by the world itself.

Lesson: *Don't live near the world. Abide in Christ.*

REVIEW	
Sunshine	= Good Times
Thunderstorms	= God's Pending Judgment
Lightning	= God's Judgment on an Individual
Snow	= God's power waiting to move
Fog	= God's power causing spiritual blindness
Earthquakes	= Conflict within the Kingdom
Landslides	= Reforms within the Kingdom
Earth's Core	= Hell
Volcanos	= Spiritual Attacks on the Kingdom
Tsunamis	= Worldly Attacks on the Kingdom
Floods	= God's Judgment on the Kingdom through His Power
Tornados	= God's Judgment on the Lukewarm Church
Hurricanes	= God's Judgment on the Worldly Church, using the World

PART II

ANIMALS

FISH & MAMMALS:

The Lost & Believers

ANIMALS

The Animal Kingdom is *huge*.

There are millions of species in the world, far too many to discuss in the limited space of this book.

Yet, when I say the world "animal," most likely your mind first imagines something that would be classified as a mammal, like lions and bears and dogs. Next, you remember reptiles, which then naturally reminds you of amphibians. And of course, thoughts of amphibians only lead us to consider fish, and finally we fill in the last category: birds.

These five, mammals, reptiles, amphibians, fish, and birds, are the basic categories of all vertebrates — and while technically a sea sponge is an animal (and so are tapeworms) vertebrates are typically what you and I would consider animals. As would have ancient man, so they are what we will discuss here.

Oh, and don't forget those pesky little insects. We'll talk about those too.

But before we get started, an important note. We'll see that many times animals serve as duplicate symbols for things already discussed in the plant life section. In the introduction, we postulated that if God had encoded a symbolic message in Creation, that the symbols we interpreted would have to be consistent, meaning one thing cannot represent two different things — and we have been faithful to that principle with our interpretation.

Yet, we never said there could not be two different symbols representing the same thing. In fact, throughout Scripture, God uses multiple symbols for the same thing. For example, the Lion of Judah and the Lamb of God both represent Jesus. So, God has no problem communicating this way.

Actually, we've already seen several examples of duplicated symbols, but I believe there is *a lot* of overlap between the interpretation of animals and plants. The difference lies in which characteristics God is trying to emphasize.

With regards to plants, I believe His emphasis is how different kinds of believers interact with the rest of the Kingdom (roots in the soil). With animals, I think His emphasis is more on the distinctive personalities and distinguishing characteristics of believers.

That said, let's dive in.

THE SENSES

O kay, so consider what makes animals different from trees. Besides the ability to move around, I mean.

Biologically speaking, there seem to be limitless differences, but one that stands out above all is the ability to sense the world around them. Of course plants have some minor sensory ability, but they don't have eyes to see, nor ears to hear. They can't taste or smell either.

Since these are the abilities unique to animals, we need to interpret the basic senses of sight, hearing, and smell before proceeding.

Vision

"So that 'seeing they may see and not perceive...lest they should turn, and their sins be forgiven them.'" (Mark 4:12)

S ince vision is the ability to see light, and light represents truth, then vision must represent the ability to discern truth.

Interestingly, animals have differing sight abilities. We humans see in three colors and experience the wide range of their combinations. This is called being *tri*chromatic. If you know anything about the way televisions work, you know that the many colors you see on the screen are actually just combinations of the fundamentals: red, blue, and green.

In art, all paint colors can be derived by mixing red, blue, and yellow. Our eyes work the same way.

However, many species don't see the world in the same way we do. Fish do see in three colors, but their colors are different from ours and they don't have the brainpower to experience the clarity we do.

Some reptiles see in color, but they don't have the brain power to discern hues like humans, others see in black and white.

Primates see in three colors like us, but other mammals see only two, which is called *di*chromacy. This does *not* mean they see in black and white — they just have access to fewer color variations, which actually results in their being unable to distinguish shades of gray.

Lastly, birds are *tetra*chromatic, which means they have four kinds of cones in their retinas, i.e. they see four kinds of color, even ultraviolet. This could be considered a kind of "heavenly vision."

Regardless, we'll touch on each animal's vision capabilities when we get to that section, but for now know that vision equals the ability to discern truth.

Lesson: *Not all have an equal ability to discern truth.*

The Blind

"Yet the LORD has not given you a heart to perceive and eyes to see and ears to hear, to this very day." (Deut. 29:4)

Those individuals who are physically blind to light are symbolic of those people who are spiritually blind to truth. This does not mean that the physically blind are also spiritually blind. One is merely symbolic of the other.

Since nobody with perfectly good eyes makes themselves blind on purpose, it is clear that all blind people are made blind by God. They're either born blind or are the victims of an accident, an illness, or an assault, all of which would be acts of God as far as the blind individual is concerned.

In the same way, nobody blinds themself to spiritual truth. They are blinded to it by the action of God. (John 12:40, 2 Thess. 2:10-12, Exodus. 9:12)

All the miracles Jesus performed during His ministry, from healings to the miraculous provision of food, to the controlling of weather, to the raising of the dead, were also performed by Old Testament prophets.

Except for making a blind man see.

For centuries before Christ, rabbis taught that one of the signs of the Messiah would be that He could heal the blind since this was a miracle that no other prophet had ever done.[17]

Of course, Jesus did heal the blind on numerous occasions. Symbolically, this shows that only God Himself can open the eyes of those who are spiritually blind to truth.

Lesson: *Prayer is more effective than arguments in opening the eyes of the spiritually blind.*

---

[17] Jacob Prasch, *Three Messianic Miracles*, http://moriel.org/MorielArchive/index.php/author/prasch/three-messianic-miracles (accessed on Sept. 20, 2013).

The Four Miracles Required of the Messiah, http://messianicgentiles.blogspot.com/2007/04/four-miracles-required-of-messiah.html (accessed on Sept. 2013).

Hearing

"I spoke to you in your prosperity, But you said, 'I will not hear.'
This has been your manner from your youth,
That you did not obey My voice." (Jeremiah 22:21)

"He who has an ear, let him hear what the Spirit says
to the churches..." (Revelation 2:7a)

Throughout Scripture, there are numerous passages equating "hearing" with "obeying." To hear is to perceive God's Voice, to perceive God's Word. To perceive God's Word is equated with obeying His voice. Scripture indicates that a failure to obey is due to someone not being given "ears to hear." (Mark 4:9-12, Matthew 13:9-16)

So, to hear means to obey God's Word, and we'll see that animals have a wide variety of hearing ranges, just as we see a wide variety in levels of obedience among believers.

Lesson: *Ask for obedience. He will give you ears to hear.*

Smell

"Beloved, do not believe every spirit, but test the spirits,
whether they are of God; because many false prophets have gone out
into the world." (1 John 4:1)

To smell is essentially to sense gases. When you smell something, you're smelling particles floating in the air. Since we've consistently interpreted all gases throughout as being symbolic of one kind of a spirit or another, from the Holy Spirit to the almost poisonous human spirit, then the sense of smell can only represent the discernment of spirits.

Spiritual discernment is different from the discernment of truth, which was represented by vision. To discern truth is to know whether something is true or false, and to be able to understand spiritual truths.

To discern spirits is to instinctively understand the source of something. It's the ability to know whether an idea is from the Holy Spirit or the world. Whether a leader has godly intentions or selfish ambition.

Surprisingly, many non-believers appear to have this ability as well. They can instantly tell if someone is a Christian or not, though they might not understand what they're doing. The difference is their affinity. A worldly person will detect a Christian and react negatively.

I'll never forget a story some missionary friends of mine once told me. Years ago, they ran a Christian bookstore in a medium-sized town in England, and one day a young man and woman stumbled into their shop. They may or may not have been half-drunk in revelry, but it was only a matter of seconds before the couple stiffened as they sensed the Christian Spirit inside the store. Then, they shrieked and fled as if being chased.

Thankfully, we believers have an even better sense of "smell," though some of us put it to use well and others seem to have their sinuses eternally stopped up. Be sure and put yours to use.

Lesson: *Do not accept things at face value, but test the spirits behind them. Seek to smell what's really going on.*

FISH

"Why do You make men like fish of the sea?"
(Habakkuk 1:14a)

"Then Jesus said to them, 'Follow Me,
and I will make you become fishers of men.'
They immediately left their nets and followed Him."
(Mark 1:17)

Given that we've already interpreted the ocean as symbolizing the world, it only follows that fish would symbolize people who inhabit the world, who belong to it, rather than the Kingdom.

It's important to say clearly that though the oceans represent the world, they are not evil. God lovingly created each and every fish and certainly enjoyed designing them, for there is such a variety in their kinds and beauty in their style. He called His creation good.

You will notice in Genesis 1 that God does not originally call the ocean *waters* good, though he does call the establishment of land good. Yet, when He gets to the creation of fish, He not only calls the fish good, but He blesses them.

Therefore, the atmosphere of the world (ocean water) is a hostile environment for inhabitants of the Kingdom, it means death for them, yet God still loves those non-believers (fish) who inhabit the world.

Fish are cold-blooded.

This means they have no internal mechanism for staying warm or heating themselves up. Their body temperature will always match the temperature of the water around them.

This distinction from warm-blooded mammals (inhabitants of the land) is crucial. Scripture says, *"for the life of the flesh is in the blood"* (Lev. 17:11), and we have already interpreted heat as being a symbol for love.

Therefore, through their cold-bloodedness, fish symbolize that non-believers have no internal source of love. How much love they feel is completely dependent on their surrounding environment.

If you put a non-believer in a loving home, they will feel loved. If you place them in a hate-filled society, they will become bitter and hateful. They have no power within themselves to counteract the influence of society around them.

As opposed to a Mother Theresa, who continually showed self-sacrificing love to the least of India's society in spite of the misery surrounding her day in and day out.

And as the oceans are only warmed by the direct impact of the sun's light, so are the "temperatures" of societies around the world fully dependent on how much of Christ's truth has permeated them.

Remove Christ's truths from a society and you get Nazi Germany, bitter, cold, full of hate. Retain Christ's truths within a society, but divorce them from their Author, and you get Sweden.

Still, oceans are always colder than the land they surround. The world will always be a less loving place than the Kingdom, and as ocean water sucks the heat from even a warm-blooded body faster than air, so will even a believer struggle with his or her internal level of love in a very cold society.

Fish have scales.

Yes, almost all fish have scales, including sharks. Sharks' scales are just so small they are almost invisible to the human eye, and thus look like skin. Even those few species who do not have scales all over their body, have them in limited areas. There are a rare number who have none, but they are very few.

Scales serve to protect the fish from predators, barnacles, and disease. In fact, shark scales are so proficient in protecting against disease that a new product modeled after shark "skin" has been deployed in hospitals to prevent the transference of infection by doctors from one patient to another.[18]

Scales also aid fish in swimming. They increase flexibility and reduce drag in the water much like the dimples on a golf ball allow it to travel farther. In short, fish can swim faster, maneuver better, and make quicker turns because they have scales instead of skin.

The oceans are truly a fish-eat-fish world. It's not just sharks that are the predators of the deep — the large majority of fish species eat other fish as a part of their regular diet. This means the life of a fish is a constantly threatened one, much more so than say a squirrel in the forest. The squirrel is alert, but he is not under constant threat of being eaten at the same levels that a fish is.

It took me a while to realize what fish scales reminded me of, but then it clicked — *medieval chain-mail body armor.*

The world is a much more dangerous place than the Kingdom (You don't have to worry about getting mugged at church). Scales are symbolic of God equipping non-believers with a spiritual defense mechanism that also allows them to maneuver quicker in the world, a "street smarts" if you will.

I know this is somewhat subjective, hard to put a finger on, but it is nevertheless true. Non-believers are used to living among other non-believers and thus are used to being taken advantage of and hurt. This makes them much more skeptical and "hard-skinned" than your average believer. These spiritual "scales" are what makes them initially skeptical of the motives of believers and the reason believers must bear testimony for long periods of time before this skepticism can be alleviated.

Bacteria and other disease agents have a much easier time surviving in water than they do the air. This is symbolic of the fact that it is much easier to pick-up false teachings and other harmful spirituality in the world than in the Kingdom. This skepticism that is natural to non-believers, while it prevents them from easily embracing the gospel, it

---

[18] Medical Design, *Shark Skin Shows How to Keep Surfaces Clean,* http://medicaldesign.com/materials/shark_skin_shows_0608 (accessed Nov. 11, 2013).

also protects them from too easily embracing false teaching. If they did not have this skepticism (scales), you would see non-believers flocking in droves much faster to the New Age religion and other pagan influences rather than retaining a lot of the vestiges of prior Christian influence on the general culture.

For example, American culture has clearly reached a post-modern phase, yet many non-believers still retain a belief in "do unto others" rather than embrace the mantra of "kill or be killed" as post-modern, evolutionary thought teaches, which also used to dominate the Roman Empire.

Still, it's only a matter of time before most fish either get sick or get eaten.

Fish have gills.

Gills are similar to our lungs in that they remove oxygen from their environment and transfer it to the blood. The primary distinctions are that gills are external organs, not internal like lungs, and gills have the ability to extract oxygen from water instead of air. Of course, gills are *not* capable of extracting oxygen from air, *only* water.

Internal lungs symbolize a believer's ability to receive breath from the Holy Spirit (oxygen) inside of them. External gills represent the fact that non-believers can only live because of the presence of the Holy Spirit's influence in the world around them. Fish cannot live in water that has not been oxygenated. They cannot breath ocean water (the world), they can only extract oxygen from the water.

We tend to think that the world is devoid of the presence and influence of God's Spirit, yet this is not true. The difference between the Kingdom and the world is the level of the presence of the Spirit. Remove His influence completely from anywhere and life is no longer possible.

Theologically, this concept is known as *common grace*.

Fish don't experience the Law of Gravity the same way we do.

Water is so effective at reducing the effects of gravity that astronauts train for weightlessness in giant aquariums. (The Law of Gravity, you will recall, represents the sinful nature.)

Do fish experience gravity? Of course they do, but the water surrounding them prevents them from *perceiving* its impact or even existence.

Fish float around blissfully unaware they are slaves to a force they don't even know exists. Until they take a leap from the water toward the sky, that is. Then, for one brief moment they experience the reality of what land animals know every day.

They don't soar above land animals, they are forever stuck below the surface, unaware of a higher world.

In the same way, because they are so completely immersed in the world, non-believers are unaware of their sinful nature. They know they cannot fly, but have no expectations that they should be able to. Since everyone around them is held down and struggles in the same way they do, non-believers have no concept of a different life. They're not happy, but they don't think anything else is possible.

Only after a person is reborn in Christ and becomes a member of the Kingdom (land) do they become aware of this spiritual force that keeps them from soaring.

Some fish have air bladders.

Fish can extract oxygen from their blood and pump these bladders full of air. They use their bladders to help them maintain buoyancy within the water.

In other words, if they want to rise toward the surface, they fill the bladder with more air, or squeeze it out to sink.

This shows how non-believers can keep themselves from sinking further into the world. They are not indwelled by the Holy Spirit like a believer (like a mammal breathing air), but must extract small teachings of the Holy Spirit that exist in the world's culture.

Just as the ocean is not devoid of oxygen, so is the world not devoid of the Spirit's influence, otherwise the world would be hell.

If a non-believer (fish) wishes to "rise" within the world, they can retain and "inflate" themselves with the teachings of the Spirit. If they do not retain that which they have gleaned subconsciously from the Spirit, they sink further into the world.

This is evidenced by non-believers who act ethically and morally even without being saved by Christ. Their superior morality tends to cause them to rise within society, and it clearly keeps them from sinking into things like drug addiction.

Some fish swim in schools.

These schools are tightly organized. They synchronize their swimming so that each member of the group moves at the same speed and in the same direction. This schooling behavior is believed to provide a variety of advantages.

It's important to point out that schooling behavior appears almost instinctive, subconscious. In the world, we see people in our culture behave this way as well.

Group-thinking reigns.

Traditionally non-Christian cultures (Think: China, India, Africa) tend to promote the importance of the group over the rights of the individual. Remove Christ from the influence over someone's mind, and they lose much of their ability to think for themselves. Instead, they simply accept what the rest of their "school" thinks as truth.

The irony is how many non-believers think it's actually Christians who are engaged in mindless group-think, but this assumption by them is just another example of group-think they have accepted. The proof in the pudding is how the greatest scientists, musicians, and inventors were all Christians or Jews who did what they did for the glory of God. It's been a while since our last Albert Einstein or Isaac Newton.

Strangely, this group-think mentality among those of the world protects them just as swimming in schools protects an individual fish from getting separated into the mouth of a shark. If non-believers did not participate in group-think, the result would be complete anarchy, since there is no other force to direct them into sensible behavior.

Fish have a sixth sense enabled by something called a lateral line system.

This system is similar to radar, and consists of a line of special cells running the length of their backs that can sense the smallest movements or pressure changes in the surrounding water. This allows fish to detect prey, predators, and even the behavior of other fish for the purpose of schooling. Fish rely on this system much more than vision, and they can even navigate well through dark or murky waters because of it.

"Fish that were experimentally blinded were able to reintegrate into the school, while fish with *severed lateral lines* were unable to re-integrate themselves. Therefore, reliance on functional mechano-reception, not vision, is essential for schooling behavior." (Pitcher, T., Partridge, B., & Wardle, C., 1976. A blind fish can school. Science, 194(4268), 963-965. doi:10.1126/ science.982056, emphasis in italics mine.)

Once again, we have another symbol for the sixth sense, the street smarts, that non-believers possess, allowing them to navigate the world instinctively with no requirement for wisdom.

Jenny is a young lady living in New York City. She always makes sure to turn both deadbolts and hook the chain on the door to her apartment before tossing her keys into a dish on the table. She sits down to watch TV after a long day at work, a job that does not satisfy, but if she can get just a little more money, she knows her problems will go away.

A televangelist comes on the screen, and she immediately turns the channel, not fooled by his promises or fake smile (lateral line system, scales). Sometimes she wonders how these fundamentalists still exist in this day and age. Everyone knows what horrible, mean people they are (group-think).

The next channel has some guy talking about alien abductions. She changes again, not believing a bit his wild story (lateral line system, scales). Still, there has to be life on other planets somewhere, doesn't there? The universe is just so big, after all (group-think). She also thinks Oprah was right about us being more connected to the universe than we think (group-think).

All people are basically good, aren't they? (Group-think) Well, maybe not her father who left her mother last year for another woman. She hasn't talked to him since (cold-blooded), but maybe she should be the first to give him a call. Somebody has to make the first move. 'Do unto others', right? (Gills, air bladder)

The doorbells rings and she is sure to check the peep hole before undoing the locks, making sure it is the delivery man with the take-out Chinese she ordered. You can't be too careful these days... (lateral line system, scales).

Even though less than .01% of the earth's water is fresh water, 40% of all fish species live there.

This represents that non-believers are attracted to the movements of God (rivers) even though they are not reborn themselves. Every week, millions and millions of people attend church who do not have a personal commitment to pursue God or follow Christ.

These are nominal Christians, Christians in name only. People who have an affection for God, yet have not been reborn. They don't know Jesus Christ as their personal Savior and Lord — they've never asked for forgiveness of sins nor submitted to his lordship. Fans, not followers.

These are the freshwater fish.

Lesson: *Don't waste time complaining about fish being fish. Instead, be a fisher of men and bring new creations into the Kingdom.*

Salmon

"Do not love the world or the things in the world. If anyone loves the world, the love of the Father is not in him." (1 John 2:15)

Ruth 4:21 says "*Salmon* begot Boaz, and Boaz begot Obed..." — just kidding.

Most people know what makes salmon so unique among the fish of the world. They're *anadromous*, meaning they migrate from the ocean to rivers in order to spawn.

Salmon are born in a freshwater river. Then, they move to the ocean, where they mature. When it's time to have little salmon babies, though, they return home to the river of their birth, leaping over obstacles and even up waterfalls to get there, many times traveling hundreds of miles to do so.

Salmon represent those nominal Christians who grow up attending church only to abandon it as young adults for the world (the ocean), embracing a life of parties and worldliness. Yet, when they mature enough that they are ready to have children of their own, they suddenly panic and flee back to the church of their youth, even overcoming tremendous obstacles and making radical changes to do so, because they are determined to protect their children from the environment they have embraced.

Rick grew up in church, and he had a decent family life. He came from well-to-do country club stock and was taught all the traditions of his prosperous, traditional church.

When he left home for his Ivy League college, those weak traditions slid off his back as he dove into a world of fraternity parties and sowing wild oats. He entered the corporate world and continued to drink heavily, with clients or without, even engaging in drugs from time to time, not to mention dalliances with females. It's what was expected of a young executive responsible for the entertainment of clients.

Rick soon met Laura, a corporate attorney, and they got married. He was promoted to partner in his firm and next came discussion of children, which they soon had.

Private school was considered an absolute necessity to protect their new treasures from the same influences they had so recently embraced. They did not want their kids exposed to drinking and sex so early and feared the public schools would do that.

Soon, Rick noticed he and Laura had subconsciously tamed their own lifestyles to the point of boring for the same reason. It occurred to him that he needed to go back to church so his kids would receive the same teaching and Sunday school lessons he had growing up. Anything to protect them from the craziness of the world.

He didn't embrace what he now considered the foolishness of his youth, he had no intention of jumping on the gospel bandwagon, but any tool they could use to shelter their children was worth the effort.

Lesson: *Sheltering your children from the world without helping them become a new creation in Christ is fruitless. They will soon embrace the same things you did if they don't have the power of God.*

Freshwater Eels

"Flee also youthful lusts; but pursue righteousness, faith, love, peace with those who call on the Lord out of a pure heart."
(2 Timothy 2:22)

Freshwater eels are *catadromous*, meaning they *live* in fresh water but migrate back to the *ocean* in order to spawn. This is the *opposite* of salmon. Freshwater eels are really the primary group of species that does this.

And they look more like snakes than they do fish...hmmm.

They represent the type of person who was not raised in the church, but rather was fully of the world growing up.

At some point in their adult life, they made the decision to begin attending church because they prefer to surround themselves with it. Yet, they never care to conform themselves to the church life around them. They like being in it, but they don't want to give up their worldliness. They don't deceive others — their distinctive worldliness, like the snake-like appearance of the freshwater eel, makes their identity clear.

And since they have no real commitment to the life of the church, much less actually following Christ, when it is time to have children and the pressure begins to be a faithful father, or a good Christian mother, they simply return to the world from where they came because it's easier.

Mary grew up poor. Her parents dealt drugs, and their home had always been the center of their business, so she'd never really known a stable environment until she discovered the church down the street.

She loved the warmth of the people who went there, the way they made her feel accepted without judging. It didn't matter that she didn't fully embrace what they wanted her too. She still got high every weekend, but she was sure to come sober on Sundays. Their approval felt too good to miss.

Still, when she got pregnant, she began to worry. Once her baby was born, she knew she had to leave. She didn't know how to be a good mother, and it was going to show. Soon, they *would* begin judging her when she didn't raise her daughter right. They would want her to learn all kinds of things, do all kinds of things their way, and she wasn't sure she was ready for that kind of commitment.

She just wanted their approval, but if she stayed, they would soon see through her facade. She decided she needed to leave while they still thought well of her. It was easier. Not so much responsibility.

Lesson: *Humble thyself. Choose the harder path.*

Great White Sharks

"Violence covers them like a garment.
Their eyes bulge with abundance..."
(Psalm 73:6b-7a)

Have you ever looked into the beady, black eyes of a shark? They're lifeless, dead, devoid of any sliver of a soul behind them. They are unique among animals, even other fish, whose eyes don't speak to such blank, opaque emptiness.

Sharks are without a doubt the top of the food chain in the oceans. They have been described as the perfect killing machine with rows upon rows of razor sharp teeth that automatically replace themselves, even if you were to knock out a hundred at a time. Rub a shark's skin one way and it feels smooth as silk. Rub it the wrong way and it will cut you.

I am convinced that the Great White Shark is God's symbol for the mafia boss. Just look at a picture of a Great White head on and you can't help but imagine John Gotti.

This type of man did not just come into existence in the 1920's with Al Capone. The description would have fit certain noblemen in medieval England, warlords in Somalia. Today we have not just the Italian mafia, but the Chinese, Russian, Japanese, and Mexican cartels. Human traffickers, drug lords. They're all the same and men like them have existed throughout history. Larger than life exploiters of others.

Sharks have very large brains and mafia bosses are very intelligent. 67% of a shark's brain is dedicated to the olfactory sense, which is why they can smell a drop of blood up to a mile away. They can also hear a fish struggling in the water from a mile away or more.

Their lateral line system is very finely-tuned — they can detect small differences in the electrical pulses emanating from a fish's muscles and know if it is weakened or not. They can even sense tiny changes in water pressure *anywhere* around them and react instantly.

If those facts alone were not enough to classify sharks as the perfect hunters, science has established that sharks, in fact, do not feel much pain.[19] They don't have the same pain nerves that we do, so if their prey fights back, *they don't care.*

Mafia bosses are also finely-tuned hunters, cruising the world in search of their next prey. They have hundreds of minions at their disposal (teeth), ready to do violence wherever they direct. We have romanticized many of these kingpins, especially the Italian ones for some reason, but they are not romantic creatures. Like the eyes of the shark, they are dead inside, soulless, uncaring, only concerned with their own survival and ready to tear apart whoever crosses their path.

In addition to being hunters of the weak, Mafia bosses are very difficult to take down, as the FBI would readily confirm. Just as a shark heals very quickly from wounds, so do these crime lords heal quickly if

---

[19] R. Aidan Martin, *Do Sharks Feel Pain?*, http://www.elasmo-research.org/education /topics/s_pain.htm (accessed on Nov. 11, 2013).

part of their criminal enterprise is wounded. If they lose underlings (teeth), those underlings are instantly replaced by others (and as the shark grows, its teeth do as well). Just as sharks rarely get sick or tumors, so does the warlord naturally resist infiltration from traitors.

Sharks do not possess an air bladder, which means they must constantly be on the move with water passing across their gills to stay alive. Mafia bosses do not retain any of the teachings or influence of the Holy Spirit. They must constantly be on the move through the criminal world, or they will be squeezed out and die or be killed by another mafia boss.

(Interestingly, dolphins are capable of killing sharks, but we'll study them later.)

Lesson: *Stay away from sharks of all kinds.*

Bull Sharks

If you decide to take a dip in the Mississippi River, be aware, you could be setting yourself up for a shark attack! Yes, Bull Sharks have been spotted in the Mississippi River as far north as Illinois, and they are responsible for the disappearance of a number of children.

Bull sharks also live in the Potomac River, Lake Pontchartrain, Lake Nicaragua, the Ganges, and numerous other fresh-water bodies. They are a species of shark that lives as easily in freshwater as it does the ocean. The movie *Jaws* was inspired by a flurry of bull shark attacks in a small freshwater creek in New Jersey back in 1916.

Bull sharks would symbolize those mafia bosses who are so shameless and bold that they regularly make themselves present in the Kingdom without even attempting to disguise their form, such as the Italian mob boss who regularly attends mass at a Catholic church even though everyone knows who he is.

Or perhaps these represent those priests who are guilty of abusing the children of their flock.

Flying Fish

"Jesus answered them, 'Most assuredly, I say to you,
whoever commits sin is a slave of sin.'"
(John 8:34)

lying fish do actually fly.
I saw them do it myself one time when I was snorkeling off the
coast of Costa Rica. I was shocked by how long they could go.
They'd leap from the water right next to our boat and then fly on and on.

They don't just jump out of the water and glide for a few seconds.
They flap their enlarged fins and fly at high speeds for long distances.
The record flight time for one of these fish is currently 45 seconds.

Flying fish are beautiful to watch.

Usually, the reason they're flying is to escape predators.

They symbolize non-believers who work desperately to escape the
dangers of the world under their own strength.

Some non-believers recognize the life they see in the Kingdom for
the blessing it is. They also see the state of the world as it is. Without a
transforming submission to Christ's authority and forgiveness of sins,
they, in their own power, work like crazy to better themselves and live
the life of a believer. And they will succeed for a time, seemingly
overcoming the world.

Yet, because they cannot "breathe" the air of the Kingdom, because
they have not been transformed into a new creation (from fish to
mammal), they find themselves soon pulled back into the world.

They may keep trying, but they will never truly escape until they
have been transformed.

Lesson: *If you find yourself beating your wings uselessly, working*
and working to escape your sinful nature to no avail, submit to Jesus
Christ as Lord and Savior and rely on His power to transform you and
overcome.

Fishing

"When He [Jesus] had stopped speaking, He said to Simon,
'Launch out into the deep and let down your nets for a catch.'
But Simon answered and said to Him, 'Master, we have toiled all night
and caught nothing; nevertheless at Your word I will let down the net.'
And when they had done this, they caught a great number of fish,
and their net was breaking." (Luke 5:4-6)

When scuba divers speak of the beauty of the oceans, they're referring to the fish, the coral, the plants. They're referring to the life within it.

On land, we can be inspired by natural scenes *independently* of the life around it. A majestic mountain, a beautiful waterfall, a desert scene, the waves at the beach — they're all beautiful in of themselves. On land, plant or animal life simply compliments what is already beautiful. The Kingdom is beautiful in of itself.

On the other hand, without the beauteous life within it, the oceans are a bleak, barren, obscure world, and would not be described as beautiful.

In the same way, non-believers are the beautiful part of the world. They are what God loves.

That Scripture uses fish as a symbol for non-believers is well-known. Jesus called on His disciple to become "fishers of men."

Fishing is symbolic of evangelism, bringing the non-believer from the world into the Kingdom. Fishermen, then, are symbols of evangelists.

Two primary things can be noted about fishermen:

First, fishing is what they do, it's their occupation, and it has a way of getting in their blood, so to speak, so they cannot imagine doing anything else. Secondly, they receive their own sustenance from what they catch in addition to what they provide for others.

Evangelists can be kind of pushy sometimes with other believers. They are unique among the occupations in the Body of Christ *in that they cannot imagine doing anything besides evangelism.* All other uses of their time seem a waste to them. While the teacher or the preacher will also *sometimes* evangelize, the evangelist often cannot conceive of anybody doing anything worthwhile if it's not evangelism.

Evangelists also draw sustenance from their work and provide sustenance for others as well. Pastors receive salaries from their congregations, every single member of which is there because somebody evangelized them, somebody reached them with the Gospel. Without the evangelist, nobody working for the Kingdom would eat.

There are a seemingly infinite number of fishing techniques used by fishermen around the world, and while the truth is that different fishing techniques work better for some species of fish in some parts of the world, and others are designed for others, many fishermen feel like *their* technique is the best and really the only one that all fishermen should use.

In the same way, there are many, many different ways to reach people with the Gospel: Door-to-door evangelism, relational evangelism, seeker-friendly services, short-term mission trips, long-term missionaries, Christian radio, books, websites, home Bible studies, television programs, and even movies. Different methods work better for different kinds of people, yet how often do we think our particular method is the very best? (Really the only one others should use too.)

Lesson: *Remember that God wants us to fish. And that He loves all the fish of the seas, just as He does every person in the world, whether they know Him or not.*

MAMMALS

"Or do you not know that your body is the temple of
the Holy Spirit who is in you...?"
(1 Corinthians 6:19a)

Mammals symbolize the wide variety of believers in God's Kingdom.

As we study mammals as a group, and remembering fish, we notice right away that believers differ from non-believers in several key ways.

Mammals breathe air.

First and foremost, just as mammals breathe oxygen from the atmosphere instead of water, believers breathe the Holy Spirit who indwells them. We don't absorb influence of the Spirit from our surroundings like water passing over gills. He is *within* us.

Mammals are warm-blooded.

This means believers have an internal source of love (heat) within themselves. When God recreates a man or woman through His Son, birthing them into the Kingdom, He creates within them a spiritual mechanism that sources love from God independently of their environment. In short, a follower of Christ has the ability to remain loving in a cold society. A non-believer does not have this ability.

Now, if you happen to be a non-believer reading this and take offense at that statement — and perhaps you might say, "Isn't it actually the church that is judgmental and hateful?" — you would be wrong.

First, you should recognize that it is hard for you to understand something you have never experienced. As a non-believer, you have never been a believer to know what that is like. Believers, on the other hand, were non-believers at one point in their lives, and they understand the difference in the reality of their daily life. Since you do not have this internal mechanism sourcing love to you supernaturally, you cannot truly conceive of what I mean — you naturally want to transmit your own experience onto all others.

Furthermore, if you know someone who calls themself part of the church, but speaks hatefully, you should politely ask them to demonstrate how exactly they are following Christ in their daily life. My bet is they call themselves a Christian, but they aren't actually following Him, or they would reflect the love He showed.

And keep in mind that the definition of love is not sweet smiles and tactful words — it's willingly sacrificing your own needs for the good of someone else, even if you bear a grim face as you do it.

Second, I would point out that the atheistic societies of the world have never produced a Mother Theresa, a person who sacrifices all worldly comforts and blessings in order to minister to those most suffering in this world, and church history is full of examples of Mother Theresas. You may *wish* to believe there are non-Christians who do this, but such people simply do not exist.

I'm not speaking about the momentary fire-fighter who runs into a burning building, or the soldier that throws himself on a grenade to save his friends. I'm talking about the rarest kind of person who is *constantly* willing to sacrifice *everything*, every day of their lives, moment after moment, in order to show love to strangers who cannot pay them back.

I know numerous self-sacrificing Christians who minister like Mother Theresa, giving of themselves selflessly without receiving anything in return. In fact, I always know I can rely on my brothers and sisters in Christ to be there for me in a pinch if I'm in need. They will show up in droves.

Non-believers will do altruistic acts from time to time, and non-believing parents of course often sacrifice of themselves for their children. Yet, since it is far too common in India and Thailand (non-Christian societies) for parents to sell their daughters into prostitution, and since non-believers who become momentary altruistic heroes seem to exist in much higher numbers in places like the United States (Christian societies), we can see that this is actually just the *air bladder effect*. These non-believers are simply acting under the influence of the society around them.

Believers aren't better than non-believers, they're just redeemed. They've submitted to God and He has literally re-created them spiritually. He has built into them new internal, spiritual mechanisms, one of which is this spiritual "warm-bloodedness," this ability to love when others don't love you back.

Mammals have hair.

All right, I have to admit, whatever in the world hair could possibly symbolize initially threw me for a loop.

However, it's one of the main characteristics unique to mammals. Neither birds, nor fish, nor reptiles, nor amphibians have it, only mammals, and yet *all* mammals have it. So, it clearly must have some distinctive, symbolic meaning associated with believers.

Then, while writing this very section, I looked across the coffee shop where I was sitting and noticed a gentleman with grey hair. Of course, that led to thoughts of my own head, which certainly saw much more hair in my youth than it does now.

Both changes are the result of age.

Then, it occurred to me that hair is to mammals as leaves are to a tree. Maturity.

Hair represents how believers in Christ have changing levels of spiritual maturity. They experience spiritual growth, unlike non-believers (fish). Non-believers do not and cannot grow spiritually. The scales of a fish don't turn grey as they age.

Hair is different. A baby is born without hair. As a boy grows into a man, his facial and body hair increases, and he may start to grow a beard. A girl usually grows her hair longer and longer as she matures. Both men and women earn grey hair along with wisdom (And some men have the added bonus I inherited of a clean top). Hair changes in tune with age, a very clear indicator of the symbolism of hair.

Animals experience similar processes. Many mammal babies are born with less or even no hair, though they usually gain their fur very quickly. Many animals also show a bit of grey hair amidst their fur when they reach an advanced age. Others experience a change of color as they mature.

Regardless, hair symbolizes spiritual maturity, or lack thereof.

(Baldness is not to be interpreted as a loss of spiritual maturity, but instead is a *change* to one's hair that comes with age, therefore indicating higher maturity — otherwise, we'd have to worry about the prophet Elisha.)

Hair on mammals performs a variety of functions relating to warmth, protection, touch, and even beauty. Hair follicles on both humans and animals have highly developed systems for helping to retain heat.

Think goose bumps. An animal's hair will stand up or flatten itself based on the surrounding temperature and the animal's need for heat. This is symbolic of the fact that as believers mature, they are more capable of retaining love (heat) within themselves than when they are immature.

Hair protects and senses as well. Hair follicles are highly sensitized to movement or stimulation, even the movement of air, and hair keeps dust out of our eyes.

Therefore, a mature believer has a more highly developed sense of discernment (clearer vision). Mature believers sense more easily bad teaching or unwise reasoning when they hear it. They're also more able to sense the movement of the Holy Spirit (air flow). Non-believers cannot sense the Holy Spirit's movements at all (No hair, and they live in the world).

Maturity determines the spiritual beauty of a believer much as the physical beauty of men and women is affected by their hair. Proverbs 16:31 says *"The silver-haired head is a crown of glory, if it is found in the way of righteousness."* and 1 Corinthians 11:15 *"But if a woman has long hair, it is a glory to her."* The grey head of a man reflects his spiritual wisdom attained with maturity and a woman's long hair symbolizes the spiritual beauty of her spirit.

Mammals give birth to live young.

When speaking about live birth vs. eggs, we must speak in generalities. Almost all mammals give birth to live young, but there are a couple of species that lay eggs. Almost all fish lay eggs, but there are a few that approach what could be considered a mammal live birth.

Reproduction can only be symbolic of having children or discipleship. I think it's probably symbolic of both, considering our children are the ones we disciple more than anybody else (whether we mean to or not).

Like trees, every animal species can only reproduce according to its own kind, speaking to the fact that believers and non-believers can only produce disciples who are like them. And yes, non-believers disciple others in their ways, whether they mean to or not, especially their children.

The main difference between live birth and eggs is one of intimacy and protection. Eggs are left in nests or attached to the stem of a water plant, etc, and are always vulnerable to predators. Also, the egg is laid with all the nutrients it needs — the mother simply guards it from there on out. (Though in some species, the mother abandons it.)

In mammals, the young develop inside the womb, constantly receiving nutrients directly from the mother in a much more intimate way (at great discomfort and effort to the mother), and they remain protected within the womb from predators until they are ready to stand on their own (again, in general).

This difference speaks to the fact that, in general, believers are able to have more intimate, connected relationships with their children and protect them longer than non-believers.

I repeat, *this is a generality*. As a few species of mammals lay eggs, so are there some believers who just aren't very good at the child rearing/discipleship thing. And there are some non-believers who do succeed in raising their children in intimate, connected relationships, but more often than not, the children of non-believers are much more susceptible to predators.

The reason being a couple of things we've already discussed. Believers have an internal "love mechanism" that allows them to love sacrificially even when the world around them is cold. Believers are also indwelt with the Holy Spirit and have access to supernatural strength and wisdom. These two factors are what give believers the advantage in connected, protective child rearing.

You will notice the truth of this difference in our modern-day culture wars. Christian parents almost universally cry out against the corrupting influences of Hollywood and MTV and shield their children from worldly things. Secular parents, for the most part, don't raise the alarm or fight against such things. It's not that secular parents don't care about their children, it's that they don't fully appreciate the dangers these predators pose to their "eggs."

Mammals have three ear bones.

Whoopity-doo, you say? What's the big deal?

At first, I wasn't sure what the big deal was myself, but given the fact that these three ear bones are one of the five main distinguishing features of mammals cited by biologists, I thought it bore studying.

It turns out that those three little ear bones make a *tremendous* difference in our hearing abilities.

Basically, fish and reptiles do *not* hear as well as we do. Their ears can generally pick up frequencies ranging between 100 Hz - 2,000 Hz, with a tolerance for only lower volumes. Humans on the other hand can hear ranges as low as 20hz and as high as 20,000 Hz, and we can tolerate significantly higher decibel volumes. A crocodile could not handle a rock concert, for example.

Beyond that, the three ear bones belonging to all mammals allow for a much finer tuning of hearing. We can distinguish words, direction of the sound, etc. Fish and reptiles only hear low frequencies and cannot distinguish small variations in frequency the way we can.

"He who has ears to hear, let him hear!" (Matthew 11:15) Jesus said this quite often to the crowds he taught, hinting that those who would believe have an ability to "hear" that non-believers do not. This is symbolized by the hearing abilities of mammals.

We can detect nuances of language, spoken words, while a fish or a crocodile would only hear a *whomp, whomp, whomp* like Charlie Brown's teacher.

Believers can hear spiritually, they can discern spiritual truth where non-believers cannot make sense of the same "sounds." To be perfectly clear, to truly hear someone means you have understood and acquiesce. Spiritual hearing is more than discernment — it is obedience.

To sum up, the distinguishing features of mammals teach us that believers, as opposed to non-believers, are indwelt with the Holy Spirit (air-breathing), they have a supernatural ability to love others (warm-blooded), they can mature spiritually (hair), they have the ability to obey spiritual truth (fine-tuned hearing), and in general, they tend to have more connected, protective relationships with their children (live birth).

There are eight primary groups of mammals.

They are: carnivores, dolphins/whales, hoofed animals, rodents, bats, primates, marsupials, and elephants.

We're going to examine some samples from each group, but for the first time, I'm going to give you a cheat sheet of sorts so you can see where we're going.

Lesson: *The spiritual advantages of believers are supernaturally inspired.*

Lion	=	Jesus, King of Kings
Carnivore	=	Church Staff/Levite
Dolphin/Whale	=	Missionary
Hoofed Animal	=	Serving Believer
Sheep/Cow	=	Meditating Believer
Pig	=	Greedy Believer
Giraffe	=	Scholar Believer
Camel	=	Abrasive Believer
Horse	=	Warrior Believer
Dog	=	Discerning Believer
Cat	=	Ego-Centric Believer
Rodent	=	Gnawing/Fellowshipping Believer
Bat	=	Prayer Warrior
Primate	=	Teacher
Marsupial	=	Sheltering Believer
Elephant	=	Leader

Lions

"But one of the elders said to me, 'Do not weep. Behold, the Lion of the tribe of Judah, the Root of David, has prevailed to open the scroll and to loose its seven seals.'" (Revelation 5:5)

"The lion, which is mightiest among beasts and does not turn back before any."
(Proverbs 30:30, ESV)

Lions are majestic.

They are not hard to interpret — just stare at the face of one, a male with a full mane, and you cannot help but be awed by his power. There is a distinct impression of majesty.

The Bible refers to Jesus as the Lion of Judah. Without a doubt, lions symbolize the kingly believer, and there's only *one* King in the Kingdom of God, Jesus the Messiah.

Much has been made of the fact that male lions will often stay with their cubs while the female lions of the pride do the work, hunting for food. However, the males will get involved when the prey is large enough to present a worry for the smaller females, or when the pride needs protection. Interestingly, male lions are *more likely* to share the kill with his young cubs than the females are.

Is this not comparable to how Jesus lets the Church, His bride, serve as His hands and feet, His agent of action in the world? Yet, when a situation becomes overly difficult for the Church, Jesus supernaturally steps in and helps.

An example of this is in missions. For centuries, missionaries have traveled the world sharing the Gospel, serving as Christ's mouth, hands, and feet. Yet, when missionaries turned their attention to the Muslim world after September 11th, they found themselves facing an angry, intolerant philosophy in Islam, where those who would spread the Gospel or those who would give themselves to Christ would be subjected to violence and death. So, Jesus stepped in.

Accounts of random Muslims around the globe having dreams about Jesus suddenly skyrocketed. Across the Muslim world, missionaries tell stories of men and women unexpectedly showing up at their doorstep that had never had any previous contact with the missionary, all saying that Jesus had told them in a dream to go find the missionary.

As many as 50% of Muslim converts to Christianity in the last ten years are estimated to be a result of such dreams, and there have been a *lot* of converts. (Muslims assign great value to dreams.)

This is the King helping His Bride when the prey is too difficult. And He is generous in sharing the provision, more so than competing "females" (churches of different denominations).

Truly the lion is the king of the jungle, he's at the top of the food chain, and the Bible itself compares this symbol to our Lord and Savior, the King of Kings, Jesus Christ.

Lesson: *Be in awe of our King. Respect Him.*

First Order
Carnivores

"Speak to Aaron and to his sons, saying, 'This is the law of the sin offering...[it] shall be killed before the Lord. It is most holy. The priest who offers it for sin shall eat it...everyone who touches its flesh must be holy...all the males among the priests may eat it. It is most holy.'"
(Leviticus 6:25-29)

Obviously, numerous kinds of mammals are carnivores. Given that we have shown mammals to be symbolic of believers, interpreting carnivores is, at first glance, hard. Do carnivores represent believers thriving off the slaughter of other believers within the Kingdom?

I don't think so.

When it came to fishing, Jesus clearly took that as a symbol for evangelism, yet aren't those fish actually eaten? Is Jesus saying that evangelists are destroying and devouring those they evangelize? No — especially since He used the illustration to call others into evangelism.

He's teaching that as the fisherman receives his sustenance from the fish, so is the evangelist provided for from the fruit of his work.

I think the initial perspective is what's wrong. We can view the act of a lion taking down prey as destructive, but do you hold that view when you eat a steak? Do you view yourself as a horrible destroyer of beings, or are you thankful for the provision and view the life of the animal that died as a necessary sacrifice so you can live?

Indeed, we have no reservation in calling Jesus the Lion of Judah...*but lions are carnivores.*

A different perspective might be to view such an act as a sacrifice on the part of the one to provide for the sustenance of the carnivore.

Thus, the symbol would be that carnivore believers are those who receive their daily bread from the sacrifices of other believers.

Yes, dear pastors, please forgive me. I know the image is not a pleasant one, but as carnivores make up only 5% of all mammals, the percentage is similar to that of Levites as compared with the rest of Israel, or the typical percentage of staff as compared with the laymen of a church.

What I absolutely do not wish to imply is that the pastors or the staff of a church do violence to others. *This should never be said!* The men and women who dedicate their entire lives to serving God's Kingdom are humble and have the hearts of servants, loving others at a great cost to themselves.

That truth, however, would be comparable to Jesus' title as the Lamb of God, which is often given in contrast to his title of the Lion of Judah. In other words, Jesus is described simultaneously with both images, one appealing to His self-sacrificing, loving nature, the other His kingly nature and role as the head of the Kingdom.

The same dual description can be applied to pastors and other leaders of the Kingdom. They are humble servants, loving others sacrificially, and there are other animal symbols that speak to this. The various kinds of trees describe other aspects of these leaders, their fortitude and core nature. The symbol of the carnivore speaks to their role as leader, living off the sacrifice of others (the tithe).

A note is due here for those who rail against "organized religion." If by organized religion, you mean an established church body that has a full-time pastor and/or staff, then you are way off base.

In specific revelation, the Bible, God made it clear that He intended for His people to have full-time ministers, the Levites and the priests. In general revelation, i.e. nature, He's made it clear through the symbol of carnivores that there are to be full-time ministers who live off the sacrifices of others.

So, full-time church staff is the clear will of God.

As laypeople, it is our job to support them in every way.

Lesson: *If you are a lay person, give your full tithe with joy. If you are a minister, appreciate the sacrifices offered up by your congregation for it is their very life.*

Second Order
Dolphins

*"You shall also make a covering of ram skins dyed red for the tent, and
a covering of tachash skins above that." (Exodus 26:14)*

Dolphins are not fish.
They are *mammals* who live in the ocean. They breathe air,
they are warm-blooded, and they bear live young instead of
laying eggs. They have skin and hair, not scales, and they even have
three ear bones just like the rest of us mammals. Dolphins are clearly
not *of* the ocean, but they were designed to live *in* the ocean.

"...do not be conformed to this world..." (Romans 12:2)

Dolphins symbolize missionaries, believers who are living in the
world (ocean). They receive their sustenance from the life of the sea just
as the missionary earns his livelihood by his work in the world.

Everyone loves dolphins. They are not only beautiful and talented,
but they are extremely intelligent creatures. They can be trained to do
amazing acrobatic feats, and they are the ocean's friendly face.

Fish are not "friends" with man, and sharks are downright hostile,
but everyone smiles when they see a dolphin. Dolphins are known for
guiding ships (other missionaries) through danger and even rescuing
humans from sharks or drowning.

Dolphins have sharp eyesight and better hearing than humans.

In the same way, missionaries are usually hyper-aware of the
goings-on in the community around them, much more so than the
average believer in a dominantly Christian society (great eyesight).
They have to be in order to survive.

They also have a very high obedience level (hearing). It takes a very
obedient believer to give up their family, friends, and entire way of life

to go minister in another country. They wouldn't do it if they didn't hear God calling them.

Dolphins can and do kill sharks.

As crazy as it sounds, they have a special ability to recover from large, gaping shark bites.[20] Yes, that's right, a shark can bite a huge chunk out of a dolphin, and not only will the dolphin not hemorrhage, but it will also remain free of infection, heal quickly, and even heal well enough that the original shape of the dolphin is preserved.

On the other hand, sharks can't resist dolphins. Dolphins are smarter, faster, and maneuver better. When one of their group is in danger, dolphins can and do slam their snouts into a cartilage-filled shark over and over until the shark is damaged enough that he dies. Even one blow is often enough to stun the shark or knock it unconscious. Surprisingly, the vicious shark is helpless against a dolphin.

This beautifully portrays one of the ways in which missionaries fight against the influence of powerful criminal elements in this world.

Yes, this is not the primary occupation of a missionary, just as a dolphin's priority is not seeking out sharks to destroy, but when a missionary perceives a human trafficking crime boss is threatening the safety of some young ones in their care, they will take the warlord on.

The crime boss may try to attack with his minions (teeth), but the missionary often displays an almost supernatural ability to outmaneuver and resist the "bite" (quick healing). As the dolphin attacks with his snout, so does the missionary use his mouth as the primary weapon, i.e. the words of his mouth.

Dolphins protect.

Dolphins stay with sick or injured dolphins, even helping them to the surface to keep breathing. Their protective nature is not limited to

---

[20] Karen Mallet, *Dolphins' "Remarkable" Recovery from Injury Offers Important Insights for Human Healing* (Georgetown University Medical Center), http://explore.georgetown.edu/news/?ID=57991&PageTemplate ID=295 (accessed on Sept. 20, 2013).

just other dolphins, but they will even protect other species and have been observed circling around helpless humans to protect them from approaching sharks.

This depicts how missionaries are protective of the helpless in the world. Throughout the history of the world, it has always been Christian missionaries who have started the orphanages, free clinics and hospitals. It was Christians who began the abolition societies of the world two hundred years ago and who are still fighting slavery today.

Dolphins communicate.

They emit a wide range of complicated whistles, trills, and clicks for a variety of purposes. They use the lower range frequencies to talk to each other, and the higher frequencies for echolocation, a sonar similar to that used by bats.

Missionaries are also *highly* communicative. Much of what they do involves communication. They communicate regularly with other missionaries about technique, coordinating efforts, etc. They also talk endlessly with those they are trying to witness to about Christ. This is their sonar. The results of a thousand conversations reveal those who are receptive to the Good News.

Dolphins also help humans fish.

For thousands of years, we humans have trained dolphins to help us, most often in the realm of fishing. For example, in Santa Catarina, Brazil, dolphins regularly work together to drive schools of fish into the nets of fishermen waiting along the shore.

What a beautiful picture of missionaries moving the lost of the world toward the Kingdom where they are finally "brought to shore" by the evangelists (fishermen).

I've always been fascinated by the Tabernacle. You may or may not be familiar with it and its furnishings, but many Bible translations say that God ordained the top covering of the Tabernacle to be made of badger skins. Yet, modern scholars think it should actually be translated *dolphin skins*, or *manatee skins*. See below:

"This word [badger] is found in Ex. 25:5; 26:14; 35:7, 23; 36:19; 39:34; Num. 4:6, etc. The tabernacle was covered with badgers' skins; the shoes of women were also made of them (Ezek. 16:10). Our translators seem to have been misled by the similarity in sound of the Hebrew *tachash* and the Latin *taxus*, "a badger." The revisers have correctly substituted "seal skins." The Arabs of the Sinaitic peninsula apply the name *tucash* to the seals and dugongs which are common in the Red Sea, and the skins of which are largely used as leather and for sandals. Though the badger is common in Palestine, and might occur in the wilderness, its small hide would have been useless as a tent covering. The dugong, very plentiful in the shallow waters on the shores of the Red Sea, is a marine animal from 12 to 30 feet long, something between a whale and a seal, never leaving the water, but very easily caught. It grazes on seaweed, and is known by naturalists as *Halicore tabernaculi*."
(Source: http://classic.net.bible.org/dictionary.php?word=badger)

Josephus seems to confirm that dugong skins were used for the top covering by saying, *"and great was the surprise of those who viewed these curtains at a distance, for they seemed not at all to differ from the color of the sky."*[21]

So, what is the significance of this? In the Tabernacle, a layer of goat skins was covered by red-dyed ram skins, which in turn was covered by the sky-blue dolphin skins. This means that from inside God's house, we see sinners (goats) covered by the blood of the ram (which is actually an invisible layer sandwiched between the others). Yet, from the outside of God's house, the world sees those who carry the Great Commission (missionaries, dolphins), and their color imitates the color of God the Father (sky).

Lesson: *Support missionaries in whatever way you can.*

---

[21] Josephus, *Antiquities of the Jews, Book III*, Chapter 6.4

Whales

"Then Jonah prayed to the Lord his God from the fish's belly."
(Jonah 2:1)

"Praise the Lord from the earth, you great sea creatures and all the depths" (Psalm 148:7)

Much of what we said of dolphins remains true for whales, but we can't move on without discussing those beautiful whale songs. Whale songs are easily the most beautiful sound recorded from the ocean depths.

It pictures missionaries lifting up worship to their Creator from within the world. Just as the oceans are devoid of music without the whale, so is the only true music to be heard in "the world" the worship initiated within the heart of the missionary.

Note: In light of our interpretation, it no longer seems random that Jonah, who was called by God to become a missionary to the city of Ninevah but refused to go, was swallowed by a *whale*. It's almost like Jonah tried to flee the Kingdom (Israel) into the world (ocean) until God forced him to get retrained by a *big* missionary (whale), at which point Jonah repented and became a missionary himself.

Third Order
Hoofed Animals

"Be diligent to know the state of your flocks, and attend to your herds."
(Proverbs 27:23)

Y ou know, hoofed animals are probably a lot more interesting than you realize.

Together, they make up one of the eight primary groups of mammals. Next to rodents, hoofed animals are the largest species group in the mammal kingdom, which symbolically indicates that the largest parts of our congregations are represented by rodents and hoofed mammals. The latter are also referred to as *ungulates* (I know — strange name).

We'll discuss rodents later. For now, note that the two main differences distinguishing hoofed animals from other mammals is: 1. Their tendency to form herds, and 2. That they can be *cultivated.*

These are the *herders* of the Body of Christ, believers that don't necessarily think independently, but instead go with the flow. I know that sounds negative, but is anyone really willing to argue that "herd thinking" doesn't go on in the life of the Church?

It's not a negative, but a description. God did not create everyone to be a leader. Obviously, the majority of believers have to be followers or we would just have chaos.

Herd believers stick close together and look to each other for an indication of which way to go.

In herds, there is usually a *control animal* whose behavior is imitated by all the others.

Within a congregation, herd believers will also usually have a few individuals to whom they look for guidance in what opinion to form, which movement to back, etc.

Herd believers are easy to panic and stampede.

I was recently made aware of a situation at a local church where there had been a very public disagreement between the pastor and the elder board. The result, unfortunately, was a general desertion of the people to other churches. A church that was once considered the most popular local branch among a certain denomination suddenly became a ghost town with only a handful of believers showing up on any given Sunday.

From what I understand of the case, there was a solid group of supporters for both sides of the argument, and I'm sure both the pastor and the elders felt they had sufficient reason to cause a stink, but it's irrelevant since *all* the attenders left anyway, and very quickly.

Instead of sticking through the problem and working it out as a family, at the first sign of a threat, the believers of that body literally stampeded to find safer parts of the Kingdom (land). My guess would be that their body had an unusually high percentage of herd believers.

Many pastors understand the power of momentum. This is a result of the herd factor. Wherever there is access to the power of God (water) in the Kingdom and safety from threats, herds will gather.

Herd believers feed on grass.

While rodents gnaw on wood, hoofed animals eat grass. Since we have identified grass as being symbolic of lukewarm or weak believers, this indicates that herd believers primarily feed on the "lighter" teachings.

They don't go deep, but chew on the superficial aspects of Christian theology and limit themselves to that. They know the Gospel and the basics of living a moral life, but they don't pursue "strong meat." This matches well with their tendency against independent thinking.

Blades of grass represent the weak maturity of the "grass" believer, and this is where the "herd" believer receives his or her nourishment, from normal, everyday actions with other, equally superficial believers. They pattern their lives on what they see the majority of other believers doing and that is sufficient for them.

Herd believers are cultivated.

Everything we've said so far about herd believers sounds negative, but *hoofed animals are the only animals that serve a significant economic benefit to humans.* Herders around the world cultivate them, growing herds for meat, milk, and clothing. The large majority of animals we manage or try to use for our benefit are hoofed animals.

Cultivation is easily equated with discipleship. Jesus speaks to us of this in the analogy of the Good Shepherd and the sheep. He cares for us as a shepherd does a flock. He disciples us, provides for us, protects us, and leads us to still waters. He *cultivates* us.

Herd believers are not bad. In fact, cultivation shows that herd believers are *the most useful* to a church, just as hoofed animals are the only ones cultivated in the physical world. If you are a leader in a church, you should consider purposefully cultivating herd believers.

Just because they tend to flock and herd and avoid independent thinking does not mean they cannot be discipled. Lead your flock to a well-watered field full of strong, nutrient-rich grass and you will have an extremely strong, healthy herd. Simply remember that a herd must consume grass, so the healthy teaching that you wish to impart must be broken down into simple, easy-to-understand parts for them to ingest. And that if you wish for the entire herd to be strong, you must strengthen the entire herd at the same time. Herd believers do not feed each other, so you cannot focus all your efforts on one and hope he or she will turn around and feed others.

It is often said that 20% of a congregation does 80% of the work. This 20% are the herd believers. They are the workhorses (oxen, horses, camels) — the servants of the Kingdom. So, don't neglect them!

Lesson: *Don't undervalue the herd believer.*

Even-Toed Hoofed Animals

"Among the animals, whatever divides the hoof, having cloven hooves and chewing the cud—that you may eat." (Leviticus 11:3)

It would be impossible to discuss hoofed animals without discussing the dietary laws of Scripture, specifically God's command that only animals that chew their cud *and* have cloven hooves are to be considered "clean" and edible. On the flip side, animals that do not have cloven hooves, or that do not chew their cud, are deemed "unclean."

For the record, cloven hooves correspond to what scientists call "even-toed ungulates," i.e. even-toed, hoofed mammals. Scientists have also recognized that there is a *big* biological difference between even-toed hoofers and odd-toed ungulates (animals without cloven hooves), and the difference is not just an extra toe.

With the exception of the pig, almost all cloven-hoofed animals chew their cud. This means after they chew some grass and swallow it, their stomachs (they have four) process it, and then they *regurgitate* it. The new substance is called "cud."

These animals munch on this partially-digested cud again, extracting even more nutrition from the same food.

It's kind of gross, but it's what they do — and it's highly efficient. They get a lot more nutritional value from every single mouthful than others.

The first reason God commanded His people to only eat these animals is they don't compete for the same food sources as humans. They are extremely efficient when they eat, and they transform that which humans can't consume (arid grass) into viable food for humans (milk, meat).

Simply put, *whatever people eat, they cultivate large herds of.* Therefore, since pigs *do* compete for the same food sources as humans, when a people group cultivates pigs, they automatically become poorer as a result.

This chewing of the cud, chewing every bite of food twice, is symbolic of herd believers meditating on the things of God. They might receive their spiritual food in simple bites (grass), but they will later "regurgitate" it for themselves to meditate upon again.

Herd believers get much more value out of every teaching than other believers. Because of this, they are the most efficient and the easiest to feed.

In fact, the scientific name for these animals is *ruminants*, from which we get the verb "to ruminate." Ruminating on something means to meditate upon it.

In other words, the idea of meditation, as used in the English language, was inspired by these creatures.

Lesson: *Ruminate on the things of God.*

Sheep

"But when He saw the multitudes, He was moved with compassion for them, because they were weary and scattered, like sheep having no shepherd." (Matthew 9:36)

"What man of you, having a hundred sheep, if he loses one of them, does not leave the ninety-nine in the wilderness, and go after the one which is lost until he finds it? And when he has found it, he lays it on his shoulders, rejoicing." (Luke 15:4-5)

Sheep are Jesus' favorite symbol for His people.

He used the example of the Good Shepherd and His flock often, and the spiritual symbolism built into sheep is so great that whole books have been written on the subject.

I highly recommend reading *A Shepherd Looks at Psalm* 23, by W. Phillip Keller for a deeper understanding of why Jesus used sheep as symbols for us. Since Mr. Keller's work has already addressed this topic so well, I will just emphasize two characteristics here:

Sheep are simple-minded.
They literally have to be led to new grass or they will starve to death after consuming everything around them. They get lost easily, and without a shepherd to protect them, they are prime candidates for any passing predator's next meal.

Frankly, while many hard, scientific evidences have been discovered that effectively disprove the Theory of Evolution (that is, macro-evolution, one species evolving into another — not microevolution, otherwise known as adaptation), the existence of sheep has to be another that is rarely mentioned. Such helpless creatures could have never made it on their own for millions of years without the aid of humans to care for them. Just not possible in an evolutionary context.

This sheepish simple-mindedness is very appropriate for us as God's people. He has to constantly lead us to our next meal (spiritual meal). We stray so easily, blissfully unaware of dangers lurking over the ridge — and often we're not even smart enough to keep ourselves from falling into ruts or pits.

It also demonstrates how much God cares for us. How intimately He is aware of our needs, watching out for us, protecting us. What a beautiful picture!

In spite of our simple-mindedness, however, **sheep recognize the voice of their shepherd.**
A flock of sheep knows its shepherd and they will not respond to the voice of another. You can mix two or three flocks in the same pen, mingling them for an extended period of time, but when one of their shepherds arrives at the gate and calls out, his sheep, and *only* his sheep, will come out of the pen. The other flocks will remain where they are until they hear the voice of their shepherd.

In the same way, we know the voice of our Savior. We recognize it and we follow when we hear it. Sometimes, we may hear other voices that seem to be saying the right things, but we instinctively resist responding because we don't recognize the Spirit behind that voice.

How do we know when God is speaking to a people? Look at those believers who are regularly seeking God through daily prayer and daily Bible reading. They will be aligned in their opinion of what is right and what should be done, even if they don't know each other. This is because they are the most attuned to the voice of their Shepherd.

Note: This does not work with believers who just claim the name of Christ, attend church regularly, or say they're followers of God. They must be actively engaged in the daily spiritual disciplines.

Lesson: *Trust in the care and protection of God.*

Pigs

"Do not give what is holy to the dogs; nor cast your pearls before swine, lest they trample them under their feet, and turn and tear you in pieces." (Matthew 7:6)

Most herd believers meditate on their spiritual food, but not pig believers. They greedily gobble up all they can get, continually processing and processing, but never meditating.

Most livestock have four stomachs, but pigs have only one. They are omnivores — which means they will eat everything. Literally, *everything.* Including trash and feces.

Because they scavenge so much garbage, even eating rotten meat, their meat tends to be filled with parasites and sources of illness that humans can contract. This is the second reason that God declared animals like pigs (and other carnivores) "unclean." Their meat is extremely unhealthy.

For thousands of years, people have died from disease contracted through eating pork. It's only in recent years, in the United States and other developed countries, that pork has become "safe" due to care with regards to what cultivated pigs are fed and modern meat processing methods. Still, some people get sick even now.

Pigs symbolize *greedy* believers. You know, the kind of believer that is always demanding attention and time from a church's staff, requiring programs be started to meet their needs, asserting their opinions above those of others.

While all the other cloven-hoofed animals are servants, *pigs are happy to be served.* And for some ungodly reason, some churches feel the need to cultivate these believers, when they should really be culled.

Pigs are intelligent.

They are known to be one of the smartest animals on earth. Yet, unlike elephants, dolphins, and primates, scientists cannot verify if they are self-aware. Why?

Because they don't care.

Elephants and primates will look in mirrors and touch their own faces. They will also notice if something looks different about their reflection and show concern. They are self-aware.

On the other hand, studies have shown that pigs can indeed understand the concept of mirrors because they'll use them to find food, but they refuse to do anything to show they recognize their own reflection. They are only concerned with the mirror if it reveals a hidden source of food. They just don't care about anything else.

This is true of the greedy believer as well. They don't care to take the time to evaluate their spiritual state, to better themselves, or consider that they might need to change. What's going on inside of them is of no relevance compared with finding the next meal.

Pigs are greedy.

Even piglets, as cute as they may be, are known for blatant, overt greediness. We'll give pigs their due as far as smarts goes, but really, the main way pigs reveal their intelligence is through the cunning and creativity they utilize to hog all the food for themselves. Pigs are smart enough to follow another pig they think has found something to eat, and that pig is smart enough to realize he's being followed and employ deceptive tricks to throw the other guy off the track.

Pig believers are the same way, they use all their spiritual talents to improve a church's ability to serve them. Meaning, they use intelligent sounding arguments and emotional manipulation to get attention and drive the creation of unnecessary programs that meet their specific needs.

Pigs are fat.

The average adult pig consumes *five pounds* of food and drinks *fourteen gallons* of water *per day*. I repeat, *per day*.

The greedy believer hogs a similar level of resources within the Body of Christ in contrast with other, more efficient servant "herd" believers.

Pigs have a highly sensitive sense of smell.

They are excellent hunters of food and can use their snouts to scrounge and dig up hidden food. So much so that European connoisseurs use pigs to locate hard-to-find truffles.

Smell is the symbol for discernment of spirits. This means pig believers have the ability to sense the spirit of a church and detect sources of spiritual food. Because of this, pig believers are prone to become church hoppers. They are constantly hunting for food for themselves — they sense when a church has something to offer them, and then move on when that source runs out.

Pigs are lazy.

They love to lie around in the mud. Believe it or not, they also like to drink alcohol if given the chance. They'll even smoke cigarettes and watch TV.[22]

This, again, speaks back to how pig believers are all about being served and getting for themselves. They don't typically give back. They lie around in the Life of the Kingdom (mud), lazily content to let others do the work. Because of this trend, they also have a propensity to develop worldly habits, thus becoming *worldly* believers because they don't have a heart to give back to God.

---

[22] Natalie Angier, *Pigs Prove to Be Smart, if Not Vain (New York Times)*, http://www.nytimes.com/2009/11/10/science/10angier.html?_r=0 (accessed on Nov. 12th, 2013).

Pigs have small lungs compared to their body size.

Because of this, pigs easily contract sicknesses like bronchitis and pneumonia.

Of course, selfish pig believers have less contact with God's Spirit (small lung capacity), otherwise they would not be so selfish!

The susceptibility of pigs to illness of the lungs is symbolic of how the greedy believer easily contracts spiritual disease.

Wild pigs have tusks.

This means that, in their natural state, greedy believers are fighters. Which, of course, only makes sense. If you don't have a combative nature, then you aren't going to be the type to squeal and fight for attention.

The Bible consistently uses animal "horns" as symbols for leadership, and the Hebrew word used for a tusk is the same as horn (See Ezekiel 27:15). Therefore, tusks, like horns, should be considered symbols of leadership.

Unfortunately, this means that pig believers may often be found in leadership roles.

However, we'll note that cultivated pigs don't have tusks because their herders cut them for safety! Therefore, in a healthy church body, the dangerous nature of pig believers is recognized and they are prevented from holding leadership positions.

On the other hand, if they strike out on their own, they'll regrow their tusks and you may find the pig believer soon leading a crazy, little fledgling church where they are the constant center of attention.

Pigs can squeal louder than a supersonic airliner.

Yes, that's right, pigs have been recorded squealing at decibel levels louder than a jet. The British government has even issued *official* warnings to pig farmers that they should wear earmuffs!

This also fits with pig believers. If they didn't squeal, how would they get the attention they want? You know that man or woman that is constantly complaining about *everything* in all your church's congregational business meetings? They might be a pig believer.

Pigs don't sweat and they can get sunburned.

Believe it or not, pigs actually prefer cleanliness, but in the summertime, out of necessity, they roll in the mud to protect their skin and keep cool.

Pig believers don't feel a natural compulsion to engage in fellowship (rolling in the mud, i.e. life in the Kingdom), but when life is throwing them some strong challenges (summertime), they will seek out other believers in earnest in order to get relief from their burning burdens. Again, greedy believers use fellowship to get, not to give.

Pigs can be prickly.

Pig hair is actually called bristles. It is very coarse and prickly to the touch. Since we've established that hair represents maturity, then this symbolizes how fellowship (touch) with a selfish believer can be "prickly." It is often not the most pleasant of experiences to hang out with a Christian who is only out to meet their own needs.

Pigs are scavengers.

We've already mentioned this, but to focus on the point, pigs are constantly ready to eat, searching for food, and will eat anything and everything they find.

Therefore, pig believers have no filter on the teachings they take in. They consume any and every spiritual message without discrimination, be it garbage or the best of sermons.

Pigs have poor eyesight.

Specifically, it is believed they have trouble focusing their eyes, so everything may constantly appear blurry to them.[23]

We've said that pig believers have an excellent sense of smell, i.e. they can discern the spirit of a church and know if they're in the right place or not, but they have trouble processing the truth (focusing vision) they receive in that church.

---

[23] http://animalbehaviour.net/JudithKBlackshaw/JKBlackshawCh3e.pdf (accessed on Nov. 12th, 2013).

They don't stop to meditate on what they hear (They don't chew their cud) — they just keep processing more on top of more regardless of its quality or whether it meshes with what they already know.

The result is the capability of absorbing nourishment while at the same time allowing spiritual parasites and disease to take root in their spiritual flesh.

Pig meat is unclean.

It is because of the eating habits we have already described that God declared pig meat "unclean." In reality, it is full of parasites and other pathogens that can do us harm if consumed.

This means that in addition to being "prickly" in casual fellowship, pig believers can cause us true spiritual harm if we enter into a more substantive fellowship with them. The staff of a church (carnivores) may find their congregation filled with spiritual disease if there is a high percent of greedy believers among them.

Let us be clear — *the difference between clean and unclean is* not *believer vs. unbeliever* — both clean and unclean are mammals (believers). I think the tendency when observing a pig believer would be to assume that they are not justified by faith. However, there *are* justified believers who are simply selfish and don't reflect the spirit of Christ well.

Pigs are self-sufficient.

If a pig is released into the wild, they will survive on their own, no problem. They don't need social interaction like horses. They don't need to be led to food like sheep. They go wild fairly easily.

So, we can take courage from this. If you have a greedy, selfish believer in your congregation, and the need arises for them to be removed from your local body for whatever reason, we probably don't need to worry about them surviving on their own. They'll be just fine.

Lesson: *Seek not to get, but to give.*

Giraffes

"The heart of the prudent acquires knowledge,
And the ear of the wise seeks knowledge."
(Proverbs 18:15)

Among the even-toed ungulates, giraffes are the opposite of pigs. Even though very few people ever eat giraffe meat, their meat has actually been declared kosher by leading rabbis because the giraffe chews its cud and has cloven hooves.

When choosing food, giraffes are much pickier than swine. They only eat from the tallest sources, preferring the leaves of the acacia tree.

Giraffe believers are the *scholarly* believers. A *scholar* is distinct from a *teacher*. Teachers study to pass their knowledge on, scholars study for the sake of study.

Our symbolic interpretation is secured by the source of the giraffe's food. While other herd believers glean sustenance by consuming the fruit of the grasslands, i.e. interacting with the maturity of weaker, less prominent brothers and sisters in Christ, the scholarly believer studies the "great ones." The giraffe believer takes his sustenance from the works (leaves) of Karl Barth, Bonhoeffer, and Tozer (trees).

Because giraffe believers get their nourishment from such rich sources, they are "kosher" within the Kingdom, though fellowship with the scholarly believer can have a strange feel to it, which might explain the unpopularity of giraffe meat.

Giraffes live in the savannah *wood*lands — they primarily eat acacia tree leaves.

This means that scholar believers don't like being in a church that is dominated by either superficial believers (grass) or strong, prominent disciples of Christ (trees). They prefer a mix. They want room to move around, but they need nourishment from the more mature disciples.

These giraffe believers prefer "acacia" leaves. Acacia is the wood that God commanded to be used for the construction of the tabernacle and the Ark of the Covenant. It is probable the crown of thorns was made of acacia branches, and possible the burning bush was an acacia as well. The common denominator for each of those things is God's covenant with His people. The Ark represents the Old Covenant, and the Crown of Thorns the New. Symbolically, I would interpret this to mean that Christian scholars like to study (chew on) the covenants of God.

If you think about it, doesn't a cursory glance at the major topic discussions of scholarly theologians verify this?

Giraffes have camouflage patterns across their bodies, and they are quiet, elegant animals.

If you were to visit any given church on a Sunday morning, you would not notice the scholar believer. He or she would not stand out from the crowd. Their personality is usually going to be somewhat introverted and quiet. They are not the ones who stand on the corners proclaiming their truth like exhorters, or desperate to share what they know like teachers. They don't stand behind the pulpit and lead like a pastor. No, they blend in as if camouflaged, quietly munching their acacia leaves.

Giraffes have long necks. They're the tallest of animals.

This is a statement of their prominence in the Body of Christ. In spite of their camouflage, once you've seen the giraffe, you're amazed by his height.

The same goes for a giraffe believer. Those believers around them who have seen through the camouflage, who know them, will be well aware of their specialness within the Body and how they stand "taller" than most, only partaking in the highest forms of spiritual food.

Giraffe believers have to develop the ability to partake in such food. They have to grow long spiritual "necks," massive, elongated support structures for their current thinking (head). For example, to understand St. Augustine or Immanuel Kant, you must already have an extensive knowledge of all of Scripture. To fully understand the Reformation and the teachings of Martin Luther, you must already have a thorough understanding of church history up to that point. This knowledge (neck) directs their thinking (head).

Giraffes have sharp vision, hearing, and smell.

They excel in all three of the main senses. This means scholarly believers have an excellent ability to perceive truth, obey God's Word, and discern spiritual matters.

Giraffes form very loose herds.

A herd of giraffes is defined by a group that stays within less than a kilometer of each other and moves in the same general direction. These herds are *very* loosely formed. Giraffe herds can easily break up, mingle with others, and then reform into a new herd. The male to female ratio is unimportant. Herds have been observed that were almost exclusively male, and others almost all female. Also, giraffe herds have no true leaders.[24]

This does seem to be the modus operandi of scholars in general, and so the Christian scholar would naturally follow the same trend. Scholars form loose alliances, and those alliances will last as long as they share common theories, understanding, or interpretation of data. If certain members of an allied group of scholars adopt a new theory, or develop a new interpretation of significance that the other members don't share, the alliance will dissolve, and members will form new alliances with other scholars who do share their ideas.

This characteristic of giraffes stands in stark contrast to the habits of elephants, but we'll take a look at them later.

The skin of giraffes resists sunburn, and they can close their nostrils against sandstorms.

Again, in contrast with elephants (and pigs), giraffes' skin resists sunburn. They don't have the need to bathe themselves in mud.

This symbolizes that a giraffe believer is capable of dealing with the loving challenges of God (heat from the sun) without needing fellowship with other believers to handle it. They don't need to immerse

---

[24] Hayley Ames, *Giraffe Behavioral Characteristics*, http://www.ehow.com/info_8132323_giraffe-behavioral-characteristics.html#ixzz27VLlKoka (accessed on Nov. 13th, 2013).

themselves in the life of the Kingdom in order to cope, and it's a good thing given their quiet, introverted nature. This is a supernatural provision by God.

The specialized ability to shut their nostrils against sandstorms, or any other blown-about debris, is another of those provisions. When the Spirit of God blows believers about the Kingdom, perhaps rapidly switching out the believers who attend a certain church — and sometimes He does so in a distressing way — the scholarly believer has the ability to shield himself from having his own inspiration (breath) impacted by the shocking developments within the church's life that rattle everybody else.

Giraffes don't need to drink very often.

Because they get so much water from the acacia leaves they eat, they can go up to a month without drinking directly from a water source. Though, if they do have access to a pool, they usually won't go more than three days.

This represents a defining aspect of the giraffe believer's nature. They receive much of the life God offers through their studies. That's how they tap into His power.

In general, they don't need a local movement of God (river) to thrive as other believers do. Yet, if God *is* moving near to them, they will partake, but they still won't feel the need to be as constantly involved as others.

In addition, giraffes don't need as much food as other herbivores. This is because the acacia leaves have very high concentrations of nutrition and giraffes have a very efficient digestive system.

The studies of scholarly believers are so "nutrient-rich," spiritually speaking, that they don't need to ruminate nearly as much as other herd believers.

Giraffes have special features that protect them when they are drinking.

You may have never thought of the danger a giraffe risks every single time he bends over to take a drink of water, but think about it.

Such a long neck contains a *lot* of blood, and their powerful hearts are accustomed to pumping hard to get that blood all the way up into their heads. So, what would you normally expect to happen if a giraffe bends their neck down until their head is suddenly lower than their heart? A fast rush of blood to the brain resulting in a super-stroke — and a dead giraffe.

Because of this risk, giraffes have something called a *rete mirabile*, which is an unusually complex jumble of arteries that prevents blood from rushing forward in a straight line. They also have *seven* different valves in their jugular veins, which prevent the blood headed to the heart from flowing back into the brain.

Scholarly believers face a risk of having a rush of life (blood) suddenly explode their thinking (brain) when they stoop to partake in the life of the Kingdom. Getting down and dirty, getting involved in the messiness of Kingdom life can have a way of messing with one's *theories*.

The practical struggles of our brothers and sisters in Christ, the emotion of seeing their pain, or watching God move in completely unexpected ways can all burst our spiritual hypotheses of how the spiritual life is supposed to go. Thankfully, God has provided special spiritual mechanisms within the giraffe believer to keep their minds from being harmed and their more detached understandings intact.

Giraffes fight with their necks.

When two male giraffes are battling for dominance (not for the right to lead the herd — it's usually over the right to mate with a female), they use their necks. Zoologists call it necking.

During one of these battles, giraffes will either use their necks to slowly push against the other one, or they will ready themselves and then sling their necks at each other with great, powerful blows.

We have already identified the neck as the body of knowledge that moves our thinking (head), so this would have to be scholars debating with their respective knowledge levels. Which, of course, is how scholars battle. Sometimes, the reason is to prove their worthiness to make disciples (procreate).

Giraffes have ossicones.

These are actually smallish, bony horns on the top of their heads. Sometimes they will use these to fight too, but they prefer their necks. We don't have to assign our own interpretation for horns — the Bible does that for us.

There are numerous examples in Scripture where animal horns are used symbolically in prophecy, and they usually represent "power" or "authority."

So, scholar believers are portrayed as having some level of leadership or authority in the Kingdom, yet small amounts of it (small horns).

This is true. We respect our theologians, we defer to them for questions of spiritual orthodoxy, but we don't follow their instruction as strongly as we would a pastor or an exhorter.

Lesson: *Appreciate the unique giftedness of each kind of believer.*

Odd-Toed Hoofed Animals
(Never thought you'd get excited about odd-toed ungulates, did you?)

Well, maybe you're still not, but let's change that!

We already went over the even-toed guys, highlighting pigs and giraffes who stand out among them. Of those even-toes, pretty much all of them (except the pig) are considered clean meat for consumption by biblical standards.

The odd-toes are not. Odd-toe basically means no cloven hoof. And there's a good reason God declared them "unclean." They don't have the four-stomach system like a cow or a giraffe.

Cloven-hoofed animals (even-toes) reprocess and chew their cud so thoroughly that no parasite can survive, but horses and many other odd-toes just have one stomach. Like us, they constantly process their food without chewing their cud, digesting it as it passes through the intestines.

Camels, on the other hand, have three stomachs, and they *do* chew their cud, *but the lack of that fourth stomach is just too crucial.* Missing that one final stomach allows parasites to get through and be present in their flesh. Those same parasites can then be passed on to humans.

Horses too. Horse meat also tends to be full of sickness and parasites dangerous to humans. (See, and you thought it was just our love of horses that prevented horse meat from appearing in grocery stores — which only makes the French seem crazier.)

In fact, all meat from odd-toed hoofed animals is potentially unhealthy for humans to eat. So, God had a very good reason for His rule.

I think He also had another good reason. Of the three "unclean" examples we're looking at here — pigs, horses, and camels — one thing these animals all seem to have in common is a higher intelligence. Pigs are known for their smarts, and both horses and camels are clearly more intelligent and have more personality than your average cow, deer, or bison.

Is it possible that God, out of His love, made these creatures "unclean" because He knew He'd also made them more aware, more capable of suffering when slaughtered for their meat? I don't have an authoritative answer for that, but I'm guessing that might be another reason for the distinction.

Horses

*"Have you given the horse strength? Have you clothed his neck
with thunder?...He mocks at fear, and is not frightened;
Nor does he turn back from the sword." (Job 39:19;22)*

Horses represent the warrior servants of the Body of Christ. This identification is pretty easy considering the obvious roles horses play in our society. They've served as cavalry mounts in the military, they've toiled in front of plows, and cowboys wouldn't be anything without their steeds. They're warrior/workers.

The *warrior* believer is hard to specifically identify. I don't have a label to assign like missionary, pastor, or teacher — they're part of the laypeople — but I do know one when I see one.

Horses are workers.

Horses prefer to live in the wild, but they can be domesticated and willingly engage in a wide variety of tasks.

This tells us that the horse believer is going to be someone who *gets things done*. They do not ruminate and meditate on thoughts like other herd believers. This doesn't mean they aren't intelligent. On the contrary. Horses are very intelligent animals, so this would mean that the horse believer is as well. They're just not about thinking, they're about doing.

Horses are fighters.

There is a reason that horses have served so often in the armies of the world. They have a very strong fight-or-flight response. While they will flee when startled, or if they perceive the threat is too great, they are also just as likely to stand and fight, especially if their foal is in danger.

If you see a horse flaring its nostrils with its ears pulled back, watch out!

Horse believers are similar. They will back off if needed, but if the situation merits, they will dig in and fight. Especially if they perceive a fight is needed to protect others in the Body of Christ.

Horse believers are some of the most useful servants of God in a congregation. They get the work done, and if something threatens their spiritual family, they will rear up and fight.

Horses are strong and beautiful.

This means horse believers are going to be some of the most admired among their church body. They are admired *because* they are strong, and people generally want to around them.

Horses are social animals.

Horse herds have much stronger bonds than, for example, those of giraffes. They need constant social interaction with other horses. A horse might come to accept a human as a companion instead, but they will still need regular attention from the human to be okay. When isolated for extended periods of time, horses develop serious psychological problems.

Warrior believers (horses) are very different from *scholar* believers (giraffes) in this regard. A scholar believer is introverted and content to keep to himself, doing his own thing, but a warrior believer will push for strong social interaction with others; they are extroverted. They will lead small groups, serve as greeters, or put together a food drive.

You won't find horse believers spending much time on theological discussions, though they are nevertheless highly faithful and dedicated. They just know what they believe, and they believe what they believe. Since that has been settled, now they're about getting things done.

Horses have the largest eyes of any land mammal — they also have excellent vision.

This means the horse believer has an excellent ability to discern truth. Perhaps this is the reason they don't have the need to "chew" on it over and over? They've already understood it.

While researching horses, I came across blogs recommending people only approach a horse from the front if they're holding potentially "scary" items in their hands. The reason being that horses have a strong binocular vision in the front, but less-focused, predator-aware vision on the sides. Thus, if you have something in your arms that might spook them, approach from the front so they can see clearly what it is.

This means that if you know any horse believers and have an unexpected truth to share with them, you would do better to just tell them directly instead of trying to converse about it in a round-about way. They could misunderstand your point and react angrily to something you did not intend.

Horses also have an excellent sense of touch.

I would interpret this to mean the horse believer has a superior ability to interact with the rest of the Kingdom. This interpretation fits very nicely with their need for high levels of social interaction, meaning they not only need social interaction, but they are good at it, and that fits in well with the fact that horses are beautiful, meaning people admire the horse believer.

From horse racing to more leisurely horseback riding, people love horses. I know I've always loved cowboys and the Old West and the idea of riding into a town to save the day astride a powerful mustang.

Yet, I'm allergic. That's right, I'm allergic to horses. I know, I know, you're probably laughing at this great sadness of mine. Oh well. (I wonder if that means that I would admire a horse believer but they would not like me, or maybe they would like me, but I wouldn't get along with them...Probably neither.)

Regardless, horses are one of the world's favorite animals, and so are horse believers among the Body of Christ.

Lesson: *Cultivate horse believers to have a strong, effective church.*

Camels

"The camel, because it chews the cud but does not have cloven hooves, is unclean to you..." (Leviticus 11:4b)

I once knew a man — I'll call him Charles. Charles was an institution. He'd been teaching a systematic, dispensationalist Bible study at the church I was attending then *for years*. You could easily characterize this church as a *desert* church. It was *not* dead, plenty of life going on — we sent at least 30 to 40 young people from our congregation into full-time ministry over a period of 7 years — but God's invigorating power was not flowing through it in the way I've observed at other churches.

Now, while our congregation was a very loving congregation (heat in the desert), Charles was not a loving individual. He was clearly an intelligent man, he knew Scripture like the back of his hand, and if you happened to be one of the students that admired him and accepted everything he taught without objection, you were one of his favorites. However, if you questioned or disagreed with his teaching — and he did not always have the best principles for biblical interpretation — you would be peppered with rapid-fire scriptural challenges and treated gruffly from then on out.

For years, Charles had been faithfully doing what he viewed as his service to God, conducting his semi-popular Bible studies regardless of the state of the church, for good or for bad. He did not seem to notice if God was moving in the church or not, but trudged on year after year with no reward or even knowing if his ministry had born fruit.

As soon as I began studying camels, my mind flew back to my memories of Charles. I believe he exemplifies the *camel* believer perfectly.

You are probably aware that camels can go for long periods of time without water, but you may not have realized just *how well* camels can do that. They don't actually store water in their humps; that's fat. Later, when in need, they convert the fat to energy and for every gram of fat converted, they are able to extract one gram of water due to a reaction with oxygen.

Some camels in the Sahara have been known to go all winter without water.

They have special body features that allow them to withstand a dehydration that would kill the rest of us. For example, they are the only mammals that have oval-shaped red blood cells that allow their blood to keep flowing as it thickens with less water. Their nostrils are specially designed to retain water vapor when they exhale, and the same is true for their kidneys and intestines. Camels are so efficient in their water management that they can get all the water they need just from eating green plants and never taking a drink.

This would seem to indicate that a camel believer like Charles is able to extract enough of God's power from his interactions with other believers (sparse plants) that he has no problem thriving in a desert church. He does not need to experience God moving directly (water) to keep trudging along for extended periods of time. However, he also does not release any of God's power back into the church as he exhales, which by the way, was exactly how this man's ministry felt.

Camels have extremely thick hair.

You'd think that would make them hotter, but studies have shown that their coat actually protects them from the desert's heat, insulating them. A camel that's been shorn sweats 50% more than a camel with a full coat, and sweat, of course, greatly hinders their water retention.

This thick coat symbolizes strong spiritual maturity in a camel believer, and Charles was certainly very mature, though it did not result in him exuding love. In fact, in a strange way, just like the camel, it was his extreme "maturity" (hair) that seemed to insulate him from the loving nature of the rest of the church. Yet, he never overheated himself, he never became overwhelmed with love, but remained emotionally distant.

Camels have an unusually durable immune system — and so did Charles. Spiritually, I mean. He showed sharp discernment in many instances. And when not, when his quirky theological stances caused him to embrace some insidious false teaching, he seemed to have the ability to resist any negative impact of it on his spiritual walk and remained faithful.

Camels can eat a lot of different kinds of foods.

They have very hardy stomachs, and Charles was capable of extracting nourishment from all kinds of minute teachings, many of which would not necessarily edify the average believer.

Some of the differences between camels and horses are striking and worth mentioning.

Compared with horses, camels can carry more weight, are smarter, quieter, and don't need to be shod.[25]

Horses require much more care. Charles was more like the camel. He didn't require any care — no one had to manage him. He just did what he did on his own. He was capable of carrying greater spiritual burdens than most. I've already mentioned he was very intelligent, and he tended to keep to himself.

On the other hand, horses respond better to directing cues. Horses have simpler saddles, and camels are just physically harder to ride. Camels are harder to persuade to leave home or their herd. They don't like new places, and camels can be hard on fences.

Again, a perfect description of Charles. He did *not* like anyone telling him what to do. He felt like he was serving God directly and bucked under authority. He was also a man of routine and did not want to engage in new activity.

Of course, we've all heard of camels spitting on people. They are docile and sweet if well-treated, stubborn and angry if not. (I've already described Charles' personality.)

---

[25] C. Wright, DVM, *Camels Vs. Horses*,
http://camelphotos.com/CamelVsHorses.html (accessed on Nov. 14th, 2013).

Camels are working animals that provide milk, meat, and hair for clothing.

Charles was certainly a working servant of God — *no one* would accuse him of failing there. His primary act of service was to teach, which represents the giving of milk and meat in the sense that Paul uses the symbols in the New Testament.

Yet, the Old Testament does not declare camel meat to be kosher. And this is also what I observed: Those students that most absorbed the hard teachings that Charles shared with his classes seemed to develop unusual quirks in their personal theologies, quirks that Charles himself was able to avoid. The effect of eating unclean meat.

Camel hair is very coarse — at least the outer layer is. Charles' spiritual maturity certainly came across this way. His teaching style was abrasive. He did not encourage, but challenged constantly. Prickly just like camel hair.

Yet, the innermost layer of camel hair can actually be quite soft. Which might explain why those who were truly closest to Charles loved him.

Lesson: *Work to appreciate the gifts of the abrasive believer.*

Dogs

"Beloved, do not believe every spirit, but test the spirits, whether they are of God..." (1 John 4:1a)

I saw a true crime show once where a child had been kidnapped from a hotel room. The police had no clues, so they brought in a bloodhound. After a single sniff of the kid's clothing, the dog took off, hot on the trail. Amazed, I watched as the hound followed the scent to a local highway and then raced up an entrance ramp to the interstate.

I thought *oh well, that ends that,* but no, that dog wanted to keep going. The officers realized the abductor was traveling in a car and had gotten on the interstate. So, they loaded the blood-hound up in the police vehicle and let him out at every exit ramp to see if he would keep going down the highway or take the exit.

The officers explained that the human body sheds more than 40,000 skin cells per minute, and some of those skin cells will always escape through a car's air conditioning system or other gaps, even as it travels down a road. The bloodhound's sense of smell is so sharp he can follow that trail.

I wish the end of the story was a good one — the bloodhound did eventually take one of the exit ramps, and he led the authorities to a field in the middle of nowhere. The child was found (unfortunately it was too late). The good news is the same bloodhound picked up the scent of the perpetrator and off he went again. They caught the guy, a total random stranger.

I know it's a sad story, but I've never forgotten the keenness of that dog's sense of smell.

Who doesn't love dogs? They're faithful, always happy to see you, and they make great companions. They are fairly intelligent and are some of the most socially adept animals.

What strikes me most about dogs is their senses. We are all aware that dogs have an excellent sense of smell, but did you know that the average olfactory (smell) bulb in a dog's brain is forty times larger than that of humans? The olfactory cortex dominates their brain in the same way the visual cortex dominates ours. That means they smell things with the same vividness and detail that we see with our eyes.

And among the dog breeds, bloodhounds have even greater olfactory capabilities. The average dog may have 125 million - 220 million smell receptors, while the bloodhound has over 300 million. The average dog's sense of smell is estimated to be between one hundred thousand to one million times better than a human's, but a bloodhound can smell up to *one hundred million* times better than us.

So, the sense of smell is symbolically equated to the gift of spiritual discernment. That means a dog believer is a *discerning* believer. These believers can smell bad theology from a mile away. To be clear, spiritual discernment is actually a discernment of spirits (smell) as opposed to discernment of truth (vision).

Dog believers can sense the heart of someone better than anyone else, sometimes before the other has even opened their mouth. They instinctively know whether a person has good intentions or not, whether their motives are pure, and whether their speech reflects the Will and Word of God.

They understand these things without fully understanding *how* they understand these things. They would claim it's because of years of studying the Bible, or chalk it up to experience, but the truth is that spiritual discernment is a gift of the Holy Spirit. Their spiritual brains have been given this ability supernaturally.

So, the next time a discerning brother or sister in Christ tells you they smell something fishy, and you don't sense the same thing, don't just blow off their words. Pay attention to the warning as the pioneers of old would have listened to the sudden growling of a dog in their camp as he peered out into the darkness, or his ceaseless barking at a stranger that no one knew.

Dogs have excellent hearing.

They can hear in ranges up to 60,000 Hz, which means they can hear things at much higher frequencies than humans, but not quite as well as bats or dolphins.

This means that a dog believer, the discerning believer, has a high level of obedience to God's Word in their life, though not quite as high as a prayer warrior or a missionary.

Dogs have dichromatic vision.

This does not mean they see in black and white — they do have color vision — but they only have two kinds of color receptors in their eyes where we have three. This means their color vision does not see all the shades of color we see, and *they specifically have trouble seeing differing shades of grey.*

If you know a dog believer (gifted with spiritual discernment), you have probably noticed their tendency to see the world in black and white. Maybe you've even been annoyed by their inability to see the same range of greys that you see. These believers are often misjudged as being judgmental.

However, wisdom would dictate we pay attention to their view of those greys. It is not that they are deprived of the ability to see the shades of grey. It is more that they have been gifted to not be *hindered* by the shades of grey so they can more accurately tell right from wrong.

After all, if we're honest, every shade of grey either tilts to the black side of the spectrum or the white. While we might be fascinated with the wide variety of nuances, the discerning believer is ignoring that and instead focuses on whether that particular moral decision is on the side of darkness or light.

Instead of ignoring their warning as voiced by a simpleton less sophisticated than ourselves, we would do well to realize they are gifted with a vision we don't have.

Lesson: *Heed the warnings of the discerning believer.*

Cats

"And when you pray, you shall not be like the hypocrites.
For they love to pray standing in the synagogues
and on the corners of the streets, that they may be seen by men.
Assuredly, I say to you, they have their reward." (Matthew 6:5)

Obviously, dogs and cats are both favorites of ours, but they have such distinct personalities. It has been said that a dog might reflect to himself "This person feeds me, pets me, and takes care of my every need, they must be king." While the cat says "This person feeds me, pets me, and takes care of my every need, therefore *I* must be king."

I could go on for a long time about the stark difference in person-alities between our two favorite pets, but Bob Sjogren has already done an excellent treatment of the subject in his book *Dog and Cat Theology*, so why repeat it all here? If you wish to delve in more, I highly recommend Sjogren's book.

However, I will touch on the egocentric nature of cats. You don't see people using cats to herd sheep, pull sleds, find drugs in a suitcase, or to fetch the paper. Frankly, you don't see cats serving *anywhere*, in any role. No, they just sit around and preen, and sometimes they will hunt.

The *egocentric* believer is a distinct animal from the *greedy* believer (pig). While both are selfish, the greedy believer is focused on *getting things* for themselves, and the egocentric believer is focused on *being the center of things*. They want the attention of others. They are the Pharisee preening on the street corner as he prays loudly for all to see and announces how much he's given to the poor. He's about his own glory.

Unfortunately, many of us like to give attention to this kind of cat believer. They act like it's all about them and some of us fall for it, flattering them with the attention they crave. After all, if it didn't work, why would they keep doing it?

You may have guessed by now that I don't own any cats. My daughter loves them, but I'm allergic to them, so, thankfully, we don't even have to argue about it in my family.

Cats think they are lions.

At least, people often say this about them. It's telling. There is only one lion for us — the Lion of Judah, Jesus Christ. He is the center of the Kingdom.

Cat believers think they are like Him. Yet, they are so small, so unintimidating. Size represents prominence, and the cat believer is not prominent in the Kingdom. They do not typically hold positions of importance because others perceive their self-centered nature.

They try to look like the Lion in outward appearance, but their inward nature does not match, and they are missing the Great Lion's mane, which is a symbol of His crown and authority.

I'll never forget the day I tried to throw a cat in a swimming pool. Hold on, calm down...I was five and it was just my little wading pool. I thought he would have fun going for a little swim. I didn't understand why he suddenly got so tense, acting like he didn't want to try it. I mean, once he got in, I knew he'd see how fun it was.

Of course, I never got him in the water, and he left some nice scratches on my bare chest to teach me just how much **cats *don't like water.***

Symbolically, this would have to mean the egocentric believer does not want anything to do with God's power (water). Well, they'll sip from it to survive, but they don't want to bathe in it. Just as a cat prefers to lick itself clean, so does an egocentric believer prefer to make themselves look good through their own power. After all, if they bathed themselves in God's power, it would suddenly become about God, right? And not them.

Lesson: *Avoid the ego-centric believer. Do not seek glory for yourself, but seek to glorify God alone.*

Fourth Order
Rodents

"Whoever eats [gnaws] My flesh...has eternal life,
and I will raise him up at the last day."
(John 6:54)

Wait a second, wait a second...you're probably thinking about some big ol' nasty rats right now, but what about the cute squirrels in your backyard, and chipmunks, hamsters, guinea pigs, beavers, porcupines, and even nutria?

Also note that the following are *not* rodents: Bats, shrews, moles, rabbits, and weasels.

Regardless, rodents are by far the largest group of mammals, accounting for 40% of all mammal species, but individually they are very small in comparison with others.

Thus, we have an order that symbolizes the largest group of believers who have little prominence.

These are the "lay people" of the Kingdom.

Not to be depreciative in the least by that interpretation of course. Without rodents, our ecosystem would fall apart. Just as all churches would cease to function without the presence of the everyman believer that makes up the large majority of the Body.

Also, while there is great similarity among the various rodent species, there is also great diversity and uniqueness among them. In the same way, many of the men and women who make up our congregations may look similar on the surface, but they all have unique spiritual gifts and serve according to their specific purposes in the Kingdom — and they should be appreciated as such.

Without delving into more detailed articles on each rodent species, two dominant characteristics about rodents in general stand out to separate them from the pack.

Rodents have very sharp incisor teeth on both the top and bottom jaws.

These sharp teeth are ideal for gnawing on wood, breaking up food, and even fighting off predators. In fact, the name rodent comes from the Latin word *rodere*, which means "to gnaw."

This is also the primary activity of a large number of believers — to "gnaw" on the Word of God, the verbal witness they receive from others in the Kingdom represented by seeds and fruit. They gnaw on sermons, on Christian literature, and on words from other believers.

As rodents gnaw on wood not to glean nutrition, but to keep their specialized teeth sharp, so do believers "gnaw" on one another to stay spiritually sharp. *"As iron sharpens iron, So a man sharpens the countenance of his friend."* (Proverbs 27:17) Wood represents the life or substance of a believer as opposed to his witness.

Many rodent species have higher than average hearing ranges, which would symbolize that many lay people have a higher than average level of *obedience* to God's Word.

Lesson: *Never fail to appreciate the role of the average layperson. Though small, they are important.*

Fifth Order

Bats

"Now it came to pass in those days that He went out to the mountain to pray, and continued all night in prayer to God." (Luke 6:12)

In school, they taught me that bats were flying rodents. Maybe they taught you the same thing? Well, they taught us wrong.

Bats are not rodents. They are an order unto themselves, and their species are so numerous that they make up 20% of all mammal species by themselves!

Of course, they are the only mammals with a true ability to fly. (Yes, there are others that *appear* to fly, i.e. flying squirrels, but those guys are really just gliding.)

Clearly, as a symbol, bats must represent a significantly sized group of believers that have a very specialized function. Care to guess?

Let's look at the basics and see if we can get an idea.

First off, bats are primarily nocturnal. Next, their wings can only symbolize an unusual ability to resist the sinful nature (gravity), and this is mirrored by an extremely high hearing range (150,000 Hz), representing an unusual ability to obey God's Voice.

The key is their ability to echolocate. You know, *their specialized sonar*, the ability to emit sound at super-sonic (high) frequencies and use the reflections of that sound to detect the location of insects. In other words, they can *speak* in what could be considered "heavenly" (super-sonic) ways.

Bats represent the prayer warriors of the Kingdom.

Now, if you are a prayer warrior, or know one and love them, please do not be offended. Bats are not ugly, though I would say that they do appear *foreign*. My son thinks they are some of the cutest animals on earth.

Prayer warriors are an amazing type of believer. Their extreme faithfulness, their ability to stay up all night on their knees in prayer (equivalent to the nocturnal nature of the bat), intimidates the rest of us mortal men and women. Their faithful habits seem foreign to us.

Contrary to popular opinion, **bats are *not* blind**. They do have poor vision, but they're not blind. This is because they don't really need to see that well, not with such a unique sonar/hearing capability.

Prayer warriors are not blind to God's truth (light), but they don't need it to operate in the same way the rest of us do. Those believers who spend so much time in prayer often neglect the study of His Word, but they do not suffer because they have an uncanny ability to hear His Voice in prayer and *obey*.

Like birds, some bats can see ultraviolet frequencies.

Ultraviolet sight represents *heavenly* sight, so while the worldly vision may fail them, prayer warriors can see things the rest of us cannot. They have a certain heavenly sight. We'll discuss this more when we get to birds.

Bats play an important role in fertilization.

They aid in flower pollination and dispersing fruit seeds across soil. Prayer warriors do this as well. It is through prayer, through pleading to God's heart that revivals begin. God's Spirit often moves in response to dedicated, sincere prayer. The fertility of the Kingdom is impacted by the prayers of prayer warriors.

Bats wings are delicate.

Their wings are thin membranes, much thinner than birds' wings, which means bat wings can be easily torn or damaged.

This signifies that while a prayer warrior has an unusual ability to resist the sinful nature, that ability can be easily ruptured. Like all believers, they are susceptible to fall. This ability to "fly" is directly related to their super ability to obey God's Voice.

Some readers may not be aware of the distinction between the sinful nature and sin itself. To be clear, the sinful nature is the strong pull of sin upon our hearts — sin is the result of actually giving in to the sinful nature. The sinful nature could also be described as a rebellious nature. We have a rebellious nature, but if we can resist it, our actual rebellion stops.

So, we are not saying that prayer warriors are without sin — no one is without sin except Jesus — but they have been given an extreme ability to overcome the pull of the sinful nature.

To fly is to be borne upon the wind, so the image of flight is not a believer overcoming sin through their own power, but they are borne up by the Holy Spirit (the wind).

When a bat's wing is torn, it heals very quickly.

I have to imagine this means that with such a special gift of faithful obedience, if the prayer warrior stumbles, they are able to be restored quickly in their ability to fly.

Daniel is a great example of this. Of all the heroes from the Old Testament, Daniel is the one we constantly see in prayer and communion with God.

In the Old Testament, Daniel is also the only one of whom we don't know his sin. Of course, Daniel was a sinner like the rest of us, or he wouldn't be in need of a Savior, but I find it interesting that Scripture is silent on what his sins were. We know the sins of Adam, Noah, Abraham, Moses, Samson, Saul, David, Elijah, Hezekiah, Jonah, Peter, Paul, John, etc., etc.

Daniel stands out among them as constantly faithful — *and he was a man of prayer*. I believe it's because he was gifted with an unusual ability to overcome the sinful nature and obey God's voice. After all, Daniel is told several times that he is a "man greatly beloved" by God.

Lesson: *High levels of prayer are connected to obedience.*

Sixth Order
Primates

*"Having then gifts differing according to the grace that is given to us,
let us use them...he who teaches, in teaching..."*
(Romans 12:6-7)

Primates are some of the most intelligent animals on earth, and chimpanzees, specifically, are rated as *the* smartest next to humans, so let's focus on them.

Chimpanzees have complex social structures, demonstrate amazing memory capabilities, and can even communicate complex sentences to humans using sign language. They are also innovative enough to make their own tools, such as using a stick to get ants out of an anthill, or using a sharp stick to hunt for small game.

As the brainiacs of the Animal Kingdom, primates symbolize the teachers and theologians of the Body of Christ.

When we think about primates, what jumps out at us is their ability to think and learn. That's what distinguishes them from other animals.

We view theologians in a similar light, as thinkers rather than doers. Teachers are also necessarily great thinkers and they often develop spiritual "tools" for the rest of us to use.

Primates have binocular vision.

This gives them significant depth perception, which relates to a teacher's ability to understand remote subjects. A theologian can glean revelation from a study of Heaven in Scripture without having visited in person. A good teacher can perceive and understand the struggles someone from a broken family endures without having to experience the trauma themself.

Primates have opposable thumbs, which allows them to grasp things.

In the same way, teachers can grasp complicated concepts in ways that others can't. Then, they take those complex ideas and rehash them into simple tools the rest of us can understand.

Primates have fingernails, not claws.

Claws belong to the average animal, for tearing food or for defense, but claws can't hold on to things very well.

Now think about your fingernails. How do you use them? As little tools. To pick a sticker off something, to dig into an orange peel, or to scratch someone's back.

Primates don't need claws. Fingernails are much more useful to them, allowing them to pick at things.

Teachers and theologians are the same way. They have the ability to pick apart truths for the rest of us to consume.

Some primates eat meat, but most eat plants, seeds, fruit, or insects.

This shows how *some* teachers, perhaps the most capable ones (Chimpanzees), are often on the staff of a church (carnivore). Yet, the majority of teachers are volunteers and thrive instead on fellowship with other believers, the testimonies of other believers, and the inspiration of God.

Primates usually live in the forest.

This symbolizes the fact that teachers are usually found within the *mature* Body of Christ (forest). Evangelists belong to the coast as fishers of men, but teachers belong to the forest.

Most species of primates are shy of water.

This applies to both the ocean and fresh water rivers or lakes.

The ocean makes perfect sense as biblical teachers regularly instruct others to avoid the world, yet there is a strange phenomenon among teachers and theologians that bears comment.

Lay people are the first to embrace a new, spontaneous movement of God (river, fresh water). The teachers and theologians of the Kingdom are usually the last to accept God's movement as authentic.

They approach such movements with great caution, viewing themselves as the caretakers of legitimate doctrine. They have difficulty initially separating the movement of God from a movement of the world, which is their real concern. This was the struggle of many of the Pharisees.

They tend to fear spontaneous movements they cannot control, especially if lay people are embracing it, who often have less knowledge or discernment. Yet, these lay persons have a spiritual discernment that is independent of intellectual discernment. They recognize the voice of their Shepherd and jump right in.

Not that teachers don't have their role in protecting us from "bad water." Of course they do.

But the truth is, even with a fresh, crystalline river, primates fear water — basically because they can't swim. Teachers and theologians enjoy a well-structured, precise environment where they can dissect life. Movements of God are messy and by nature require a release of control. Far outside the average teacher's comfort zone.

Lesson: *Don't look to teachers to verify the movements of God. The fruit of the Spirit verifies them.*

Seventh Order
Marsupials

"Train up a child in the way he should go,
And when he is old he will not depart from it."
(Proverbs 22:6)

Ah, marsupials.
They're a different breed. I've always wanted to go to Australia to see them in the wild.

You're probably imaging kangaroos right now, but koalas, opossums, wombats, these are all marsupials — and no, they don't *all* live in Australia. Marsupials are also found throughout South America, and there could be an opossum hiding in the woods in your backyard right now.

In school, they might have taught you, as they did me, that marsupials are a distinct animal classification, equal to mammals and reptiles, but not part of the mammal family. However, that is not actually the case. Marsupials are considered a sub-group of mammals. They are one of the eight orders.

The reason is that they share every characteristic in common with mammals, with the sole exception being a placental birth. They still bear their young live instead of laying eggs, but because the mother does not develop a placenta in her womb, the baby is born *very* young and crawls into the mother's pouch where it hides and nurses until it is grown.

In fact, marsupial mothers often allow their children to stay in the pouch for much longer than is really needed.

Marsupial believers are the *shelterers* of the Kingdom.

You know, those parents who overprotect their kids beyond the realm of wisdom. We're not speaking of homeschoolers here (though many shelterers are homeschoolers). Most home-schooled children excel in college and show even better social adjustment than other students. No, *shelterers* and *homeschoolers* are mutually exclusive categories that just happen to converge at times. Many shelterers send their kids to private school, and some even stay in public school.

School choice is not the distinguishing feature of a sheltering parent, nor does the mere act of *sheltering* make one a *shelterer*. A shelterer is fearful enough of the world's influence that they hide their kid away from it for much longer than normal Christian families.

All good parents protect their kids from the world's influence, but, at the right times, most begin to slowly expose their children to it in order to prepare them. A shelterer breaks from the ranks at that point and continues to shield their children up into their late teens.

I would hypothesize that because of such a parent's obsession with overprotecting their offspring, they actually break the more intimate nurturing aspect of their relationship with the child very early on, comparable to the way in which a marsupial baby does not spend much time intimately nurtured in the womb, but is birthed early and then shielded in the pouch for far too long. In many cases, kangaroos actually have to physically dump their kids out of the pouch to get the kid to step out on its own.

In an article on homeschooling,[26] author Reb Bradley recounts the following story:

> "*When my oldest son was almost 16 we let him get his first job washing dishes at a restaurant managed by a Christian friend of ours. As diehard shelterers we wrestled with whether or not our son was ready to enter the world's workforce. We knew we couldn't shelter him forever, and so finally concluded that he should be old enough to send into the world two nights a week. What we didn't realize was that he would be working with drug-using, tattooed, partiers, and our Christian friend was never scheduled to work our son's shift.*

---

[26] Reb Bradley, *Solving the Crisis in Homeschooling*, http://www.familyministries.com/HS_Crisis.htm (accessed Dec. 27th, 2013).

Within a month it became apparent that our son's new work associates were having an effect on him. He came home one evening and asked, "Dad, can I dye my hair blue?" After my wife was finally able to peel me off the ceiling, I laid into him, reminding him whose son he was, and that I would not have people at church telling their children not to be like the pastor's son. I explained that just because he wanted to use washable dye, it didn't make me any happier. (Note that my intense reaction had to do with "outward appearances" and the impact on me.)

Of course, my wife and I immediately began to evaluate whether we had made a mistake by letting him take the job. After an intense discussion we decided to coach him more carefully and let him keep his job.

Two months later he came home from work and asked me if he could pierce his ear. Again, my wife had to peel me off the ceiling. He thought it might be okay since he wanted a cross earring — like I was supposed to be happy, because it would be a "sanctified" piercing. If that wasn't enough, he also wanted to get a tattoo! But it was going to be okay, because it would be a Christian tattoo!

As I was looking back on this experience several years later, something my son said shortly after he started his job kept coming back to me. When I picked him up the second night of work, he got in the car with a big smile on his face and said "They like me!" As I dwelt on that comment, it suddenly came clear to me – my son had finally met someone who liked him for who he was. Few others in his entire life had shown him much acceptance, especially not his mother and I. It is no exaggeration – in our efforts to shape and improve him, all we did was find fault with everything he did. We loved him dearly, but he constantly heard from us that what he did (who he was) wasn't good enough. He craved our approval, but we couldn't be pleased. Years later, I realized he had given up trying to please us when he was 14, and from then on he was just patronizing us.

The reason our son wanted to adorn himself like his work associates, was because they accepted him for who he was. He wanted to fit in with those who made him feel significant. He wanted to be like those who gave him a sense of identity. The problem wasn't one that could be solved by extended sheltering – he could have been sheltered until he was 30 and he still would have been vulnerable. The problem was that we had sent our son into the world insecure in who he was. He went into the world with a hole in his heart that God had wanted to fill through his parents."

Again, the distinctive characteristic of the sheltering believer (marsupial) is that they are so concerned with shielding their child that they forget to have a relationship with them.

This is visualized in the early birth/pouch of the marsupial.

Marsupials have high infant mortality rates.

Yep, it's true. Marsupials are born with lower immunity capabilities due to the lack of a placenta.[27]

So, to combat this, God made marsupials extremely fertile.

Ironically, in spite of the *image* of extreme care the kangaroo gives, with its joey peering cutely from its pouch, the kangaroo loses a lot more babies to the world than most mammals.

Isn't this the experience most of us have had with sheltering parents? They give a strong image of care and protection, but don't they seem to have a much higher rate of rebellion among their kids?

That's certainly the lesson Rod Dreher has for us in his article.

---

[27] Deane, EM, *Development of the immune system and immunological protection in marsupial pouch young,*

http://www.ncbi.nlm.nih.gov/pubmed/10785270 (accessed Nov. 15th, 2013).

Marsupials are fighters.

The boxing prowess of kangaroos is well-known. Opossums and wombats are also known for their ferociousness. Only koalas escape such a reputation…wait a second…actually, koalas have been known to attack humans too! (If they feel threatened.)

I would have to say that parents who overprotect their children are definitely fighters. This is a *great* quality of "marsupial" believers. If they were passive, they would not care so deeply, and there is no doubt they love their children fiercely.

Lesson: *Protect your children from the world, but be sure to connect with them in relationship as you do.*

Eighth Order
Elephants

"There is no creature among all the Beasts of the world which hath so great and ample demonstration of the power and wisdom of Almighty God as the elephant."
~ Edward Topsell, 1658

"Yet it shall not be so among you; but whoever desires to become great among you, let him be your servant." (Matthew 20:26)

D id you know that elephants are highly intelligent? You've probably heard about their amazing memories, but did you know that elephants also show a significant sense of self-awareness? Scientific observers have noted elephants displaying altruism, grief, learning abilities, mimicry, compassion, and cooperation. They engage in art, play games, use tools, and may even use language when communicating with each other.

Next to chimpanzees and dolphins, elephants are about as intelligent as you get, yet elephants seem to surpass even chimpanzees when it comes to emotional empathy and altruism. Aristotle once said that elephants are *"the animal which surpasses all others in wit and mind."*

Yet, elephants are also strong. No other land animal can hope to even come close to the sheer power brewing within their muscles. They have no known predators, excepting cases where lions may prey on the young or sick. Even lions don't dare take on a mature adult.

So, we look at the elephant and see believers who are both smart and able to carry great burdens. These are the leaders within the Body of Christ.

Elephants have trunks.

No other animal shares this feature — no other animal sports a unique, *fifth* appendage such as the trunk.

Most mammals have four legs that let them move about the earth or climb trees. Primates have four appendages, two legs for movement, and two arms that can be used both as tools and for movement.

The elephant is very different in that he has four legs for movement, and then a fifth appendage that is exclusively a tool and not for movement. So, the trunk represents a part of the elephant believer that no other type of believer has, something they can sense with and use to do work.

The elephant trunk represents a leader's *followers*. (After all, as John Maxwell says, "if you turn around and no one is following, you're not leading — you're just taking a walk".) Ask any leader, and they'll tell you that their followers are a big part of who they are.

Followers don't make up the majority of who a leader is, but they are an essential part of the leader in the same way a trunk is for an elephant.

Elephant trunks are so specialized that they can pluck up a single blade of grass, yet so strong they can rip apart the branches of a tree. The following is from Wikipedia regarding the many ways elephants use their trunks:

> *"Familiar elephants will greet each other by entwining their trunks, much like a handshake. They also use them while play-wrestling, caressing during courtship and mother-child interactions, and for dominance displays; a raised trunk can be a warning or threat, while a lowered trunk can be a sign of submission. Elephants can defend themselves very well by flailing their trunks at unwanted intruders or by grasping and flinging them...An elephant also relies on its trunk for its highly developed sense of smell. By raising the trunk up in the air and swiveling it from side to side, like a periscope, it can determine the location of friends, enemies, and food sources. The*

complete trunk can have up to 150,000 separate muscle fascicles, giving it strength and flexibility. "

I don't want to convey the sense that leaders "use" their followers, but the entire reason leaders lead is because the primary way a leader influences their world is through their followers. A leader without followers would have very little impact at all, just like an elephant stomping around without a trunk.

As elephants use their trunks for everything from showing love to defense, so do leaders do the same through their followers. The pastor of a small church may directly love others, but logistically, the pastor of a large church is unable to effectively show love to his entire congregation or community, so he does it vicariously through his followers. He teaches them to love, and they love others directly in his stead.

The sense of smell is symbolic of a discernment of spirits, and as an elephant's trunk provides it with a strong sense of smell, so does the pastor receive reports back about what's going on in the community from his congregation. Followers pass information to the leader about what's happening, new teachings that are being disseminated, threats to the people, etc.

A trunk is simultaneously flexible, strong, and precise. Leaders have extreme flexibility if they lead their followers well. They can guide a single believer to act in one place, or inspire the entire group to transform their community.

Elephants have tusks.

They use them as digging tools and also for defense. Curiously, one thing often mentioned with regards to elephant tusks is the way they use them to strip bark off trees.

Tusks simultaneously symbolize a leader's authority and ability to fight. All leaders must have fight in them, or they do not remain the leader for long. A leader is equipped to aggressively fight off an attacker, but they can also adapt this ability, using it in a more gentle fashion as a tool.

Specifically, Christian leaders have the ability to "strip the bark" off another believer (tree), digging beneath the image that a believer might want to portray (bark) in order to get at the flesh beneath, the believer's true self. To do this requires a certain amount of aggressiveness on the part of the leader, and he or she does it with their spiritual "tusks."

Elephants have tough skin.

Do I even need to ask if leaders have "tough skin?" Of course they do. Any leader receives criticism, and the bigger the leader, they more they are attacked. None are spared. Leaders have developed a thick skin that allows them to slough off such abuse — or they don't remain leaders for long.

But more interestingly, while elephants have very thick, tough skin, that skin is also highly *sensitive*. Elephants are easily sunburned. Because of this, elephants regularly coat themselves with mud baths. These mud baths also protect them from mosquito bites and moisture loss in the heat of the day. Their skin would suffer serious damage without this habit.

The love of God is symbolized by heat from the sun, though I should remind you that we have discussed how God often allows us to struggle with challenges out of *love* for us. Those He does not care about, He leaves alone until the judgment. Those He loves, He strengthens. (I know, many of you are suddenly wondering if you wouldn't prefer God to be a little more apathetic toward you.)

The larger the leader, the more God allows them to experience challenges, for their own good and for the good of their followers. However, if leaders do not constantly immerse themselves in the Kingdom (mud baths), which is the power of God (water) working in conjunction with fellowship with other believers (dirt), they will get burned. *Burned out*, to be specific.

This regular habit of immersing themselves in the life of the Kingdom also protects leaders from infection by false doctrines (mosquito bites) and a loss of God's power in their life (moisture loss).

Elephants are not able to release body heat well through their skin.

This is because their ratio of skin to body mass is so low. (Meaning they have a *lot* of thick body beneath the surface area of their skin.)

To combat this, elephants flap their big ears! Blood circulating through their ears is cooled by the air by as much as 10° F before returning to the rest of their body.

Understanding the source of their overheating problem is important. Unlike the sunburn issues we already mentioned, this is internal over-heating is due to their *own* heat production. However, if an elephant were to take a trip to the South Pole, he would not overheat, so the external temperature plays a role in conjunction with the internal heat.

In general, Christian leaders, as opposed to non-believing leaders, and we are talking about true Christian leaders here, swell with love (internal heat). As Moses loved God and Israel, so do most pastors love God and their flocks dearly, and the amount of love God puts in their heart overwhelms their ability to distribute it. Christian men and women in leadership positions are not physically capable of sharing all the love within them because of the limitations of any one human's contact with their world (skin).

Yet, as already mentioned, leaders are burdened with challenges, and Christian leaders are burdened in this way because of God's love (external heat). The "mud baths" (bathing in the life of the Kingdom) only help save their outer layer from burning. It allows them to continue to appear energetic and humble (looking dirty is humbling, and life in the Kingdom is messy and muddy), but it does not address the fullness of the internal spiritual struggles a leader may face since fellowship with others can never really heal the deepest parts of their soul.

In order to not overheat, Christian leaders must turn to obedience to God's Voice (flapping ears). They find that neither accomplishing great feats, nor loving people, nor doing good works is ever enough to satisfactorily express the love inside them back to God. And fellowship with others is never enough to fully relieve them of their burdens.

Eventually, they find the only way they can be fully comfortable is through obedience. The Spirit (air) receives their love through obed-ience and they are relieved.

I personally experienced this recently. For a long time, I have had a strong heart to minister to others through several ministries in which I'm involved — yet, we have faced countless struggles just getting things off the ground at times.

(Which makes *no* sense, right? If we're about God's business, shouldn't He make it easy for us to succeed?)

Yet, He is so mature that instead of instant success, He prefers to not miss the opportunity to grow us in the process through challenges.

Regardless, at a time when I was faced with high levels of frustration and ambiguity, I sought Him in prayer. His answer was to ask for better obedience in completely unrelated things (or seemingly so). I asked for specific guidance on issues, He responded with a general "Obey."

Though it did not give me the practical guidance I wanted, I knew I would get no further answers until I did obey, and so, I chose obedience.

In that moment, when I realized that I had actually begun to obey His Voice in new ways, though I had no more clarity on decisions or plans than I had before, the stress of not knowing the future was suddenly relieved. I experienced a new peace with God, which in the end was a much bigger relief than I would have ever gotten from a few answers.

Now, I'm not sharing this story to stake a claim on some great leadership ability for myself — I'm not that special. Yet this experience of mine struck a chord of similarity, and I would equate it with an elephant flapping his ears.

This heightened obedience for leaders is absolutely necessary. Without obedience, a leader soon falls, and when an elephant falls, it shakes the earth.

Elephants swim well.

As opposed to primates who fear the water. Which demonstrates a big difference between a Christian leader and a Christian teacher. Of course, all leaders teach, but their primary role is to lead, not just teach.

While teachers will be cautious and even fearful of the movements of God, leaders are *looking* for movements of God and are usually ready to jump in once they discover one.

Elephants are self-aware.

Scientists have verified that elephants can see a reflection in a mirror and recognize that they are seeing themselves. Few other animals can do this. In fact, if an elephant sees new markings on itself in a reflection, it will begin to touch them with its trunk to figure out what they are. If the same experiment is done with invisible paint, the elephant does not pay it any attention.

A requirement for any leader is that they be self-aware. Leaders who don't know themselves, who don't know their own strengths and weaknesses, make poor leaders indeed.

Elephants have great hearing and smell, but poor eyesight.

This would symbolize a strong ability to obey the Word of God (hearing) and discern spirits (smell).

All great men of God do obey God well, and strong leaders have great discernment when it comes to people and their motivations, so great pastors or other Christian leaders would necessarily do both well.

On the other hand, visionary leaders can and often do lead without a strong ability to understand the smaller nuances of truth (poor eyesight). Meaning, a Christian leader can lead as long as they are faithful to God and understand the people they're leading.

Some pastors are visionary leaders, others are teachers. Book knowledge and a detailed understanding of theology is necessary to be a teacher, but not a leader.

Elephants have very sensitive networks of nerves in their trunks and their feet.

When trying to listen hard, they will actually plant their feet firmly and lay their trunks along the ground to sense vibrations. It's this ability, rather than their large ears, that helps them hear so well.

This means that much of a Christian leader's ability to obey and discern is derived from their interaction with their followers (a pastor's interaction with his congregation). They receive and collect vital information from other believers that helps guide them in the right path.

Elephants are known for their trumpet calls.

They use a wide variety of calls to communicate different things to other elephants.

Of course, good leaders are communicators. A trumpet call could be viewed as the image of a leader casting a vision for his people, calling them to something higher.

Elephants are emotional.

They show grief and even hold primitive funeral services when one of their family dies. They enter bouts of rage — and when they're *that* mad, they can crush even a rhinoceros. They've also been observed doing things that could only be described as *vindictive*.

These are all negative emotions (anger and sadness), and we'll see shortly that elephants are also capable of positive ones, but there is no doubt that elephants feel strong emotions.

Leaders are often passionate people, though good leaders have learned self-control along with that passion, but it is difficult to rally people to follow and buy into a vision if there is not a strong *emotional* call from the leader to engage.

Elephants are altruistic.

In India, one elephant that had been trained to lift logs from a truck bed and insert them into pre-dug holes suddenly hesitated and refused to put a certain log into a hole. Investigating closer, his handlers realized that there was a dog sleeping in the bottom of the hole. As soon as they got the dog out, the elephant happily tipped the log up into it.[28]

In her book *Coming of Age with Elephants*, Joyce Poole documents a story about a remarkable case:

> *"A ranch herder was out on his own with camels when he came across a family of elephants. The matriarch charged at him and knocked him over with her trunk, breaking*

---

[28] Craig Holdrege, *Elephantine Intelligence*, http://www.natureinstitute.org/pub/ic/ic5/elephant.htm (accessed Nov. 15th, 2013).

one of his legs. In the evening, when he did not return, a search party was sent in a truck to find him. When the party discovered him, he was being guarded by an elephant. The animal charged the truck, so they shot over her and scared her away. The herdsman later told them that when he could not stand up, the elephant used her trunk to lift him under the shade of a tree. She guarded him for the day and would gently touch him with her trunk."

It is also known that when one elephant is injured, elephants that aren't even related to it will come to help if able.

In the same way, Christian leaders will often come to the aid of others in need. They feel an instinctive protectiveness for their own flock and even others who are helpless.

I'm sure you've run across leaders who were full of themselves and willing to use others for their own gain. Such leaders though, even if you find them in the church, are not *really Christian* leaders because they're obviously not followers of Christ.

A leader who follows Christ has a strongly altruistic nature. If they didn't, why would they bother leading? Leading is hard, full of challenges and criticism. If you're not in it for your own glory, then you might as well just stay at home in peace.

Unless, of course, you have this altruistic nature within you, driving you to care for others at your own expense.

Lesson: *Encourage the Christian leaders in your life. Their role is vital and they're not in it for their own gain.*

Final Note on Mammals

There are obviously *so many* animals we did not even get a chance to look at — just as the Kingdom is filled with such a wide variety of believers. Books and books could be written on them. So, if you have a favorite animal that we did not mention, now that you understand the fundamentals of the symbolism, why don't you try to take a stab at it yourself?

Also worth mentioning is that many real-life believers may see in themselves a mixture of several of these animals. That is okay.

R E V I E W		
Vision	=	Discernment of Truth
Hearing	=	Ability to Obey
Smell	=	Discernment of Spirits
Fish	=	Non-believer
Fishing	=	Evangelism
Mammal	=	Believer
Lion	=	Jesus, King of Kings
Carnivore	=	Church Staff / Levite
Dolphin/Whale	=	Missionary
Hoofed Animal	=	Serving Believer
Sheep/Cow	=	Meditating Believer
Pig	=	Greedy Believer
Giraffe	=	Scholar Believer
Camel	=	Abrasive Believer
Horse	=	Warrior Believer
Dog	=	Discerning Believer
Cat	=	Ego-Centric Believer
Rodent	=	Gnawing/Fellowshipping Believer
Bat	=	Prayer Warrior
Primate	=	Teacher
Marsupial	=	Sheltering Believer
Elephant	=	Leader

BIRDS & INSECTS:

Angels & Spirits

BIRDS

"And it shall be, when you hear a sound of marching in the tops of the mulberry trees, then you shall go out to battle, for God has gone out before you to strike the camp of the Philistines."
(1 Chronicles 14:15)

Birds fly.

That right there puts them in a completely different category. Clearly distinct from every other major animal group, they are the only animals that easily defy the Law of Gravity, soaring through the heavens with little effort. They truly operate in a *different realm* from the rest of us.

They have a different perspective too.

From overhead, they can see the entire landscape. The daily happenings of life on earth seem so much smaller when viewed from up high. It's a more correct perspective than ours, which is born of our innate sense of self-absorbed self-importance.

So, what do birds symbolize?

Spiritually speaking, birds would have to represent beings who are not bound by the sinful nature (gravity), who operate in the heavens (sky), who see things from a different perspective than us, and often remain unseen by us as they soar in a different realm.

Which, of course, would have to mean…Angels.

When I first considered birds and what they might represent, I honestly didn't have a clue. But the ability to defy the sinful nature without limitation was a big hint. *No human,* neither believer nor non-believer, can do that.

The fact that angels are routinely portrayed in Scripture as having large wings was another big clue — quite an obvious one frankly. Slap myself on the forehead, why didn't I think of that sooner?

Angels are also a part of creation and the spiritual realm, so it stands to reason they have to be represented by something, and birds make perfect sense.

While we don't know a lot about them, we do know that angels number in the millions, if not billions or trillions. With that many angels, and knowing God's character and His love for variety, surely the diversity of roles, appearances, and functions of angels must be as wide as the numerous types of birds.

Scripture does not give us detailed explanations of the daily life of angels, what they do or why they exist. The word angel means *messenger*, which is the primary context in which they're seen in the Bible. We are also given glimpses of their role in the worship of God and their ministry before his throne. We're afforded very brief descriptions of their wars, and informed that some angels rule over entire countries. And we know that some of them have fallen from grace.

As I approached this section of the book and began researching angels, I was quite surprised to find that both Christian and Jewish theologians have a much more developed systematic understanding of the roles and ranks of angels than I knew.

Beyond the *seraphim* and *cherubim* who minister before God's throne (of whom most of us are aware), there are the *erelim* (the "thrones"), living beings who represent God's justice and authority in the cosmos. There are also the *dominions*, the *powers*, and the *principalities*, all ranks of angels who rule over specific earthly territories, influence the political sphere, and inspire art and science, all, of course, under God's direction.

In fact, in Ephesians 6:12, when Paul says *"For we do not wrestle against flesh and blood, but against principalities, against powers, against the rulers of the darkness of this age, against spiritual hosts of wickedness in the heavenly places,"* he is referring to these ranks of angels commonly understood by the rabbis of his day. These are technical terms referring specifically to angels, and in this context, they would be fallen angels.

Scripture purposefully manages very tightly all information about these beings. We are not to worship angels, call on them, try to communicate with them, or otherwise involve ourselves with their doings. Their realm is not our realm, and if God wanted us to be aware of theirs and be able to navigate it, He would have revealed much more than He has. It's very dangerous for a believer to insert themselves into a spiritual world they do not understand, as is seen in Acts 19:11-17.

Yet, at the same time, God chose to reveal something of angels to us — I think for the purpose of reminding us how small we are and how little we understand of what He is doing.

As we dive into the topic of birds, I believe they can be a window into garnering extra understanding of the different types, roles and characteristics of angels. However, we should be careful to not establish any *absolute* theology or understanding solely from a symbolic interpretation. When it comes to angels, Scripture does not give us much material with which to confirm our interpretation, so we should study birds with an *interested* eye, but not an *absolute* one.

"Their wings stretched upward; two wings of each one touched one another, and two covered their bodies."
(Ezekiel 1:11b)

Birds have feathers.

Feathers serve several purposes. First of all, they are what allows a bird to control his flight. Without them, it would careen about wildly.

Feathers are also the glory of a bird — many of them are vividly colored and patterned in beautiful displays like the parrot or the peacock. Others provide camouflage as in the case of the owl.

Regardless, feathers are what make a bird's personality visible, whether it be an intimidating, predatory Eagle, a pure white dove, or a gorgeous cockatoo. Without feathers, all birds become uniformly pitiful-looking creatures. (Just imagine a plucked chicken.)

Feathers also help a bird retain warmth and provide water-proofing.

Now, we have established that hair in mammals and leaves on trees both represent maturity. Also, the scales of a fish, being indicative of a non-believer's skepticism, could also symbolize a type of maturity, if you will. Therefore, it is tempting to interpret feathers for birds in the same way.

But, *can angels mature?*

Here is what we do know: there are millions upon millions of angels engaged in a variety of functions. God did not create mindless robots when He created humans. Since angels can fall, that would seem to indicate they are also not mindless creations, but intelligent and capable of thought.

In the Book of Daniel, we see that it took Michael the Archangel three weeks to overcome "the Prince of Persia," referring to enemy angels opposing Daniel and the Jewish people. Why does God allow these types of battles in the heavenly realms? When He can simply speak a word and end all conflict, why would He allow His angels to endure such struggles?

This is one case where the reason cannot be to benefit us. Frankly, we have been kept almost completely in the dark regarding such angelic fights. That is the only battle on which we have any detail, and it's hard to believe that God would allow an entire unseen war in the heavenly realms and only release a few details about one battle if the only purpose was to teach us an object lesson about spiritual warfare.

Struggle provokes spiritual growth, and it seems much more likely that the heavenly war's purpose is for the benefit of Michael and the angels who serve God faithfully.

My conclusion is that angels must be able to mature.

How does maturity arrive without a struggle against the sinful nature?

I don't know. As a human, that's outside my realm of experience to understand. Perhaps that's why the heavenly angelic struggle takes the form of a war. Their struggle is not against internal sin, but external sin.

In fact, baby birds do begin life with soft, fluffy feathers that keep them warm but do not allow them to fly or swim. When they get older, these feathers fall out and are replaced by the more glorious adult feathers.

This is another indicator that feathers do in fact symbolize maturity just like hair and leaves.

So, then are there young angels? Or all they all ancient? Are new angels created by God on a regular basis just like new human babies? I don't know the answer to that. You don't either.

Regardless, that feathers represent spiritual maturity seems to be true, which would mean that an angel's strength and ability to soar, as well as his beauty, is directly tied to their spiritual maturity. Which would also make sense.

This interpretation also fits with the common belief in Christian Theology that the devil was once one of God's most beautiful creations who became an ugly creature after he fell. Such a choice, such a pride would have cost him his spiritual maturity, erasing any former glory like a plucked chicken (or, I'm sure, much worse in that case).

Feather loss is called molting. The primary causes of molting are a lack of sunlight, the presence of harmful parasites, or malnutrition.[29] The spiritual metaphor here would be that a lack of exposure to truth (sunlight or food), or bad teaching or pride (parasites) can provoke an angel to fall and lose his feathers.

Birds have hollow bones.

Like mammals, and *unlike fish*, birds breathe air. This would symbolize angels being filled with the Holy Spirit.

I don't know that I've ever heard any specific teaching on whether angels are filled with the Holy Spirit, but how would they not be? How can anyone be in tune with God's will and obey it without the Holy Spirit working within them?

It seems to me that angels indeed must be filled with the Holy Spirit just as believers are. There is evidence for this in Ezekiel 1:20, *"Wherever the Spirit wanted to go, they went, because there the Spirit went; and the wheels were lifted together with them, for the spirit of the living creatures was in the wheels."*

Interestingly, of the air that birds breathe, only 25% goes to their lungs for respiration. The other 75% is sent to fill small air sacs and the cavities in their hollow bones to help them with lift in flight.[30] Filling

---

[29] Lindsay Haymes, *Feather Loss*,
http://www.ozarksfn.com/mo-articles-aamp-stories-editorial-159/90-farm-help-missouri/2211-feather-loss.html (accessed on Nov. 18th, 2013).
[30] Maina, John N. (November 2006). "Development, structure, and function of a novel respiratory organ, the lung-air sac system of birds: to go where no other vertebrate has gone." *Biological Reviews* 81 (4): 545-79.

their hollow bones with air makes them more lightweight, able to soar, able to defy the Law of Gravity.

So, it is the power of the Holy Spirit that keeps angels from falling into the power of sin. And should we be surprised by that? No man or woman has ever overcome sin through their own power, but only through the power of the Spirit. Should we expect angels to be able to be sinless of their own accord, without God's power acting within them? No, clearly angels are only exempt from the sinful nature because of the Holy Spirit lifting them up.

Some birds migrate and travel in flocks.

As we said, there are different ranks of angels with different functions. For example, there is a clear warrior class of angels.

Birds that migrate typically fly in flocks, which are organized in formations that remind one of Air Force maneuvers. These migratory flocking birds represent God's soldiers, his heavenly armies that move throughout the heavens fighting in different places.

Birds migrate because of a lack of food or because they're looking for warmth. However, the actual moment of migration is typically launched because they sense a change in the length of the days.

We know from clear teaching in Scripture that events on earth are mere reflections of the war going on in the heavens. When a spiritual revival breaks out, when a country turns to Christ, when slavery is eradicated, when families are restored, we know it's because God's angels in Heaven are overcoming the forces of darkness.

If birds migrate south in the winter in search of warmth and food and light, then we could interpret this to mean that God's warrior angels are sent by Him to whatever part of the Kingdom is more full of love (warmth) and truth (light).

Birds use the wind to travel those long distances (they certainly wouldn't get very far fighting a headwind). In the same way, angels would surely only go to battle riding the power of the Holy Spirit.

"So he answered, 'Do not fear, for those who are with us are more than those who are with them.' And Elisha prayed, and said, 'Lord, I pray, open his eyes that he may see.' Then the Lord opened the eyes of the

young man, and he saw. And behold, the mountain was full of horses and chariots of fire all around Elisha." (2 Kings 6:16-17)

Birds have highly developed vision.

When I was a young boy, I would spot a plane high up in the sky that my father could not see, and he would call me "Eagle Eye."

This excellent eyesight in birds corresponds to the ability of angels to see better than us humans what is truly going on in the world. They have a spiritual vision that we do not.

Some water birds have special lenses in their eyes that flex when they enter water, allowing them to see just as clearly while submerged. This demonstrates that angels are also flexible and have a dominating vision in both the Kingdom and the world.

Birds can see ultraviolet.

What an amazing fact of nature! You'll be even more surprised to learn that many birds have ultraviolet patterns on their plumage — that's right, patterns visible only to other birds!

Only an ultraviolet lamp can reveal those patterns to us. Kind of weird, huh? To think that robin in your back yard might have a whole other set of patterns on its wing you've never seen.

Ultraviolet light symbolizes the truth of Christ's royalty radiating out from Himself (the sun). So, as our symbolism here continues, we see that angels have the ability to see things we cannot see. Specifically, they can see who has special "ultraviolet" markings — who has been marked by the King.[31]

Biologists categorize birds according to their form and structure, but since the ranks of angels are distinguished by *function*, I think *we* should divide the birds by their function for the purpose of this analysis.

To do so, we'll especially be looking at diet, as diet can serve as an indicator of their function.

Lesson: *Heaven and the spiritual realm are much more complex than we realize.*

---

[31] Revelation 7:2-3

Eagles

"Then I saw an angel standing in the sun; and he cried with a loud voice, saying to all the birds that fly in the midst of heaven, 'Come and gather together for the supper of the great God, that you may eat the flesh of kings, the flesh of captains, the flesh of mighty men.'"
(Revelation 19:17-18a)

Eagles are hunters. They, and other birds of prey, would clearly be analogous to warrior angels. Many passages in Scripture show angels either prepared for battle, sword in hand, or actually fighting against the enemies of God.

At the Day of the Lord, we know that Jesus will return with an army of angels behind Him. Who will possibly be able to resist their force?

With supernatural strength, the ability to see and travel in other dimensions, the ability to attack from a place in invisibility, and supernatural skill, what person could hope to stand up to an angel in battle and win?

It's about as ridiculous as the thought of a mouse fighting off an eagle.

More specifically, eagles represent the fourth rank of angels called *dominions*. Their Hebrew name is the *Hashmallim*. Dominions are powerful angels that rule entire nations and direct lower ranks of angels.

I do not think it's a coincidence that 26 modern nations use the eagle as their national symbol, including the United States, Germany, Mexico, Russia, Iraq, Indonesia, and Austria. The eagle was also a symbol used by ancient Egypt, the Persian Empire, the Roman Empire, the Byzantine Empire, the Holy Roman Empire, the Ottoman Turks, Napoleon's France, the Austrian Empire, Prussia, and even the Spanish monarchs Isabella & Ferdinand.

Seems pretty clear on this one — eagles symbolize the *dominions*.

Question: *Do we have a correct understanding of just how significant and fierce the spiritual war actually is?*

Doves

"Then the dove came to him in the evening, and behold, a freshly plucked olive leaf was in her mouth; and Noah knew that the waters had receded from the earth." (Proverbs 8:11)

The dove has always been a symbol of peace. This beautiful bird was the last bird Noah sent from the ark in search of land before they dared disembark. The dove's return with an olive branch in its mouth has signified peace ever since. Peace with God, a peace that promises future blessing for men, and Christians are aware of the symbol inherent in the olive branch.

The olive tree is a scriptural symbol for God's people (the church), and God is showing how He will bring peace and blessing to the earth through the establishment of a people dedicated to Him.

We also see the dove descending upon Jesus at His baptism, and Matthew identifies the dove as a symbol for the Holy Spirit.

Which then throws a great big wrench in the works.

How can we interpret the dove as the Holy Spirit in one place, as "peace" in another, and yet insist that all other birds represent angels?

The key is in the many appearances of "The Angel of the Lord" throughout the Old Testament. Men and women are shown to have a variety of encounters in the Old Testament, some with ordinary angels, but others are with someone referred to as "The Angel of the Lord." Many Christians believe the Angel of the Lord is actually a theophany, a manifestation of God in the Old Testament, or an appearance of Jesus Himself before His incarnation.

The Angel of the Lord always speaks as if He were God Himself and receives worship without protesting, while lesser angels correct anyone who from fear attempts to worship them. The fact that the Angel of the Lord does not correct such worship and says things like "I AM the God of Bethel" (Genesis 31:13) is strong evidence that this Angel is actually God Himself.

Also, it is interesting to notice that every single time the Angel of the Lord appears to someone, it is to declare peace or blessing, a reassurance that God is with His people.

Thus, the dove does perfectly symbolize God Himself, as an Angel, bestowing peace and blessings upon His people, and the dove of Matthew shows God's Spirit descending upon His Son to bless His ministry as it begins.

Lesson: *God primarily desires to communicate blessings and peace.*

Owls

"For the Lord will pass through to strike the Egyptians;
and when He sees the blood on the lintel and on the two doorposts,
the Lord will pass over the door and not allow the destroyer
to come into your houses to strike you." (Exodus 12:23)

Owls are also birds of prey — swift, silent predators who always catch their game. There are a few distinctions between them and other birds of prey that bear mentioning. First, eagles, hawks, and falcons all have similar appearances of body. Their facial shape gives them a firm expression, serious and militant.

With their round head and flattened face, owls look very distinct from other birds of prey. Their feathers are specially designed to be extra silent during flight. They are also nocturnal animals, stalking their prey in the blackness of night.

A few years ago, I went camping in the North Georgia mountains with my son for cub scouts. I remember lying in the tent at midnight, the cool night air turning my breath into misty vapor, listening to the distant, lonely *hooooot* of an owl somewhere up on the mountain. It was a hollow, haunting sound.

Throughout the history of the world, across all cultures, from Native Americans to Africa, to the Middle East and even Rome, owl

sightings were considered bad omens, usually an indication that someone in your family would soon die. They have been traditionally associated with bad luck, sickness and death.

It seems prudent, therefore, to determine the owl to be a symbol of
the angel of death mentioned throughout Scripture.

At first glance, it would seem the vulture or another carrion eater
might be a better fit for that. However, the angel that David saw hovering above Jerusalem while it slaughtered its inhabitants by plague does
not sound like an ugly creature, but a fearsome being determined to
carry out God's instructions. Exodus refers to the angel of death as "the
destroyer."

A vulture does not destroy — it eats that which has already been
destroyed. It eats that which is already dead. An owl, on the other hand,
is a beautiful destroyer, a bringer of death, its prey is taken alive, but
does not survive.

Today, of course, we associate owls with wisdom.

However, this association was only true for Ancient Greece and
later on, western Christian societies. Ancient Greece was a culture
obsessed with wisdom, and Christian societies have access to Wisdom
in ways that other cultures do not.

This reflects the understanding of more advanced thinkers — that
for a being to know when to visit death on whom, knowing the right
time and place for each person's end, requires great wisdom. It requires
extreme wisdom to administer death correctly.

**Owls don't have the ability to swivel their eyes independently of
their head.**

This is why God gave them the ability to turn their heads almost a
full 360 degrees!

I believe this is symbolic of how the angel of death is strictly limited to carry out the orders of God. He is not free to look where he would,
but only where the head directs him. He has no free will, ensuring that
God remains in full control over the giving and taking of life.

Lesson: *No one dies without God's direction.*

Ravens

*"Then he sent out a raven, which kept going to and fro until
the waters had dried up from the earth." (Genesis 8:7)*

Ravens are very intelligent creatures that have been viewed in ancient cultures as omens for both good and bad events. Instinct might lead us to interpret this jet-black bird as the angel of death instead of the owl, but, frankly, the reasons we associate the raven with death is its black color, the fact it eats carrion, and Edgar Allen Poe's famous work, *The Raven*.

Some cultures did view crows and ravens as harbingers of war.

However, in the Bible, we see ravens referenced in a few significant ways, none of which have to do with death, but all of which could be associated with conflict.

Noah sent a raven out from the ark until it found enough dry land it did not return. The dove, I suppose, must be a more sensitive creature because it required not only dry land, but the beginnings of vegetation before it would not return. Symbolically, God sent conflict upon the earth in judgment (raven) before He sent peace and blessings (dove).

Elijah was fed by ravens in the middle of his conflict with Ahab. The birds were *not* sent to say "Peace and blessings upon you from here on out, Elijah," but instead "I will provide for you during the conflict."

Jesus referenced ravens when he said *"Consider the ravens, for they neither sow nor reap, which have neither storehouse nor barn; and God feeds them. Of how much more value are you than the birds?" (Luke 12:24)*

Considering the fact that Jesus said He did not come to bring peace, but a sword, the raven symbolism He employs can be seen as meaning "God will provide for you in the midst of the coming conflict."

According to orthodox Christian theology, angels of the sixth rank are called "powers" or the "authorities." These are also mentioned by Paul in Ephesians 6:12 and they are understood to be warrior angels charged with being the "bearers of conscience" and the "keepers of history."

Every good story must have conflict to be interesting, and thus history is essentially the story of conflict upon the earth over the centuries. Conscience is invoked when one's actions are in conflict with the law of God written upon our hearts.

Given the raven's extremely high intelligence (ranked #5 in the world over all animals), and their biblical association with conflict, I would therefore interpret ravens as being *symbols* for angels of this rank.

Lesson: *God has not promised us lives free of conflict, but He is with us, providing for us in the conflict.*

Songbirds

"And suddenly there was with the angel a multitude of the heavenly host praising God and saying: 'Glory to God in the highest, and on earth peace, goodwill toward men!'"
(Luke 2:13-14)

Bird songs are some of the most beautiful sounds in nature. So, the songbird further confirms our understanding of birds representing angels.

In the Bible, when angels are not portrayed as warriors, or messengers delivering God's Word, we see them worshiping. This appears to be a major function of a number of the angelic ranks — the worship of their Creator.

And angelic worship is perfectly symbolized by the inspiring melodies so faithfully offered each day by songbirds.

While I was a student at Georgia Tech, as I'd walk back to my dorm from class at the end of each day, I remember how often I got to enjoy the sudden cacophonies of song trilled by hundreds of tiny birds flooding the trees that lined the sidewalks. It took me a while to realize they would only do that right before sunset. (I'm not always the most observant of people.)

Yet, it's a common occurrence. Birds erupt into loud choruses right before sunrise each morning, and again right before sunset in the late afternoon or evening. As we've already associated those times of the day with the birth and death of Christ, their chorus in the morning would correspond to the magnificent angelic chorus heard by the shepherds at Christ's birth. And I have *no* doubt there must have also been tremendous worship offered at the Resurrection.

Of course, the daily sunset chorus I enjoyed at college would then correspond to angelic worship at the time of Christ's death. Again, considering angels have been worshiping God since their creation, it's hard to imagine there wouldn't have been heightened surges of worship lifted up as the angels witnessed the faithfulness of Christ on the cross and the culmination of a major part of God' plan of salvation.

Truly, without birdsong, nature would be a much quieter, less pleasant place. Their melodies are so dominant...God clearly intends to show how beautiful to His ears the worship of angels is.

Lesson: *Worship your Creator in Spirit and in truth.*

Hummingbirds

"But the soul of the diligent shall be made rich."
(Proverbs 13:4b)

Hummingbirds are the perfect blend of science and art. My wife has a hummingbird feeder on our front porch and she loves to see the little guys visit to feed. One day after we first put it up, she thought *God, it would be so cool to see a hummingbird* — and in that very instant, one showed up!

They are tiny, yet beautiful examples of God's creation. They're inspiring marvels who seem to defy the laws of aerodynamics, beating their wings between 12 to 100 beats per *second*. They're capable of hovering in place, flying backward, *or even upside down*. Scientists are still trying figure out the specifics of how they fly since it's so different from other birds.

The rapidity at which they beat their wings requires great expenditures of energy, so hummingbirds spend 80% of their time resting. They will even go into a state called *torpor*, which could be considered a kind of hibernation state used to conserve energy. Still, they typically need to eat 7 times *per hour* in order to survive.

Outside of their fascinating beauty, you'll know them for their role in fertilizing flowering plants as they sip nectar from one and then move to another.

Hummingbirds intrigue and stump the best engineers while retaining a beauty sufficient to inspire any artist.

Given the description above, I would tend to identify hummingbirds as symbols for the seventh rank of angels called the *principalities* or *rulers*. This angel rank is referenced by Paul in Ephesians 6:12 and orthodox Christian theology credits them with distributing blessings to the material world and inspiring men and women in the realms of art and science.

As hummingbirds are a magnificent vision of the blending of art and science and are responsible for the germination of new plants, so is this rank of angels responsible for the germination of new ideas among mankind.

And our inspiration does seem to come in spurts, with long periods of rest in between new ideas, much like the feeding pattern of the hummingbird.

Not to mention the scientifically established fact that hummingbirds have a favorite color: red (the color of mankind).

I have to imagine that any angel or group of angels who is charged with inspiring mankind for the purpose of bestowing material blessings would have to love mankind. If they did not, surely they would be often tempted to withhold such inspiration, especially in view of our great stubbornness and sinful nature.

Yet, God does love us, and I suspect so do they. That soaring of the spirit you experience when you see a hummingbird, that joyful inspiration, is symbolic of the inspiration these servants of God bless us with each day.

Lesson: *God is the source of all inspiration, even when He uses angels to perform the work.*

Carrier Pigeons

"Then the angel said to them, 'Do not be afraid, for behold,
I bring you good tidings of great joy which will be to all people.'"
(Luke 2:10)

For centuries, carrier pigeons have been known to travel hundreds and even thousands of miles between two remote locations, bearing messages or medicines attached to their legs. The ability of these birds to never lose their way is astounding. Animal Planet ranks them the eighth most intelligent animal in the world.[32]

Yet, the carrying of the message is our focus here. Few other animals have been used successfully as a messaging service. And the word *angel* means "messenger." This is just one more confirmation that our interpretation of birds as representing angels is correct.

Birds vs. Mammals

So far in our study, we've commented on the following differences between fish and mammals:

Fish	**Mammals**
Breathe Water	Breathe Air
Cold-blooded	Warm-blooded
Scales	Hair

---

[32] Animal Planet, *Top 10 Smartest Animals*, http://animal.discovery.com/wild-animals/10-smartest-animals.htm (accessed on Nov. 18th, 2013).

Eggs	Live Young
Low-level Hearing	Fine-tuned Hearing

In comparison, birds have *a lot* in common with mammals — except for a couple of items.

Birds have feathers instead of hair, which indicates angels have a spiritual maturity that enables them to defy the sinful nature (gravity) and fly. They lay eggs instead of bearing their young live, which implies that angels are not designed for discipleship.

Lastly, birds have highly developed hearing and are able to distinguish things like pitch and tone, but their hearing, while quite well-developed, is still not as finely-tuned as a mammal's. This demonstrates how angels can hear and distinguish God's voice for the purpose of obedience, but they are not able to "hear" the message and repent in the same way we humans are.

Reptiles

Unlike birds, reptiles are very different from mammals. Of the five distinguishing mammalian characteristics, reptiles miss four. The only difference between them and fish is that they breathe air instead of water.

They are cold-blooded, have scales, lay eggs, and they can only hear lower frequencies — usually less than 1.5kHz (Humans can hear up to 20 kHz).

So, drawing from prior interpretations, let's translate:

Reptiles represent creatures that move among us in the Kingdom (breathe air), but are not capable of retaining love within themselves (cold-blooded). This group cannot "hear" God's Word (low hearing range), not for repentance, not even for obedience. The only difference between these beings and non-believers (fish) is the breathing of the Spirit (air) rather than the world (water).

Yet, reptiles are considered by phylogeneticists to be more closely related to birds than they are even to amphibians. In fact, crocodiles are technically more closely related to birds than they are to lizards.

Which brings us to the largest reptiles of all, the dinosaurs, which paleontologists are calling the ancestors of the birds, another major connection. (For anyone who's wondering, I believe Science has fully disproven the Theory of Macroevolution, one species evolving into another, as *not* a viable scientific theory, but that's another book for another time.)

It seems clear that reptiles represent beings that are not in good spiritual standing with God — they are too similar to fish — not to mention their general disagreeable appearance. (Yes, I know there are crocodile and snake lovers out there who would beg to differ and claim such animals are beautiful, but to be truthful, they're fascinated by their engineering, their sleekness of design, not their aesthetic beauty. Reptiles are not beautiful in the same way birds and mammals can be.)

So, there are three options. Reptiles represent either:

1) Backslidden believers
2) Non-believers living among believers in the Kingdom
   – or –
3) Fallen angels.

It's also possible they represent a combination of the three. To decipher this mystery, we'll turn to the Bible for help.

Our first major clue is in Genesis 3 — the serpent in the Garden of Eden. The Hebrew word used for serpent here is *nachash*, which literally means "the shining one," but also means "snake" in Hebrew. *Seraph* is another term for serpent used in the Bible, literally meaning "burning one," and is used to refer both to literal snakes and to the rank of angels that stand closest to God's throne, the *Seraphim*. These angels are described as resembling flying dragons. (I know, weird, right?) Add to that the fact that theologians believe the devil is a fallen *Seraph*.

So, from Genesis to Revelation we see the devil being symbolized or described as a serpent or flying dragon, and the *nachash* of Genesis 3 could have easily been a flying dragon instead of the traditional snake that we think of (We assume when God condemned him to eat dust and crawl on his belly that God was removing legs from a lizard, but it could just as easily be God removing the wings from a flying dragon — which, theologically speaking, would make more sense).

Dragons, of course, are indistinguishable from dinosaurs. We only consider dragons mythological because we've assigned them a different name. Yet, once archaeologists began discovering those enormous bones, it became quite clear that dragons did in fact once roam the earth, and the traditions of lore actually represented a forgotten truth.

The earliest traditions assign wings to these giant lizards and it is very possible this was inspired by visions or accounts of encounters with actual *seraphim*, the angels described in the Bible.

Stepping past all this conjecture, the fact that our enemy is always symbolized in Scripture by a reptile is a very strong argument for the interpretation of reptiles as representing fallen angels.

The strong physical relationship between reptiles and birds, in spite of the initial impression that they are closer to fish, solidifies our interpretation further.

In other words, our spiritual symbolism strongly separates reptiles from angels (birds) and closely identifies them with non-believers (fish), yet their skeletal structure (design) speaks to a common ancestry with the angels (birds).

This is especially true of crocodiles, which are the most dragon-like reptiles we know today, and which have the closest relationship to birds.

Beyond that, who cares? Frankly, I have absolutely no interest in studying demons or fallen angels. I don't want to know anything about them or give them any more attention than Scripture requires.

Perhaps another author will wish to study the symbolism of the details built into the design of reptiles. As for me, I will stick with birds and mammals and fish, thank you very much.

That said, to be exhaustive, we must touch on the various subcategories of reptiles to identify them before moving on.

Crocodiles

Many reptiles have a habit of living near or hiding out in water. Specifically, *fresh* water.

Crocodiles, again the most dragon-like reptile, like to submerge themselves in rivers to wait for prey that might come to the shore to drink.

In the same way, the enemies of God will sometimes camouflage themselves by hiding out within the powerful movements of God (river) to prey on believers. (Think wolves in sheep's clothing.)

Even within the churches where God is moving powerfully, there are people, teachings, and situations with which we must take much care. Beware of hidden dangers that are not part of the movement, but hiding out in the movement.

Lesson: *Jesus warned us of wolves within the church. They are real, so take heed.*

Snakes

*"Serpents, brood of vipers! How can you escape
the condemnation of hell?" (Matthew 23:33)*

Jesus called the Pharisees serpents, as did John the Baptist.
The allusion to the serpent of the Garden of Eden had to be
intentional.

Snakes consume small rodents, bird eggs, other reptiles or amphibians. Some are venomous, though most are not. All snakes either poison their prey or they crush it.

The Pharisees are typological representatives of corrupt or evil religious leaders. In John 8, Jesus says the father of the Pharisees is the devil. Symbolically, when He calls them vipers, He is calling them models of that now-wingless, formerly winged, dragon-like, fallen *seraph* angel. Chips off the old rebellious block.

Also, by calling them vipers, He is calling them poisonous, and false religious leaders do inject poison into their followers. They bite into the sheep of their fold with paralyzing or fatal false teaching. Or they slowly crush them. Or both.

Vipers have heat-sensing pits on the sides of their head. These pits help them identify their prey and guide their strike.

In the same way, false religious teachers will attack those non-prominent believers (rodents) that are showing the most love (heat) in their local church body.

I have seen this happen personally. I once served on the leadership of a smaller church, and we were approached by a charismatic pastor who said he and his much larger church would like to partner with us to help us grow. In the beginning, we were all very excited.

But then, one by one, he began chasing off members of the original congregation, but left in place any new attenders that began visiting after his arrival. He first attacked those members of our church who were the most caring among us, the most productive, spiritually speaking. Through guile and slyness, he attacked anyone who showed leadership potential and might pose a threat to his leadership.

These brothers and sisters in Christ were too humble to stay and defend themselves, so they simply moved on, though they were wounded. I was too inexperienced at the time, and his tactics took some of us by such surprise that our opposition was crippled and came too late.

Just as snakes move in sideways, slithering ways that are foreign to mammals, this man stabbed a number of our strongest members with venomous false rumors, sometimes using others to spread and magnify the lie. Once the strongest of his opposition was gone, he slowly crushed the life out of the remaining members of the original congregation. By the time his methods finally became glaringly obvious, it was too late. In the end, he gained control of an urban property worth several million dollars without paying a penny for it.

Thankfully, in all my years in ministry, in all the churches I've attended, I've only run across such a man one time. Just as it's rare to come across a snake in the woods, I am happy that this type of leader is also very infrequent.

Still, every now and then, you will stumble upon a snake. When you do...just run the other way. Unless, of course, you're ready to engage in mortal battle.

Lesson: *Look out for snakes.*

Turtles

Okay...so I really resisted giving turtles a negative interpretation. After all, some of them are so cute!

Yet, a negative interpretation for reptiles as a category requires turtles to be included in that. Still, I know how people love turtles.

Regardless, turtles are clearly cold-blooded, which symbolizes a type of person/being that does not retain God's love within himself. Clearly non-believers.

Other distinguishing characteristics of a turtle from other reptiles are their slow-moving ways and hard shells.

Instinctively, when studying turtles, I found myself reminded of a certain kind of person that I have encountered from time to time. I'll call him the "mushy-minded theologian." Or another possible name could be the "introverted elitist."

Today, we imagine wisdom behind the eyes of a turtle, probably because their expression seems so stern and detached.

Yet, truly turtles deserve no special assignation of wisdom. I've seen plenty of them squished on the highway. If they were actually so wise, like the owl, you'd think they'd know better. I mean, how wise are you if you don't realize you're too slow to cross a freeway? Unless they're secretly a bunch of adrenaline-junkie risk-takers...

No, turtles represent those who appear wise, slow and deliberative in their thinking, yet are not. Well, they *are* slow and deliberative in their thinking, *just not wise.*

Imagine your typical erudite theologian inhabiting the halls of your favorite Ivy League school. You know, the kind the Discovery Channel usually taps for its Easter specials, the "theologian" who rejects the Bible as the authoritative Word of God, teaching that it only holds an advisory role in a believer's life and is no greater than other religious works.

These men and women will give a scholarly appearance when prompted for their opinion on a matter, leaning back and folding their hands with a sigh, employing any number of technical terms for simple concepts to cloud the fact that their conclusion cannot hold up under the weight of scrutiny or the application of logic. Yet, they sincerely believe their convoluted assessments hold water.

Their stubborn streak is a mile wide — and this is symbolized by the turtle's hard shell. As a turtle cannot hear with the depth of a mammal, so the mushy-minded theologian is unable to "hear" God's voice through His Word, even though many of them *study it for a living.* Its truest sounds escape their ears for lack of ability.

Yet, they are convinced of their own intellectual superiority, and this "hardness" of spirit is seemingly impenetrable. Their pride is wrapped around their pronounced opinions, their scholarly teachings, and when confronted, they just withdraw into their shell rather than face it.

They are unable to consider a different way of thinking because they view all fervent followers of Christ as inferior. They immediately hold no respect for someone who considers God's Word authoritative. If touched, they might snap at you (and their beaks are sharp), but if confronted by something threatening (like strong logic), they simply withdraw inside the shell of their pride and position and refuse to face it.

John Crossan of the Jesus Seminar comes to mind.

And, of course, there are sea turtles, which would be similar elitist professors operating in the World rather than the Kingdom.

In ancient cultures across the globe, turtles were worshiped and assigned a primary place in mythology. The common thread of the various legends involved a giant turtle supporting the world on its back like a reptilian Atlas, or they viewed the turtle's shell as a symbol for heaven meeting earth. In this second type of myth, the curved upper portion of the shell symbolized the sky (heaven) and the flat underside represented earth. Non-Christians interpreted this myth to mean that the way to reach heaven is through the earth.

Which, of course, is *anti-gospel*. The Good News of Jesus Christ is that the way to Heaven originates from Heaven.

Perhaps it was some subconscious instinct that caused early Christians to use turtles as symbols for evil forces in war. The enlightened Greeks and Romans didn't have much better opinions — some Romans describing them as loathsome creatures, and the Greeks giving them a name that means "citizen of hell."

The negative connotation given the turtles back then was apparently due to the turtle's propensity to live in mire or swampy areas, oblivious of the filth in which they swam.

These opposing views match perfectly with our interpretation.

The false theologian is a force for evil in the constant spiritual war battled across the globe, and Christians would view them that way naturally.

On the other hand, the unredeemed of the world always celebrate their self-proclaimed scholars, ascribing so much credibility to what they say, that they tend to rest their entire worldview upon the pronouncements of their favorite "turtles." (Like pagan myths where the earth rests on the back of the turtle.)

Regardless, while the symbolism of the turtle seems to have come full circle, let's not blame the cute little guys for what they're meant to represent. They're okay to have for pets.

Lesson: *Ignore any teacher or "scholar" who denies the authority of God's Word.*

Conclusions on Reptiles

I acknowledge that our analysis of reptiles has mixed results, alternately identifying some with fallen angels and others with false believers influenced by the forces of evil. Take note that none of these represent nominal Christians that attend church regularly but have not experienced a personal conversion to become a follower of Christ.

No, snakes and turtles represent fake believers who deceive and lead astray. They appear to be believers because they seem to breathe the same Spirit we do, meaning they live in the Kingdom, but nothing else about them is like mammals. Nothing else about them is like a real believer.

Jesus told the Pharisees that their father was the devil, but He never said this about the unsaved flocking to hear His teaching and receive His healing. This is the distinction between snakes and fish.

Our conflict lies in the fact that we interpret crocodiles to symbolize the supernatural, yet snakes the natural. Maybe a resolution would be that *all* reptiles represent false believers who are children of the original, invisible reptile, the fallen dragon. Or perhaps we have already assessed it accurately. I'll let you decide.

Amphibians

*"And I saw three unclean spirits like frogs coming out of the mouth of
the dragon, out of the mouth of the beast, and out of
the mouth of the false prophet."*
(Revelation 16:13)

So, then who in the world do amphibians symbolize?

On the surface, our initial instinct is to strongly associate them with reptiles, which is a big hint. However, a little scientific study reveals that there are actually stark differences between reptiles and amphibians.

Amphibians begin their lives like fish, born in the water from eggs that were laid in the water. They breathe water through gills until they've developed their lungs and legs, at which point they emerge onto land and lose their gills.

You know, like tadpoles.

After reaching adulthood, they remain close to water and still spend much of their time in it, but they now breathe air through lungs and live on land.

Reptiles do none of that. They are born from eggs, but on land, and they experience no transforming process like amphibians.

So far, we have interpreted air-breathing lungs as being symbolic of being indwelled by the Holy Spirit, and we have clearly identified oxygen/air as being a symbol for the Spirit. However, perhaps we need to get a little more specific with our interpretation of air-breathing lungs. Perhaps lungs or gills more specifically symbolize the realm to which someone belongs. On its most basic level, what is breathed symbolizes the domain.

This only makes sense given our other interpretations. Mammals (believers) and birds (angels) belong to the heavenly realm, and fish (non-believers) belong to the world.

Reptiles (fallen angels, false prophets, false teachers) are air-breathers, which would simply point to the fact that their domain is the

Kingdom instead of the world, which fallen angels are/were, and false religious leaders and teachers appear to be.

Therefore, amphibians would have to represent people who originate in the world (seas) and undergo a transformation of sorts as they move to the Kingdom (land). Since they originate in the World, they cannot be fallen angels, because angels originate in the heavenly realm.

Amphibians represent false Christians, i.e. non-believers who have emerged from the World (water) and put on a moral appearance to live as if they were part of the Kingdom (land), but underneath they are the same creature.

Scripture says that when we come to Christ, we are born again, made a *new creation*. A comparison to this would be like seeing a fish pulled from the water and killed, which somehow provokes the birth of a mammal on the beach. No connection between the two. After the fish has been fished, he dies. Just as our old selves die to sin. The new birth as a spiritual "mammal" follows, and we become alive to Christ.

Amphibian believers are *not* a new creation. Yet, in a sense, they *have* changed, of course. They no longer appear worldly, but have an appearance of godliness. Yet, there was no new birth. Instead, in their own power, they have transformed themselves to reflect the *morals* of someone who lives in the Kingdom so they can fit in the Kingdom (land), but they do not bear the *fruit of the Spirit*, i.e. show the selfless, Spirit-inspired love that a follower of Christ shows (warm-blooded). They have never died to sin, so they have never become alive to Christ.

Thus, in the Book of Revelation, the symbolic frogs that emerge from the mouths of the dragon, the beast, and the false prophet (Rev. 16:13) could be seen as a false spiritual revival coming from their words.

Paul also seems to describe a land overrun by amphibian believers in the end times. In 2 Timothy, he says *"that in the last days perilous times will come: For men will be lovers of themselves...having a form of godliness but denying its power...for of this sort are those who creep into households..."*

Furthermore, Revelation 16:13 describes the frogs as representing "unclean spirits," which would also match our interpretation that a frog symbolizes a nominal Christian who is Christian in name only and has not been transformed by the saving work of Christ. Their spirits are not alive, their spirits have not been cleansed by the Blood of Christ.

Jim has been a salesman at his local car dealership for years, and he's one of the best. When he was first starting out, he noticed that many of the dealership's customers, being in a rural area, were regular church attenders.

He also noticed that many of them would enter the dealership skeptical of its salesman, ready for someone to try to pull a fast one on them. When one particularly friendly customer invited him to attend the town's main church one Sunday, he decided to go along.

He soon began attending more regularly, and it wasn't long before many of the church-going customers sought *him* out instead of the other salesman since they knew him. They trusted a man who they saw next to them in the pew more than they did a stranger, and Jim's growing commissions reflected that.

He wasn't about to end a good thing, so he did his best to fit in. Plus, he'd made a lot of new friends and liked hanging out with them. He didn't want to lose those friendships either.

Though, that didn't mean he didn't pad his sales sheets sometimes to wring a little more commission out of the dealership or bad mouth an associate to make sure a customer stuck with him. It also didn't mean he didn't go out on the lake and get drunk with his worldly friends some weekends.

If he was ever forced to choose between the two lifestyles, he wasn't sure on which side he would actually land. He liked his church friends, but there was still something about them that he didn't feel comfortable with...

Amphibians lay their eggs in water, and their eggs resemble fish eggs.

This is in contrast to reptiles, who lay theirs in nests on land. Interpretation: Spiritual amphibians make their disciples in the World, not in the Kingdom. They attend church on Sunday, but lose that form of godliness at work on Monday. Thus, they influence their co-workers in worldly ways. In the case of Jim, he may influence a younger salesman to imitate his tactics, but he won't be discipling new Christians at church.

In contrast, false religious leaders and teachers (reptiles) make their nasty disciples within the church.

For the most part, **amphibians have four legs and *walk* or *hop* across the land,** but scientists typically describe the movement of reptiles as *crawling* along their bellies, even with regard to crocodiles and turtles.

This could be interpreted to mean that the average false believer (frog) acts and looks a lot more like a true believer (mammal), but the average false religious *leader* acts and looks a lot more like their father, the slithering serpent.

Frogs are cold blooded.

Which means "amphibious" non-believers don't have the super-natural ability to retain love within themselves, but can only be filled with as much love (heat) as is available in the society around them.

Frogs have a very low hearing range.

This shows how nominal Christians do not have the ability to obey (hear) God's Word like actual believers, even though they are living in the Kingdom.

Frogs have no scales.

Nor do they have hair. Instead, they have a thin, delicate, and highly absorbent skin. In fact, a significant amount of an amphibian's breathing is done through its skin (some species do *all* their breathing through their skin). This is symbolic of the fact that, like fish, these non-believing inhabitants of the Kingdom rely on breathing the Spirit's influence from their surrounding environment rather than being fully indwelled by Him.

(You don't believe the Spirit can fill non-believers? Plenty of scriptural examples exist saying He does. Matthew 7:22-23 comes to mind: *"Many will say to Me in that day, 'Lord, Lord, have we not prophesied in Your name, cast out demons in Your name, and done many wonders in Your name?' And then I will declare to them, 'I never knew you; depart from Me, you who practice lawlessness!'"*)

The delicate skin of a frog is symbolic of how a false Christian has no spiritual maturity. No hair to symbolize Godly maturity. No scales either, to symbolize the worldly, cynical maturity of non-believers.

This is because nominal Christians have embraced a feel-good form of Christianity. They do it for social reasons, or because it seems like a good idea, or because they intellectually sympathize, but they have not experienced a heart-felt repentance of sin and passionate submission to God's will. So, they never grow spiritually mature (hair), but they lose the healthy cynicism generated by the world (scales).

They believe it when Christ said He came to give life abundantly, but they don't have access to the supernatural power that actually produces that abundant life in them, empowering them to overcome the world. So, they lose the cynicism that protected them, leaving themselves vulnerable — just as frogs are easily poisoned by simply exposing their skin to something toxic.

Nominal believers don't have the ability to discern falsehood or spiritual danger and defend against it like a believer does. They are easily poisoned.

Lesson: *Make sure you have truly submitted to Jesus Christ as Lord and Savior.*

INSECTS

"Are they not all ministering spirits sent forth to minister for those who will inherit salvation?" (Hebrews 1:14)

Insects are a conundrum.

We seem to have covered all the spiritual categories already...so what could they possibly represent?

Well, we'll begin as we have with every other biological group so far: Identify their basic characteristics and see if anything jumps out.

Taking a good hard look at the little buggers, insects just seem *foreign*. We feel a certain affinity for other animals, identifying with them, but insects are a whole other matter.

We do *not* identify with insects (the fanatical entomologist notwithstanding). Perhaps because they don't seem to have any personality? Sure, fish don't show much personality either, but insects act like emotionless drones.

Step out onto your back porch and look around. You won't immediately notice the insects — unless one happens to fly right past your face. You see the sky, the trees, maybe a bird or squirrel, but you don't notice the insects unless you *look* for them.

Their world is normally invisible to us. Yet, if I gave you a special set of insect-locating goggles, you'd probably be shocked by the hundreds of thousands of blips suddenly showing up in your field of vision.

So, they are foreign and invisible.

Many have wings, though some don't. Like hummingbirds, numerous species serve by pollinating plants. Others help aerate the soil so plants can grow better. Still others aid in decomposition. Yet, many others are nothing more than pests who consume crops to the farmer's great frustration.

I feel a certain hesitancy with assigning absoluteness to an interpretation of insects — probably because we have so little knowledge of the spiritual realm — yet, it only seems natural to return to the themes we discussed concerning birds and reptiles.

First off, insects are cold-blooded (yes, they have blood, it's just not red) and they lay eggs, both of which clearly identify them as not being believers. They may walk on water in some cases, but they don't live *in* water, and they breathe air, both of which indicate they are not of the "world," but of the spiritual realm.

Their lack of hair[33], feathers, or scales indicates they have no spiritual maturity, yet strangely, the presence of wings indicates they are not subject to the sinful nature.

We are starting to get the picture of angelic "drones," beings who serve the Kingdom with little or no self-will, yet serve it in indispensable ways (i.e. pollination, aeration, etc.)

There is also a dual nature among insects that seems conflicting — the blessing of bees vs. the pest of the boll weevil. The beauty of butterflies as opposed to the revulsion of cockroaches.

The parallels between them and birds and reptiles are strong, some insects matching aspects of birds, others reptiles. The main difference, of course, is size. Insects are just smaller, and as we've already pointed out, they tend to remain invisible to us under most circumstances unless we're searching for them.

Size, we've said, is a symbol of prominence. Therefore, insects should represent spiritual beings, angels or fallen angels, or even ranks we're unaware of, workers of the Kingdom who are less prominent than those angel ranks represented by birds.

Most species of insects do fly, which solidifies their parallel to birds.

Most unusual though is their hearing. Insects can hear both extremely high frequencies as well as ultra-low frequencies. They do not have the three-ear-bone system of mammals — theirs is much simpler. Yet, they can hear frequencies that no other creatures on earth can hear. Not even whales or bats.

---

[33] Many insects have "hair-like" structures called setae or chaetae. These are not hair follicles, but unicellular outgrowths from their exoskeletons. http://en.wikipedia.org/wiki/Setae (accessed on October 14th, 2013).

To summarize the key characteristics of insects, we have described non-prominent spiritual beings, servants of God who are not subject to the sinful nature, have no spiritual maturity, yet are finely attuned to hear God's voice. Such beings would be designed for pure, unwavering obedience to God.

Do such beings exist? Perhaps we have evidence of them in 1 Kings 22:

> *"And the Lord said, 'Who will persuade Ahab to go up, that he may fall at Ramoth Gilead?' So one spoke in this manner, and another spoke in that manner. Then a spirit came forward and stood before the Lord, and said, 'I will persuade him.' The Lord said to him, 'In what way?' So he said, 'I will go out and be a lying spirit in the mouth of all his prophets.' And the Lord said, 'You shall persuade him, and also prevail. Go out and do so.'" (1 Kings 22:20-22)*

I can't help but notice that throughout the Old Testament, including in the same book of Kings, angels are always called angels (1 Kings 19:7), but in the passage above "a spirit" is referenced, a spirit who becomes a "lying spirit," which is a role we've never seen *angels* performing before.

There is a similar use in 1 Samuel:

> *"But the Spirit of the Lord departed from Saul, and a distressing spirit from the Lord troubled him." (1 Samuel 16:14)*

Again, the book of Samuel also uses the term "angel" elsewhere for those who are clearly angels (2 Samuel 24:16). Psalms 103 and 104 have a curious distinction in their refrains:

> *"Who makes His angels spirits,
> His ministers a flame of fire." (Psalm 104:4)*

"Bless the Lord, all you His hosts,
You ministers of His, who do His pleasure." (Psalm 103:21)

Notice that angels and ministers are two different terms used in two different Psalms. Perhaps it's because the word "angel" is referring to the greater ranks and "ministers" is referring to lesser ministering spirits, which might be symbolized in Creation by insects?

I have no evidence for that other than the verses above and the fact that all of our other interpretations so far have clearly matched the teachings of Scripture. In fact, perhaps this ambiguity with regard to insects now further proves our other interpretations to be right since it demonstrates we are not stretching the symbols, grasping to make everything fit.

Insects do represent something, of that I am sure, I just don't think we have personal experience or Scriptural revelation to understand exactly what.

Regardless, there are a number of things about insects we should consider.

First, insects make up the large majority of the species of the world.

This would imply that if we are right about the existence of God's "worker bees," then they are super-numerous. More than we can probably imagine.

Second, the benefit of insects is primarily related to fertility.

Insects are viewed as beneficial with regards to pollination, aeration of soil, and decomposition, all of which deal with keeping the land fertile. This would indicate these beings are primarily charged by God with keeping the Kingdom fertile. *"Are they not all ministering spirits sent forth to minister for those who will inherit salvation?" (Hebrews 1:14)*

Third, insects consume the leaves of plants.

Since we have interpreted leaves to represent the maturity of a believer, then this would symbolize these servants of God as being dependent on the maturity of believers. This could explain spiritual warfare, why God responds when believers grow in maturity and turn to Him in humble prayer. Not that He couldn't and doesn't act without that, but we all know He chooses not to act many times until we turn and repent, or choose to have faith.

It could be that He has determined these spirits responsible for fertility should be dependent on the maturity of believers to succeed. Sure, I know it's speculation, but it's a thought.

Fourth, we are not truly revolted by *most* insects.

Yes, insects seem foreign — we don't feel a particular affection for them — but we're not revolted by wasps or ants. We may fear or avoid them because they sting, or bite, or get in our food, but we're not disgusted by them. We're not really disgusted by beetles either. Grasshoppers may give us the creeps, but only the ladies who are afraid they'll jump in their hair.

We even feel love for some, like dragonflies, or lightning bugs, or those cute little ladybugs. We're fascinated by others, like the praying mantis.

We don't like flies and consider them dirty (as we should), but this is similar to our feelings about vultures, which are birds.

We absolutely hate mosquitos because they hurt, they suck our blood, and they give us disease, but could they not be comparable to the lying spirit God sent to infect Zedekiah with deception? (1 Kings 22:24)

We *are* truly revolted by cockroaches, however, but more on that in a little bit.

There are at least thirty-three different biological *orders* of insects, but *the large majority of insect species fall into just four of those orders.* The rest of the orders only contain a smattering of species.

The first of the main groupings of insects is the *Coleoptera,* otherwise known as beetles. This group accounts for 25% of *all animal species on earth* and 40% of all insect species! So, there are a *lot* of different kinds of beetles.

The other major groupings are the *Diptera,* which are all the various kinds of flies, the *Hymenoptera,* which are bees, wasps, and ants, and the *Lepidoptera*, which you would know as butterflies and moths. Again, the primary function of all four of these orders is to make the earth more fertile.

Lesson: *God's spiritual realm is more complex than we understand.*

Locusts

Well, now that we've said that, locusts and grasshoppers are not part of the "big four," and they're not responsible for increased fertility. They belong to a smaller order called the *orthoptera*, and they *eat* plants, not help them.

All grasshoppers and crickets consume plants, but let us focus on the locust here since that is the biblical symbol we are most familiar with.

"Then the LORD said to Moses, 'Stretch out your hand over the land of Egypt for the locusts, that they may come upon the land of Egypt, and eat every herb of the land...'" (Exodus 10:12a)

Farmers hate them. Under the right conditions, locusts can reproduce very quickly and develop into huge swarms that can consume every plant within hundreds of square miles in just days.

In the Bible, locusts are associated with judgment. Massive clouds of swirling dark bodies moving in to block the sun and descending upon the farmer's field meant certain doom.

Naturally speaking, locusts would represent spirit-beings that consume the production of the Kingdom.

So, is it possible that God would create such spirit-beings for the purpose of consuming people's production in judgment? I think the answer is a most definite yes.

As a businessman, I can assure you that I feel the effects of spiritual "grasshoppers" all the time. No matter how hard you work to protect your production, it seems like there are always little things nibbling away at it.

I believe this is probably a healthy process, as irritating as it may be, because it encourages continual growth and hard work. This normal everyday occurrence is comparable to the occasional grasshopper and cricket nibbling on the leaves of the forest. They don't kill the trees or plants, they just encourage the tree to keep making new leaves. It is a stimulator of maturity (leaves).

Locusts, however, arrive in such massive swarms, they don't encourage new growth. They just kill and destroy. They denude the land and leave it barren. They are a true judgment, a removal of fertility — and thankfully, they are infrequent.

A farmer could be compared to a pastor trying to produce a harvest in his fields. When the judgment arrives, he watches helplessly as the spiritual "locusts" block out the truth (light) of the love (warmth) of Christ (sun) and strip his flock of their maturity (leaves).

It's hard to abide in faith, to retain maturity, when one feels they are under supernatural judgment from God Himself.

Yet, such a pastor should realize that the locusts did not target his field alone. He and his flock were simply victims of living in the larger land.

Locusts don't target individuals, they target entire regions. The individual suffers for corporate sin.

We saw this occur over and over again in Israel as described in the Book of Judges. While Israel in general became faithless and required a national judgment, there was always a faithful remnant among them. Yet, that did not save the faithful from suffering economic and physical oppression along with their brethren under the Midianites, the Philistines, and others.

The United States as well may be due to suffer such a judgment soon. Given the fact the many Americans have switched their worship from God Almighty to a tiny green paper god that can be incinerated with a lighter, an economic locust judgment seems most fitting.

Truly, a spiritual locust swarm would be as devastating as a physical one. To overcome, one must retain their faith and spiritual maturity in spite of it.

The good news with regards to locusts is the promise of Joel 2:25-26: *"So I will restore to you the years that the swarming locust has eaten...You shall eat in plenty and be satisfied..."*

Lesson: *Work to lead your culture to repentance so you don't suffer under judgment with them.*

Cockroaches

"And as you go, preach, saying, 'The kingdom of heaven is at hand.' Heal the sick...cast out demons." (Matthew 10:7-8)

"For everyone practicing evil hates the light and does not come to the light, lest his deeds should be exposed." (John 3:20)

Interestingly, cockroaches are *not* part of the beetle order. They're a distinct order unto themselves. Since we naturally seem to hate them so much, I would interpret that to mean that there are "orders" of these spirits that have fallen from God's grace and that the cockroach represents one of these orders. Perhaps there is a difference between demons (fallen spirits) and fallen angels?

Not only have cockroaches taken on a disgusting appearance, but unlike most other insects, they have very little hearing ability. This is further symbolic confirmation because this represents an inability to hear and obey God.

They also *choose* not to fly — most cockroaches do have wings and can fly — but when threatened, they don't use them. Instead, they scamper away. This represents one of God's spirit being's willful decision to make itself subject to the sinful nature.

Anyway, next time you see a cockroach, now you have double reason to squash it.

Bees, Wasps, & Ants

These are the *Hymenoptera*, representing warrior/worker spirits that are highly organized, armed with weapons, and go about God's work very efficiently. God's armies must be huge.

Butterflies

Butterflies are absolutely beautiful, which is why so many people like to study and collect them. Their wing patterns are so unique and fascinating, I cannot refrain from drawing one more parallel to angels and the beauty we understand them to have.

Butterflies and moths, which can also be beautiful, are charged with fertility. Thus, these *Lepidoptera* could possibly represent spirit beings who are responsible not only for keeping the Kingdom fertile, but for inspiring its beauty.

Final Note on Insects

Of course, we've only touched on the basics of insects. There is so much specified knowledge with regards to the inexhaustible variety of species, the interpretations could conceivably go on and on.

However, given our operating theory that these represent ranks of spirits unknown to us, going into any further detail would be tricky. I really hate to delve into pure speculation (though some may think that's all I've been doing in this book). I'd rather stick with interpretations that can be confirmed by Scripture.

COLORS

In this book, we began with the fundamentals and slowly worked our way into more and more complexity, but now it's time to swing around full circle and wrap things up with a discussion of the most basic of the basics: Color.

We know light represents truth, and that in physics, white light is the sum of all the colors of the rainbow. Therefore, the different colors we can see symbolize individual truths that together make up the Greater Truth.

Blue

"You shall make a veil woven of blue, purple, and scarlet thread, and fine woven linen. It shall be woven with an artistic design of cherubim."
(Exodus 26:31)

Thankfully, the Bible pretty much gives us the answer on this one: *Blue is the divine color.*

Blue represents God symbolically. All ancient peoples had this association for the color blue, which we mentioned back in the section on the sky.

This is the reason God commanded the veil to be made with those three colors: blue, purple, and red. The colors of the veil are also a symbolic message and the blue part of the cloth signifies God.

We not only see the color of the sky as relating to God, but also the color of water (God's power). Truthfully, neither the sky, nor water have a "color." If you look at a small amount of either, they seem invisible, transparent. Yet, if you step back and take in the sky or a lake as a whole, you see God's color.

In the same way, up close and in small doses, we can miss God's presence or power, but when we step back and take in the whole tapestry of events, we see Him as the truth of a matter (light) reflects off His presence and actions to reveal His nature.

You may have never thought about it, but colors convey feelings. They are not flexible things that artists can use to portray whatever mood they wish.

For example, if an artist wants to paint a canvas that creates a mood of sadness, they simply cannot choose to dominate their work with scarlet red or electric yellow. When someone is sad, we say they are "blue" for a reason.

Blue feels cool and refreshing.

I believe God chose this color to represent His nature because He is our refuge. He wants us to view Him as our refresher, our Redeemer from the burning trials of our lives. When you are parched, dying for a drink, do you wish for a red-hot cup of tea, or a cool, blue glass of water?

Through this color, God speaks of His peace, His ability to give Life, His refreshment for all. Blue is a color of safety and healing.

Blue also speaks of sadness, and I think it speaks of God's sadness over our plight here on earth, our hardships and struggles with sin, our separation from Him. The color blue seems to speak simultaneously of God's heart of compassion for us as well as His being the source of our solution.

It's also refreshing to know that surveys show the most popular color in the world is blue.

Lesson: *Seek refreshment in God.*

Purple

"And they clothed Him with purple;
and they twisted a crown of thorns, put it on His head..."
(Mark 15:17)

Purple is the color of kings. This is a well-known fact of the ancient world, that royalty would wear purple robes as a statement of their position. Wealthy families would sometimes too.

Scholars often cite the rarity and expense of purple dye as the reason for this, but the truth is more ancient. Blue is the divine color and red is the color of man. Mix them, and you get purple.

The king is viewed as above the rest of the masses, he is the divine-man, even sometimes called that literally. Thus, purple was the chosen color of kings.

Lesson: *Bow before Christ as your King.*

Red

" 'Come now, and let us reason together,' Says the LORD,
'Though your sins are like scarlet, They shall be as white as snow;
Though they are red like crimson, They shall be as wool.'"
(Isaiah 1:18)

Red is the color of man, and again the Bible doesn't leave any interpretative room on this one. The name Adam, the name God gave the first man, means *man* or *mankind* in Hebrew. It comes from other Hebrew words, namely *adom*, which means "red," *adamah*, which means "earth," and *dam*, which means "blood."

God made man from the earth, and according to tradition, unlike animals, you could see the blood through man's skin. The association of man with red is strong.

These three colors (blue, purple, and scarlet) complete the picture God painted on the veil in the temple separating the Holy of Holies from the rest of the temple.

The veil is a chromatic symbol of the person Jesus Christ, God (blue) coming in the form of a man (red), who is the King of Kings (purple), the only true God-King who has ever been. And at the moment of Christ's death on the cross, the veil tore in half, starting at the top (God's end) and ending with the bottom (man's end). I have to imagine the veil was blue at the top, red at the bottom, and purple in the middle.

Think red and you think of fire, hot, bloody, bold, and brash. The emotions it provokes are the reason that brothels around the world have adopted it as their symbol (Red-light districts). When you see a red lightbulb glowing outside a door, what feelings do you encounter? Do you get a sense of clean refreshment, or dark suspicion? Does it give you the sense that something good is going on behind that door, or something more carnal?

Sin, sexuality, and murder are all commonly represented by the color red. Which makes perfect sense — without God, man is helpless before his sin.

We'd be remiss not to note that the universal color of communist and socialist movements around the world is red. These movements purport to be "movements of the people," and indeed these philosophies leapt from the mind of man and not God. It is the sinful, economic religion of anarchists the world over, born of envy, founded in blood. Red is certainly the most appropriate color for their flags and they seem only too happy to self-proclaim it.

Red also provokes thoughts of "hot" and "fire," and to cool off, we immediately think of a need for something blue. Man's salvation from fire is God.

Lesson: *Seek God to overcome sin.*

Yellow

"And you shall know the truth, and the truth shall make you free."
(John 8:32)

The sun gives us our primary hint for the color yellow. We already discussed in the section on the sun *why* the sun looks yellow. Regardless, as the source of all our light, it symbolizes Jesus as the source of God's Truth in our world.

This means yellow is the color of God's Truth.

The feeling yellow gives us is that of happiness. It feels bright and energetic, full of light, and that is what it speaks of: Light.

God's Truth does bring happiness. It breaks our chains. It breaks through the dimmest of days and renews our energy. It electrifies us.

Lesson: *Seek God for energy and renewed strength.*

Green

"...I have come that they may have life,
and that they may have it more abundantly."
(John 10:10b)

Now that we have identified all the primary colors, the rest becomes easy. Green is a combo of blue and yellow. That would symbolize a combination of God and His Truth. What does that produce?

Life.

Yes, green is the color of the *life that God produces*, and all of nature confirms this interpretation.

Haven't you ever wondered why almost every single plant on the face of the earth is green?

I have.

I mean, if you look out your window through most of the year, you're going to see a wide and inexhaustible variety of shades of green. Green must be God's favorite color since He chose to paint everything with it.

In fact, scientifically speaking, the green color of trees is produced by chlorophyll, which is the chemical that allows a tree to receive energy from sunlight (God's Truth), and chlorophyll would not be there without the presence of water (God's power). So, even in the science, it's blue mixing with yellow to form green.

So, what feelings does the color green provoke in us? It seems to evoke a sense of cool vibrancy. Green feels alive, yet in a cool, non-burning way. It feels like thriving life.

Lesson: *Seek God to live.*

Orange

*"There is a way that seems right to a man,
But its end is the way of death."
(Proverbs 14:12)*

The personality of the color orange is to be garish. It's bright and bold and feels energetic, but in a slightly jarring way, certainly more muted from the bright energy we get from yellow.

If we continue to follow our symbolism thus far, then as orange is a combination of yellow and red, it would represent a combination of man with God's Truth. This means orange symbolizes *man's perversion of God's Truth*.

Perhaps we might call it man's truth. In fact, man's truth can give a certain energy. Self-help books might help a little. But in the end, there is something jarring about it, something not quite right. It is not the pure truth.

Lesson: *Seek the pure, unadulterated truth of God.*

Black

"Then Jesus spoke to them again, saying, 'I am the light of the world. He who follows Me shall not walk in darkness, but have the light of life.'" (John 8:12)

The color black represents darkness, which in turn represents lies and deception. We've already gone into so much discussion on darkness, we really don't need to go over it again.

But, a word of warning for those who might be inclined to interpret the colors of black and white into discussions of racism. *There are no people on earth with truly black or white skin, only varying shades between pink and brown.*

Lesson: *Walk in the Light with Christ.*

White

"After these things I looked, and behold, a great multitude which no one could number…standing before the throne and before the Lamb, clothed with white robes…" (Revelation 7:9)

"But when the king came in to see the guests, he saw a man there who did not have on a wedding garment. So he said to him, 'Friend, how did you come in here without a wedding garment?' And he was speechless. Then the king said to the servants, 'Bind him hand and foot, take him away, and cast him into outer darkness; there will be weeping and gnashing of teeth.'" (Matthew 22:11-13)

White is such an easy color to soil. Spill a drop of coffee on a white shirt, and you'll get comments all day. (Yet, you can almost drain an entire cup on a black shirt and not have it show up.)

Only the bravest of souls ventures out dressed in white.

Throughout Scripture, white is a symbol for righteousness. Our sins are blotted white by the Blood of the Lamb. When we arrive in Heaven, we will be given white robes that represent being covered by the Blood, the work of Christ on the Cross. His righteousness, not ours.

The application of God's full Truth (white light) produces righteousness.

Side Note: While surveys show that *blue* is the most popular favorite color among the people of the world, *white* was the least favorite. This fits perfectly — people love to feign an affection for God, they are attracted to the idea of Him in their life, but they don't like righteousness. Nobody wants to obey.

Lesson: *Show love to God by obeying Him. Seek His righteousness.*

Brown

Brown is the color most associated with soil and dirt, so it should be considered symbolic for the Kingdom of God.

Pink

"And now abide faith, hope, love, these three;
but the greatest of these is love." (1 Corinthians 13:13)

L ast but not least, we have pink.
Pink is created when you mix red with white, which represents the mixing of man with righteousness.

Pink is also the most feminine of colors. Women around the world enjoy pink, and it is strongly associated with Love.

And guess what? If you bring a man (red) into the righteousness of God (white), do you not suddenly have a man who is now capable of love?

Yes, without the influence of God, without having been redeemed by the blood of Christ into the righteousness of Christ, we cannot love. With God's righteousness imbued to us, with a loving relationship established with Him, His love can now flow through us to others.

And to approach it from the other end, Jesus said *"If you love Me, keep My commandments"* (John 14:15). The way man best expresses love back to God is by obeying Him through righteousness. The one who claims to love God, but does not obey, does not truly love Him.

And the reason pink is a feminine color? Because God saw that it was not good for man to be alone and He created woman for him. That was the birth of love.

Pink represents love.

Lesson: *Seek to love the way God loves.*

Errors:
A Window Revealing Correct Interpretation

This has been quite a journey we've undertaken together, and you are clearly interested, or you would not have made it this far. However, you may not have engaged yet in the discovery process yourself, meaning perhaps you haven't examined something in nature and tried to interpret its symbolic meaning on your own, according to the framework we've outlined here.

If so, then you likely have not yet appreciated the full intricacy and beauty of the network of symbols inscribed in God's Creation. It is possible to read this book and close its covers with a "That's nice," yet believing that any number of different interpretations could have worked just as well.

Errors in interpretation are the best window to see just how correct, how unique our interpretation herein has been.

To illustrate, let's try to interpret a few things differently and see what happens. For example, let's say that we don't want to interpret the oceans as representing "the World." Perhaps we could say that the oceans represent the "Sea of Forgetfulness" where God casts our sins.

In that case, we could argue that the land is the Kingdom, and through the rivers, God is washing the sins of the Kingdom into the Sea of Forgetfulness, and then God's power (seawater) is drowning the sins and holding them under pressure way down deep where no one can get to them.

That *is* a nice picture.

However, then what do all the fish and other sea life represent? What lives in the sea of forgetfulness? What about the tides and the influence of the moon (God's people) on the seas? What about Jesus saying we'd become fishers of men, a clear allusion to fish representing non-believers? We would be forced to interpret that non-believers live in the Sea of Forgetfulness and we're supposed to fish them out of there...*Why would we do that?*

What about the tides, sea grass, sharks and dolphins?

The Sea of Forgetfulness is a pretty simple concept. God casts our sins there and then they're gone. Nothing would live in it. By definition, what's in it is supposed to be forgotten.

On the other hand, since we've divorced the oceans from the World, what now in Creation can represent the World? The World is a major concept in Scripture and so it has to be represented somewhere, but there's nothing left. Land equals the Kingdom and the oceans represent the Sea of Forgetfulness. Nothing to ascribe to the World.

Perhaps we could say the desert represents the World, since most of the prophets spent a time in the "desert."

But there are no fish (non-believers) there. Then, of course, that screws up arroyos and sandstorms and everything else we've interpreted in the desert with no easy solution apparent.

We're starting to see we may have committed an error.

Furthermore, the Sea of Forgetfulness isn't even a phrase from Scripture — it's from a song. The teaching is pulled from Micah 7:19: *"He will again have compassion on us, and will subdue our iniquities. You will cast all our sins into the depths of the sea."* This has been combined in people's minds with the Sea of Glass in front of God's throne, yet there is no official existing "Sea of Forgetfulness." It may be just a metaphor from Micah.

Yet, in this hypothesis, we've ascribed 2/3 of Earth's surface to be a symbol for such a minor teaching.

Then, we examine Scripture on a broader scale and we find verses like Psalm 65:7 (*"You who still the noise of the seas, the noise of their waves, and the tumult of the peoples"*) which seems to be equating the seas with the peoples, i.e. the World. We find symbolic references to salt water in Zechariah that seem to imply a final redemption of the World, and now we're becoming convinced that we were wrong. Not the Sea of Forgetfulness, but the World.

Suddenly, all the other symbolic details of the oceans make sense again.

We're starting to see that the interpretation of God's natural symbolism isn't quite as flexible as one might initially think.

But, let's try another. Let's say that when interpreting trees, instead of saying they represent individual believers themselves, we could say they represent the *fruit* of believers, which would also be the fruit of the Kingdom. That could work, right?

I mean, we know that God's Kingdom primarily consists of the hearts of believers, right? So, the soil represents the corporate Body of Christ (This is actually correct) and trees represent our *corporate* fruit.

But...trees also *bear fruit*. So, we'd be saying that our fruit can bear fruit? I guess so. Yes, when we bear fruit, that fruit does bear more fruit, so okay. We can stretch a little and make that work.

But what about the fact that trees breathe? Our spiritual fruit doesn't breathe. Our fruit is not filled with the Spirit, we are. What about capillary action and tree rings and the way wood burns? Now, I'm shaking my head trying to make everything mesh again, and it won't.

Then, we appeal to Scripture for help and once again find ourselves corrected as every single instance that a tree is used symbolically, it represents people, not the fruit of those people.

As you can see, these interpretations are not so flexible, because they all have to mesh with each other. Just as all the different elements of nature interact with each other in seemingly infinite ways, so does a symbolic interpretation of nature have to account for all the complex theological elements of Scripture that mesh with each other in infinite ways (i.e. God, Christ, the Kingdom, grace, salvation, sin, believers, the world, etc).

And then Scripture has to be shown to use natural symbols in the same way that you've interpreted.

When a mistake in interpretation is made, you suddenly find yourself stuck, unable to move forward as the symbols stop meshing together.

I welcome you to try out your own examples. Making a few errors can be a great way to see more clearly just how difficult it is to get it right.

In Conclusion

I hope you are as amazed as I am by the intricate and wide tapestry of symbolism that God wove into Creation.

At the beginning of our journey, we proposed a theory — the idea that God *might* have encoded a symbolic message in Creation, and we established certain criteria to help us know if an attempted interpretation was valid.

Throughout the course of this book, we have obviously entered into a long and extensive interpretation, so the first question is: Are our symbols coherent?

I would answer yes. We consistently applied the same meaning to the sky, the sun, light, trees, water, land, etc. throughout. Trees always represent believers planted in the Kingdom. Sunlight is consistently symbolic of God's Truth emanating from the person of Christ.

I'm sure the dedicated critic, or a better mind than mine, will find details within this interpretation that aren't quite consistent or could be interpreted in a better way. I certainly don't pretend to have the last word on any of it.

However, our purpose in this volume was to establish whether or not there even *was* a message, and then begin to interpret it. Given the laws of probability, considering that the basic elements of nature can be assigned specific symbolic meanings (earth, water, air, plants, mammals) and constantly retain those meanings during an analysis of their interactions across the natural world means, logically, that there *clearly is a message*.

Beyond just the basics, that so many *details* in our interpretation mesh so well over and over again further proves it.

At this point, I do not consider it possible to argue there is no message from God encoded in Creation. To argue such a thing pushes the limits of probability in a way equaling those who would say our existence is an accident.

Furthermore, the fact that the Bible is chock full of spiritual symbols taken from nature (sheep, olive trees, Rock of our salvation, sand on the seashore, stars in the sky, fishers of men, bread and wine) is *strong* evidence it is appropriate to use nature this way.

So, there is a message.

Now, the question becomes: *Did we interpret it correctly?*

Again, the consistency of our interpretation is a strong indicator that we did.

We did have other criteria though. Did our interpretation ever conflict with Scripture?

The answer to that is no. While certain details might challenge the beliefs of some on debatable issues within orthodox Christianity, our entire interpretation agrees with every single clear theological teaching in the Scripture.

We also supposed that Scripture would not only *not conflict with*, but would *confirm* our interpretation. This also proved true.

For example, when initially attempting to interpret trees, I recalled the passage in Genesis 1 about trees reproducing after their own kind. So, using logic, I guessed that if land represented the Kingdom, and trees are the fruit of the land, then trees would have to be believers since they are the only fruit of the Kingdom.

It was only *after* I assigned this meaning to trees that I did some rudimentary Bible verse searches and discovered just how many times the Bible uses trees as symbols for people. This may surprise you, but many of the Bible verses cited in this book were found *after* meanings of things had already been guessed through logic.

This work is the best interpretation I can derive according to the best of my abilities, and our criteria supports my view that it is highly accurate. I encourage anyone who would like to take their own stab at it, to do so.

A surprise for me through the process of writing this book was how my own study of the Bible was greatly enhanced. There are brief mentions of natural images sprinkled all over Scripture, words that we gloss over in normal readings and that have only stood out to me now that I am more *aware*.

For example, Revelation 13 makes a curious distinction between the origins of the beast and of the false prophet. In verse 1, John says he saw the beast rising up out of the sea, but in verse 11, he says he saw the false prophet rising up out of the earth.

According to our interpretation, this would mean that the antichrist comes from the world (sea), but the false prophet will seemingly come out of the Church (Kingdom, earth). Corroborating this, many prophecy scholars have said the same thing.

Going even deeper, the false prophet is described as having the horns of a lamb, but speaking like a dragon. As we've said horns represent authority, it would mean the false prophet has great authority within the Church, but the spirit coming out of his mouth is evil and not of God.

Or how about Moses leading Israel through the Red Sea? In addition to representing baptism, this can now be viewed as a symbol of God making a place for the Kingdom (dry land) in the middle of the World (Red Sea).

Or the water that poured forth from the rock in the desert, symbolizing God's power pouring forth from Christ (boulder) to quench our thirst.

Or in Isaiah 45:8,

"Rain down, you heavens, from above,
And let the skies pour down righteousness;
Let the earth open, let them bring forth salvation,
And let righteousness spring up together.
I, the Lord, have created it."

An image of God pouring forth His power from Heaven into the Kingdom to raise up believers, with the whole process being righteous and producing righteousness. God sums it up in the last line with *"I, the Lord, have created it."*

I hope you also find yourself now gleaning new insights from Scripture that never would have jumped out at you before.

There are smaller, extra-biblical observations too. Like the colors red and green serving as symbols for Christmas. Could this, even if unintentionally so, be pointing to the life (green) given to man (red) at the birth of Christ. Or life into the form of a man — the incarnation. Or both.

How about the orange and black of Halloween? Appropriate symbols — the corrupted truth of man (orange) combined with lies (black).

The pink of St. Valentine's Day representing love together with white (righteousness), an interpretation that points back nicely to the original St. Valentine's historical account.

There's so much more to write. We've just barely touched the surface within these pages. I've already discovered a treasure trove of new symbolism encoded in the human body, cells, and the Periodic Chart of Elements. And guess what? It cleanly meshes with everything we've already found like the pieces of a well-designed jigsaw puzzle.

I've seen that the symbolism holds up no matter how deep we dive into the detail of natural things, but such is the vastness of Creation that the pages of a few books could never hope to contain it all. It is my hope that many other authors would take up the challenge to see what they can see and write it out.

Of course, this book can be misused. First of all, it does *not* support the worship of created things, nor does it imply that God is one with His creation. God is separate from and rules His Creation.

This book should also not be used to beat others over the head with insights we may have gleaned. It does not carry that level of authority. It is merely offered as a guide, a tool to perceive what God might have to say in addition to Scripture (He speaks to believers in prayer and even through visions all the time, so we do know He speaks outside of the Bible), and as a tool to lend extra insight into our study of the Word.

Our interpretation of God's natural symbols should never be given equal weight with Scripture, because *it's just our interpretation.*

I encourage you to open your eyes in a new way to the world around you. If God took the time to write you a message, isn't it worth taking the time to read it?

There is a reason for the vast variety of species in nature, for the vibrant humming of a million forms of life — and the reason goes beyond just God's supremely creative nature.

The never-ending complexity of life is an expression of the vastness of God's wisdom and what He has to say. Each species is not just a word from His lips, but a book. Each element is a sermon.

I encourage you to explore it.

Acknowledgements

Authors often begin their work inspired in solitude, yet before a book can be considered complete, it has been aided and touched by many hands, each contributing to its final excellence in their own way.

First and foremost, I would like to thank my wife, Lindsay, for her love and support, for always believing in me, and for loving my books.

My sincere and many thanks to Dan Reiland, Executive Pastor of 12Stone Church, for his tireless and enthusiastic investment in me, as well as his dedication and effort to help me make this book a success. You are truly appreciated, Dan!

To Fran Stewart, for her professional and detailed copyediting, her open mind, and for such fantastic suggestions that clearly made this a book worth writing. To Matt Smartt, for creating such a wonderful work of art in this book cover. You have outdone yourself! (I doubt anyone else sees what we see in it.)

To Jack & Barbara Mason for their endless support and offerings of encouragement.

To Jim Garlow, Senior Pastor of Skyline Church — thank you for your encouragement as a writer, and may you keep fighting the good fight out there in California and across the nation!

To 12Stone Church, for opening up God's house to allow a writer a peaceful place to craft his work (And to Patti Reiland for keeping him supplied with endless amounts of coffee).

And finally, to all my friends and clients who have voiced their support and helped spread the word, may you receive a multitude of blessings as you continue the journey.

Author's Note

I am truly and sincerely humbled by the thought that God may have used me to write this book. I say "may have," but I do really know just how much He helped and inspired me.

You may have gotten the impression that I had the entire picture in mind when I began writing, but I assure you, that could not be further from the truth.

I took the exact same journey in writing this that you did in reading it — one of discovery.

I knew my goal was to examine *all* of the basics, every aspect of nature I could to complete the picture, but when I started, I had no idea what most of it would represent.

I cannot tell you how many times I reached a topic and threw up my hands saying *What in the world is that?* Birds, reptiles, and insects come to mind — not to mention dew, volcanos, sandstorms, freshwater eels, elephant trunks, and a hundred other topics. I also can't count the number of times I had no answers, no ideas, and was forced to turn to God in prayer.

Seriously.

Night after night, I found myself bowing before Him and confessing that I had no idea what such and such represented, and then...suddenly, revelation and full understanding would pierce the blackness of my writer's block.

Looking back from this end, it all makes perfect sense and seems so self-evident now. Yet, then, coming at it from the other end, it was one big mystery after another. As it was for you as well before opening the cover of this book for the first time.

Later in the process, as I got further into the book and had a firmer grasp of the basics, God changed His methods with me.

More and more, He stopped answering me directly in prayer, and I found myself having to face the keyboard the next day with a blank page and still no answers. When that happened, I had to learn to just start writing anyway. When I did, the answers just seemed to flow out through the writing process. I would end those sections astonished at how God had just worked.

By the end, this book truly became a work of faith for me. I had to not only step out in faith with the entire idea that I was onto something, but I had to have faith that God would inspire me with revelation of truth *as* I was writing instead of before I wrote. (Of course, I have gone back and revised a number of times — my first thoughts weren't always as finely-tuned in the beginning as they were by the end.)

I also had to step out in faith by taking the time to write it. In order to finish this book, I had to neglect many other areas of my life, especially ones that produce income for my family. In fact, I had ceased writing for a period of time for that very reason until God corrected me and challenged me to have faith and finish the book.

That He would provide as long as I kept writing.

And He has.

About the Author

Zack Mason loves the art of the word and the thrill of discovery.

He has served in a variety of leadership roles in both church and Christian ministry for almost twenty years. He is currently the Executive Director of SOF Ministries, an international missions agency that has conducted work in Central America, Bangladesh, Pakistan, and the United States.

His passions include history, languages, travel, missions, and, of course, books.

He currently resides with his family outside Atlanta, GA and plans to continue writing for as long as he is allowed to do so.

You can connect with Zack by visiting:

www.zackmason.com

Glossary

Note: This glossary is presented as a tool for easy translation from symbol to English. Once again, the natural symbols are just words in a symbolic language and not the actual item described.

Air -	God the Spirit
Amphibians -	False believers
Animals -	Animated Beings
Antarctic -	Loveless Church
Ants -	Warrior/Worker spirits
Apes -	Teachers
Arctic -	Loveless Church
Arroyos -	Traditions of Men
Autumn -	Golden Time of Reflection
Bats -	Prayer Warriors
Beach -	Worldly Church
Bear -	Evangelist
Bearing young -	Intimate discipleship
Bees -	Warrior/Worker spirits
Birds -	Angels
Black -	Lies & deception
Blind -	A person unable to discern truth
Blue -	God, Divinity
Bog -	Fat Church
Boreal Forest -	Austere /Authoritarian Church
Boulder -	Jesus Christ / Messiah
Brown -	God's Kingdom
Bull Sharks -	Crime lords who attend church
Bush -	Mature Believer (Less Prominent)
Butterflies -	Inspiring spirits
Camel -	Abrasive Teacher

Capillary Action -	God's Power within a believer overcoming the sinful nature
Carbon -	Humanity
Carnivores -	Church Staff / Levites
Carrier Pigeons -	Messenger Angels
Cat -	Ego-Centric Believer
Cedar Tree -	Mature & Constant Believer
Climates -	Churches
Clouds -	God's power visible within Himself
Coast -	Worldly Church
Cockroaches -	Evil spirits
Cold-blooded -	Unable to retain God's love within oneself, dependent on surrounding culture for love
Colors -	Truths
Corona (of the sun) -	Christ's Crown
Cow -	Meditating Believer
Creeks -	God's power moving through the Kingdom
Crocodiles -	Fallen angels
Crops -	Harvest of Believers
Cyclones -	God's Judgment on the Worldly Church, using the World to do it.
Darkness -	Lies & Evil
Deaf -	Unable to obey God's voice
Deciduous -	Mature & Cyclical Believer
Deciduous Forest -	Fertile / Democratic Church
Desert -	Powerless Church
Dew -	God's giving of life to the Kingdom in the face of reduced love
Dirt -	Body of Christ
Disasters -	Movements within the Kingdom & Judgments

Dog -	Discerning Believer
Dolphin -	Missionary
Doves -	Angel of the Lord / Holy Spirit
Eagles -	"Dominions" (Warrior Angels that preside over nations)
Earth -	God's Kingdom
Earthquakes -	Conflict within the Kingdom
Earth's Core -	Hell
Eel (Freshwater) -	Worldly non-believer who tries Christianity for a while, is never transformed, and eventually returns to the world
Egg -	Disconnected discipleship
Elephants -	Leaders among God's People
Erosion -	God forming the Body of Christ
Evaporation -	God removing His Power (Life) from the earth
Evergreen -	Mature & Constant Believer
Falcons -	"Dominions" (Warrior Angels that preside over regions)
Fall (season) -	Golden Time of Reflection
Feathers -	Spiritual Maturity
Fire -	Persecution/Revival
Fish -	Non-believers
Fishing -	Evangelism
Flight -	The ability to overcome the sinful nature
Floods -	God's Judgment on the Kingdom through His Power
Flower -	Spiritual Attractiveness
Flying Fish -	Non-believers who are trying to overcome the World in their own power

Fog -	God's Power causing spiritual blindness
Forest -	Body of Believers
Forest Fire -	Persecution of Believers
Fruit Tree -	Mature, Loving Believer
Fruit/Seed -	Testimonies
Gills -	World-breathing, of the world
Giraffe -	Scholar Believer
Grass -	Superficial Believers
Grassland -	Lukewarm Church
Gravity -	The Sinful Nature
Great White Sharks -	Crime lords in the World
Green -	Life produced from God's truth
Hair -	Spiritual Maturity
Hawks -	"Dominions" (Warrior Angels that preside over regions)
Hearing -	Obedience to God
Heat -	Love
Herd Animals -	Servant Believers
Hills -	Times of Success
Hoofed Animals -	Servant Believers
Horse -	Warrior Believer
Hummingbirds -	"Principalities" (Angels in charge of inspiring art & science)
Hurricanes -	God's Judgment on the Worldly Church, using the World to do it.
Ice -	God's power, frozen, waiting to move
Insects -	Spirits that perform the Lord's work in the spiritual realm (Lower rank than angels)
Kangaroo -	Sheltering Believer
Koala Bear -	Sheltering Believer
Land -	God's Kingdom

GLOSSARY

Landslides -	Reforms within the Kingdom
Law of Gravity -	The Sinful Nature
Light -	Truth & Goodness
Lightning -	God's Judgment on an Individual
Lion -	Jesus, King of Kings
Live birth -	Intimate discipleship
Locusts -	Consuming spirits
Lunar Eclipse -	Persecution / Martyrdom
Lungs -	Spirit-breathing, of the Kingdom
Mammal -	Believer
Marsupials -	Sheltering Believers
Mist -	God's power causing spiritual blindness to things in the distance (i.e. future)
Monkeys -	Teachers
Moon -	God's People (The Church, Israel)
Moths -	Inspiring spirits
Mountains -	Times of Success
Mouse -	Layperson /Fellowshipping Believer (Gnawing Believer)
Natural Springs -	God's Power flowing up from within the Kingdom
Oak Tree -	Strong Mature & Cyclical Believer
Oasis -	A church flooded with God's Power among a region of powerless churches
Oceans (Salt Water) -	The World
Orange -	Man's perversion of truth
Owl -	Angel of Death
Oxygen -	The Holy Spirit
Photosynthesis -	The process by which believers receive energy and transform the world
Pig -	Greedy Believer

Pine Tree -	Mature & Constant Believer
Pink -	Love
Plain (terrain) -	Lukewarm Church
Plant Types -	Types of Believers
Primates -	Teachers
Purple -	Royalty, Majesty, of the King, God-man
Rain -	God's Power descending upon the Kingdom
Rain Forest -	Dynamic / Pastor-centered Church
Rainbows -	God's covenant not to destroy man with water
Ravens -	"Powers" (Warrior Angels who are the "bearers of conscience" and the "keepers of history")
Red -	Man
Reptiles -	Beings fallen from or falsely purported to be of the Kingdom
Rivers -	God's power moving through the Kingdom
Roaches -	Evil spirits
Rock-Eating Plant -	Hardy & Independent Believer
Rocks (Boulders) -	Jesus Christ / Messiah
Rodent -	Layperson /Fellowshipping Believer (Gnawing Believer)
Salmon -	Nominal Christians who leave the church when young, but return to its traditions when older, especially to benefit their children
Salt Water -	The World
Sandstorms -	When the Holy Spirit uproots people from powerless churches and re-deposits them in other churches

Scales -	Worldly skepticism
Sea Plant -	Believer Living in a Hostile Environment
Seas -	The World
Seasons -	Cycles of Spiritual Growth
Seed -	Testimonies
Senses -	Spiritual Abilities
Sharks -	Crime lords in the World
Sheep -	Meditating Believer
Sight -	Discernment of Truth
Sky -	God the Father
Smell (sense of) -	Discernment of Spirits
Snakes -	False religious leaders
Snow -	God's power, frozen, waiting to move
Snowy region -	Loveless Church
Soil -	Body of Christ
Solar Eclipse -	The Crucifixion of Christ
Songbirds -	Worshipping Angels
Spring (season) -	New Birth/New Growth
Springs (of water) -	God's Power flowing up from within the Kingdom
Stars -	The Saints (Believers who have passed on before us)
Stones -	Truths
Storms -	God's Pending Judgment
Streams -	God's power moving through the Kingdom
Summer -	Deepening Maturity
Sun -	God the Son / Jesus Christ / Messiah
Sunshine -	Good Times
Swamp -	Fat Church
Swine -	Greedy Believers
Temperate Forest -	Fertile / Democratic Church

Thunderstorms -	God's Pending Judgment
Tidal Wave -	Worldly Attacks on the Kingdom
Tornados -	God's Judgment on the Lukewarm Church
Tortoises -	False theologians / False teachers
Tree Rings -	Patterns describing the rhythms of spiritual growth
Trees -	Believers
Tropical Forest -	Dynamic / Pastor-centered Church
Tsunamis -	Worldly Attacks on the Kingdom
Turtles -	False theologians / False teachers
Typhoons -	God's Judgment on the Worldly Church, using the World to do it.
Valleys -	Times of Trouble
Vine -	Missionary
Violet -	Royalty, Majesty, of the King, God-man
Vision -	Discernment of Truth
Volcanos -	Spiritual Attacks on the Kingdom
Warm-blooded -	Able to retain God's love within oneself
Wasps -	Warrior/Worker spirits
Water (Fresh Water) -	God's Power
Water Erosion -	God forming the Body of Christ through His Power
Water Table -	God's power within the Kingdom
Weather -	Movements of God
Whale -	Missionary
White -	Righteousness
Wind -	God the Spirit
Wind Erosion -	God forming the Body of Christ through His Spirit
Winter -	Hardship & Dormancy

Wood -	The substance of the lives of believers who have gone before us
Woods -	Body of Believers
Yellow -	Truth of God

Index

1 Chronicles	373
1 John	38, 208, 281, 290, 341
1 Kings	67, 407, 409
1 Peter	202
1 Samuel	407
2 Corinthians	139, 193
2 Kings	379
2 Peter	114
2 Samuel	77, 184, 407
2 Timothy	292, 400
Acts, Book of	19, 90, 125, 189, 375
Amos	19
Ancient man	21, 90, 96, 98, 277
Arable land	206
Arctic regions & snow caps	113, 171, 183, 193, **196-197**
Arroyos	174
Atmosphere	1, 28-30, 42, 44, 65, 99, 112-113, 173, 231, 254, 258-260, 299
Autumn	139-142, 217, 221, **222-224**
Beaches & coastlines	55, 74, **208-210**, 220-221, 262, 271, 297, 400
Black (color)	46-47, 229, 279, 293, 343-344, 384, **421**, 432
Blackaby, Henry	61
Blue (color)	1-2, **19-22**, 28-29, 42, 45, 69, 71, 88, 278-279, 314, **416-417**, 418-422
Boreal/evergreen forest	183, **193-195**,
Boulders	**77-78**, 79-80, 246, 431
Boundary wall	80
Brown (color)	**423**
Burning Bush	125, 329
Bushes	22, 118, 125, **147-148**, 150, 152, 189, 268, 329,
Canopy layer	185 -186
Capillary action	**114-115**
Carbon	**46-47**, 112, 116-117, 256

Carbon dioxide	111-112, 116, 158, 256
China /Chinese Christians	132-133, 179, 254-255, 288, 290
Church	58-62, 77-81, 85, **87-96**, 121-124, 145-152, 166-167, 170, 180-197, 204, 206-207, 234-240, 256, 266-268, 307-308, 310, 381, 431
Civil War	43
Clay	73, 83-84, 130
Climate	**165**, 194, 258
Clouds	20, 64, **66-67**, 133, 175, 229-230, 234, 241-242, 253, 258, 268-270,
Concentration camps	23
Corona (sun's)	33, 92
Costa Rica	185, 209, 243, 257, 296
Crops	30, **155-157**, 206, 220, 265, 405
Darkness	23-25, **36-37**, 89, 92, 124, 251, 374, 378, 421-422
Dead Sea	55-56
Deciduous trees	135-136, **139-142**, 147, 189-192, 226,
Deciduous/temperate forest	183, 187, **189-193**, 228
Desert	67, 151, **165-181**, 196, 203, 228, 338-339, 426
Desert rain	168
Destruction of the Temple	251
Deuteronomy	101, 178
Dew	241, **242**, 435
Disasters	**243-271**
Discipleship	63, 91, 109, 143, 146, 153-154, 187, 193, 303, 318, 332, 390
Discovery Channel	233-235, 396
Dormant / dormancy	140-141, 190, 216-218, 224
Earth's core	**247-250**, 251-260
Earthquakes	**243-245**, 246, 261-262
Ecclesiastes	59, 227
Eclipse	33, 91-93
Eight (number)	31, **42**, **46**, 305, 316
ELCA (Evangelical Lutheran Church in America)	180-181
Ephesians	251, 374, 384, 387
Erosion	76, **84-86**, 158, 172, 255
Evaporation	**65**, 66-68, 168, 171, 175, 194, 230

Evergreens	128, **135-138**, 139-141, 147, 189, 192, **193-194**,
Exodus	22, 280, 311, 382-383, 410, 415,
Ezekiel	55, 109, 173, 207, 325, 375, 377
Fellowship	57, 64, 74, 108, 120, 123-124, 156, 195, 238, 253, 255, 259, 266, 326-328, 353, 363-364
Fire	42, 109-110, 112, 119, 122-124, **125-127**, 128-134, 148, 151-152, 234, 247-248, 254, 256, 418
Fishing	**297-298**, 313
Fishermen	208, 283, 297-298, 313, 353, 425, 430
Flowers	141, 147-148, **152-154**, 202, 215, 217, 350, 387,
Fog	**240-242**
Forest	107, 128-134, 151, 165, 171-172, **182-195**, 202-204, 228, 264, 353
Forest fire	**128-134**, 148, 151, 234, 254
Foundations	23, 75, 78-80, 118, 121-123, 245
Fresh water	55, 59, 170, 257, 290, 292, 353-354, 393
Frozen	196-197, 216, 225, 236-239,
Fruit / fruits	82, 84, 86, 107, 109-110, 116, 120, 140-141, **143-145**, 147-148, 151, 153, 155-157, 222-223, 226, 348, 350, 353-354, 400, 427, 430
Fruit trees	141, **144-145**, 148, 153, 205
Galatians	143, 144
General revelation	2, 101, 310
Genesis	23, 42, 44, 51, 63, 69, 81 , 97, 109, 143, 215, 264, 283, 381, 384, 391-392, 430
Glucose	111, 113
God's people	73, **87-95**, 107, 129-134, 196, 230-231, 245, 252, 254, 321, 381, 425,
Grass	128-129, **148-152**, 154, 202-204, 217, 268, 317-320, 328,
Grassland	**202-204,** 228, 328,
Gravity	2, 22, **38-40**, 92-94, 114, 183, 198-200, 248-249, 255, 286-287, 349, 373, 378, 390
Green (color)	1, 69-71, 223, 278, **419-420**, 431

Habakkuk	283
Hardwood	137-138, 141
Heat	**34-35**, 42, 47, 65, 68, 81-82, 125, 128, 139, 146, 165, 167, 171, 191, 196, 219-220, 223, 249, 270, 283-284, 299, 302, 330, 339, 363-364, 394, 402
Hebrews, Book of	101, 119, 405, 408
Hell	89, **247-250**, 252-259, 394
Holy Spirit	4, 30, **40-46**, 82, 84-85, 97, 108, 116, 120, 124-134, 156, 179, 197, 219, 230, 249, 267, 269-270, 281-282, 286-287, 295, 299, 302-303, 305, 343, 351, 377-378, 381, 399
Hosannah	245
Humility	40, 45-46, 54, **84-86**, 200, 229-230, 235, 293, 364, 409
Ice	112, **196-197**, 199, 216, **224-226**, 232, **236-240**, 264, 417
Interpretation method	**1-5, 425-427, 429-433**
Isaiah, Book of	32, 34, 108, 109, 149, 165, 169, 170, 171, 172, 182, 240, 417, 431
Israel	55, 77, 87-96, 131, 165, 172-173, 205, 207, 230-231, 245, 252, 310, 315, 411, 431
Japanese Christians	131-132
Jeremiah, Book of	251, 281
Job, Book of	32, 65, 66, 73, 84, 168, 196, 224, 233, 236, 268, 335
Joel, Book of	412
John, Gospel of	37, 40, 46, 52, 57, 79, 111, 145, 146, 161, 204, 240, 259, 280, 296, 347, 394, 412, 419, 421, 423,
Jonah	315, 351
Jude	261
Judgment	20, 51, 66, 70-71, 93, 118, 136, 177, 210, 218, 221, **229-240, 243-272**, 384, 410-412
Jungle	74, 165, **182-188**
Ketisology	5
Landslides	**246-247**, 261

Law of Gravity	2, 22, **38-40**, 92-94, 114, 183, 198-200, 248-249, 255, 286-287, 349, 373, 378, 390
Lava	161, 253-255
Leviticus	309, 319, 338
Light	**23-26**, 27-30, 34, 36-37, 42, 69-71, 78, 87-92, 97-102, 107-108, 111-113, 120, 135, 141, 146, 151, 157-159, 165, 176, 185-187, 189-196, 201, 206, 216, 219, 226, 227, 230, 237-238, 258, 260, 278-279, 284, 350, 377-379, 411, 412, 415-422, 429
Lightning	229-230, **233-235**, 259, 269,
Luke, Gospel of	55, 152, 157, 205, 240, 246, 270, 297, 320, 349, 384, 385, 389
Magma	248, 250, 259
Malachi	220
Mark, Gospel of	107, 174, 208, 278, 281, 283, 417
Martin Luther	136-137, 140, 176, 246, 329
Matthew, Gospel of	27, 63, 77, 83, 92, 109, 128, 143, 146, 148, 149, 155, 243, 247, 281, 304, 320, 322, 344, 360, 381-382, 394, 402, 412, 422
Meteors	21-22
Moon	27, 33, 40, **87-96**, 97-98, 425
Mosses / lichens	195
Mountains	19, 74, 84, 174-175, **198-202**, 203, 242, 243, 246, 251, 256-257, 349, 379
Mt. Vesuvius	252
Natural springs	**57-58**, 60, 63-64, 67
Navigation	37, 59, 78, 95, 100, 289
Nazi Germany	24, 284
New York City	43, 289
Number of man	47
Oak	107, 109, 128, 135, 137-138, 141, 143-144, 205, 265
Oasis / oases	**170**

Oceans	**55-58**, 62-63, 65, 73-75, 93-94, 157-159, 179, 201, 208, 210, 255, 261-264, 270-271, 283-298, 311-315, 353, 425-426
Orange (color)	69, 141-142, 223, **420-421**, 432
Orange butenolide	129
Oxygen	21, **42-46**, 47, 111-112, 116-117, 120, 124, 126, 128, 133, 158-159, 199-200, 256, 265, 286-287, 299, 339, 399
Ozone	21-22, 44-45
Ozone layer	21-22, 44
Passover	90
Petra / petros	77-78
Photic zone	157-158
Photosynthesis	107, **111-113**, 117, 141, 183, 192, 223
Pine cones	138, 226
Pink (color)	**423**, 432
Plains	74, **202-204**, 256, 269
Plant growth	**117**
Pneuma	41
Polar regions	**196-197**
Pompeii	251-252
Prairies	74, 151, 165, **202-204**, 256, 269, 271
Proverbs, Book of	122, 219, 302, 307, 316, 328, 348, 355, 381, 387, 420
Psalms, Book of	107, 135, 149, 198, 228, 229, 243, 246, 293, 315, 320, 407, 408, 426
Purple (color)	1, 30. 71, 142, 223, 415, **417**, 418
Rain	1, 20-21, 51, 57-60, 65-66, **67-68**, 118, **168**, 171-178, 189-190, 194-195, 203, 222-223, **228**, 229-231, 246, 258, 260, 264, 270, 431
Rain forest	172, 183, **184-188**, 189-195, 228,
Rainbow	**69-71**, 415
Red (color)	46, 69, **417-418**
Red Dwarfs	98
Revelation, book of	46, 63, 87, 244, 270, 281, 307, 379, 380, 392, 399, 400, 422, 430,
Rock-eating plants	**161**

Rocks	1, 64, **75-78**, 79-82, 86, 145, 155, 161, 246, 248, 251-253
Roman Empire	131, 286, 380
Romans, book of	1, 118, 311, 352, 397
Roots	73, 82, 107-108, 113, **118-119**, 120, 128, 135-137, 145-146, 149, 152, 160, 169, 171, 186, 195, 217, 253, 265, 267, 278
Ross, Hugh	32
Rot	**121-123**, 138
Ruach	41
Salt water	**55-57**, 262, 426
Sand	**44, 83-84**
Sandstorms	**178-181**, 330-331, 426, 435
Sea plants	**157-160**
Seas	**55-58**, 62-63, 65, 73-75, 93-94, 157-159
Seasonal Affective Disorder	226
Seasons	3, 139-140, 190-192, **215-226**
Seeds	76, 117, 120, 129-133, 137-138, **143**, 144-145, 151-157, 173, 183, 217, 260, 348, 350, 353
September 11th	22, 307
Seven (number)	31, 70, 307, 332,
Shadow	25, 151, 183, 185, 201-202
Shoreline / shores	55-56, 74, 94-95, 210, 261-263, 313-314, 393, 430
Sinful nature	39-40, 92, 95, 114-115, 183, 198-201, 246-250, 255, 286-287, 297, 349-351, 373, 376, 378, 388, 390, 406-407, 412
Six (number)	31, **46-47**,
Sky	1-2, **19-22**, 27-31, 34, 39, 41-43, 57, 65-71, 88, 98-100, 108, 116, 175, 201, 230, 233, 235, 247-248, 254, 257-258, 260, 264, 268, 287, 314, 373, 397, 415, 429-430
Snow	112, **196-197**, 199, 216, **224-226**, 232, **236-240**, 264, 417
Softwood	137-138

Soil — 3, 57-58, 64, **73-76**, **81-84**, 85-86, 107-108, 116-122, 130, 132, 143-146, **155-157**, 161, 168, 171-173, 179-180, 186-195, 200, 206-207, 244-246, 253-255, 268, 405, 408, 423, 427

Soil liquefaction — 244-245
Solvent — 54
Song of Solomon — 215
Specific revelation — 2-3, 101, 310
Speed of light — 26
Spodosol — 194
Spring — **215-218**
Stars — 20, 87, **97-102**, 430
Stones — 75-78, **79-81**, 84, 122, 155-156, 161, 246
Storms — 66, 71, 178-179, 217, 221, **229-232**, 233-235, 268-269
Summer — **219-221**
Sun — 19-21, 24-25, **27-33**, 34, 40, 43-44, 65, 87-99, 125, 135-136, 155, 191-192, 201, 216, 219-220, 224, 242, 249, 260, 330, 363, 379, 380, 411, 419, 429
Sunlight — 1, 24-25, 28-29, 42, 69-70, 107-108, 111-113, 146, 151, 158, 185-195, 226, 234, 237-238, 258, 377, 420, 429
Sunshine — 227
Sunspots — 33
Swamps — **205-207**
Taproots — 169
Tectonic plates — 243-245, 259
Third Great Awakening — 43
Thunder — 20, 66, 71, 218, 221, **229-235**, 268-269, 335
Tidal currents — 94
Tides — **93-95**, 140, 425-426
Topsell, Edward — 360
Topsoil — 200
Tradition — **174-178**
Tree mass — **116-117**
Tree rings — **115**, 224, 427

Trees	1, 3, 22, 41, 46, 56, 73, **107-121**, 122, 128-134, **135-145**, 147-153, 170-174, 178, **182-195,** 202-206, 216, 222-224, 226, 234, 240, 253, 255, 265, 278, 303, 310, 328, 362, 375, 411, 420, 427, 429-430
Truth	**23-26**, 28-33, 36-37, 40, 64, 69-71, 75-82, 87-96, 107, 111-113, 115, 120, 122-125, 140, 143, 146, 151, 155-165, 173, 176, 180, 186, 192, 195-197, 201-203, 216, 219, 225-228, 230, 234, 237-242, 246-247, 258, 260, 278-280, 282, 284, 288, 304-305, 326, 330, 336-337, 343, 350, 353, 366, 377-379, 386, 411, **415-423**, 429, 432
Types of soil	**83-84**
Ultraviolet light	29-30, **279**, 350, **379**
Valleys	60, 74, **198-202**, 203, 210, 239, 241, 243, 246, 256
Vespasianus, Titus Flavius	251
Vesuvius, Mt.	252
Vines	**145-147**, 152, 187
Vitamin D	29
Volcanos	247, 249, **251-260**, 435
Water table	**63-64**
Weather	**227-242**
White (color)	26-29, 66, 69, 88, 225, 229, 236-238, 279, 343-344, 375, 415, 417, 421, **422**, 423, 432
Wind	4, **40-41**, 43, 85, 108, 125, 128, 133-134, 149-150, 172, 178-179, 197, 217, 229-230, 268-271, 351, 378
Winter	**224-226**
Wood	115, 121, **122-125**, 126, 137-138, 317, 328, 348, 427
Yellow (color)	28-29, 69-71, 141-142, 223, 279, 416, **419**, 420
Zechariah, Book of	31, 55, 110, 426